Off the Grid

Off-grid isn't a state of mind. It isn't about someone being out of touch, about a place that is hard to get to, or about a weekend spent offline. Off-grid is the property of a building (generally a home but sometimes even a whole town) that is disconnected from the electricity and the natural gas grid. To live off-grid, therefore, means having to radically re-invent domestic life as we know it, and this is what this book is about: individuals and families who have chosen to live in that dramatically innovative, but also quite old, way of life.

This ethnography explores the day-to-day existence of people living off-the-grid in each Canadian province and territory. Vannini and Taggart demonstrate how a variety of people, all with different environmental constraints, live away from contemporary civilization. The authors also raise important questions about our social future and whether off-grid living creates an environmentally and culturally sustainable lifestyle practice. These homes are experimental labs for our collective future, an intimate look into unusual contemporary domestic lives, and a call to the rest of us leading ordinary lives to examine what we take for granted. This book is ideal for courses on the environment and sustainability as well as introduction to sociology and introduction to cultural anthropology courses.

Visit www.lifeoffgrid.ca, for resources, including photos of Vannini and Taggart's ethnographic work.

Phillip Vannini is Canada Research Chair in Public Ethnography and Professor in the School of Communication & Culture at Royal Roads University in Victoria, BC, Canada. He is author of dozens of journal articles and book chapters, and author/editor of ten books.

Jonathan Taggart is a Vancouver-based photojournalist and member of the Boreal Collective. He holds a MA in Intercultural and International Communication. His photography exhibits have captured national audiences and his pictures have appeared in magazines and newspapers across the country, such as *Canadian Geographic*, *Yukon: North of Ordinary*, *BC Business*, and *The Tyee*. Among other awards, he is the recent winner of the 2012 Western Canadian Music Award album cover design.

Innovative Ethnographies

Series Editor: Phillip Vannini, Royal Roads University

The purpose of this series is to use the new digital technology to capture a richer, more multidimensional view of social life than was otherwise done in the classic, print tradition of ethnography, while maintaining the traditional strengths of classic, ethnographic analysis.

Off the Grid

Re-Assembling Domestic Life

Phillip Vannini and Jonathan Taggart

Routledge
Taylor & Francis Group

NEW YORK AND LONDON

First published 2015
by Routledge
711 Third Avenue, New York, NY 10017

and by Routledge
2 Park Square, Milton Park, Abingdon, Oxon, OX14 4RN

Routledge is an imprint of the Taylor & Francis Group, an informa business

© 2015 Taylor & Francis

Library of Congress Cataloging in Publication Data
   Vannini, Phillip.
Off the grid : re-assembling domestic life / Phillip Vannini and Jonathan
Taggart.
      pages cm. — (Innovative ethnographies)
   Includes bibliographical references and index.
   1. Sustainable living—Canada.   2. Self-reliant living—Canada.
3. Alternative lifestyles—Canada.   4. Simplicity.   I. Taggart, Jonathan.
II. Title.
   GE199.C2V36 2014
   640.28'6—dc23
   2014016461

ISBN: 978-0-415-85432-0 (hbk)
ISBN: 978-0-415-85433-7 (pbk)
ISBN: 978-0-203-74440-6 (ebk)

Typeset in in Caslon, Copperplate, and Trade Gothic
by Apex CoVantage, LLC

Printed and bound in the United States of America by
Edwards Brothers Malloy on sustainably sourced paper

CONTENTS

PREFACE

Off-grid isn't a state of mind. It isn't about someone being out of touch, about a place that is hard to get to, or about a weekend spent offline. Off-grid is the property of a building (generally a home but sometimes even a whole town) that is disconnected from the electricity and the natural gas grid. Off-grid buildings are therefore self-sufficient for light, power, and heat. But as it goes, people who live in off-grid homes also tend to be independent for procuring other vital resources, such as water and food. To live off-grid, therefore, means having to radically re-invent domestic life as we know it, and this is what this book is about: individuals and families who have chosen to live in that dramatically innovative, but also quite old, way of life. We call them "off-gridders."

Off-gridders homes are, in many cases, experimental labs for our collective future. The lessons they are learning *today* about living with renewable energy are the lessons we will all need to learn *tomorrow* in order to make our lives more sustainable, more respectful toward the environment, and less dependent on non-renewable resources. This book is an intimate look into *unusual* contemporary domestic lives, but it is also a call to the rest of us leading *ordinary* lives to examine what we take for granted about our homes, our needs, and our wants. We believe that this book will be valuable in courses on the environment and renewable resources as well as ethnography. We also hope that our work will appeal well beyond the academy.

From 2011 to 2013 Jonathan Taggart and I spent two years travelling across Canada to find off-gridders and visit off-gridders' homes. Sometimes we were able to stay with them for a short period of time. Sometimes we were allowed to take photographs and record video and audio. And sometimes we even had the chance to practice off-grid living ourselves through short stays at off-grid cabins and homes. Altogether we visited about 100 homes and interviewed about 200 off-grid Canadians, as well as many American and British expats living in Canada. In sum we were able to find off-gridders in every single province and territory of what happens to be the second-largest country on earth. This book is our story of our travels, and ultimately our narration of their experiences, their challenges, their solutions, their aspirations, their ways of life, and their own stories.

To make our work possible Jon and I had to fly on dozens of planes, ride snowmobiles, paddle kayaks and canoes, don snow-shoes, ride ATVs, sail ferries and small boats, drive on ice roads and city streets, and bike and trek across many regions of our country. To render the intensity of that kind of experience we wrote this book in the style of a travelogue. But these aren't really the pages of a travel essay; ours is first and foremost a work of ethnography. Interviews, observation, and participation in the day-to-day life of off-gridders have not only inspired us to reflect, interpret, and contextualize off-grid living in itself, but also (and perhaps more importantly) to question our collective, modern, *on*-grid way of life. Ideally, after reading this book anyone should understand much more deeply what we all usually take for granted about our modern condition in relation to comfort, convenience, and connectivity.

There is a certain irony about our fieldwork. As Jon and I zigzagged from province to province to understand the meanings of simplicity, of a more basic and Spartan life, and of an alternative way of living with modern technology, we regularly lugged with us satchel bags and panniers full of the latest visual and digital gadgets. Thanks to the material we collected, what we ended up producing in the year following our travels is a hybrid book that combines the written word together with sound clips, photography, and video. In keeping with the purpose of the Routledge Innovative Ethnography Series, we offer our readers/viewers/listeners our multiple creations, hoping that these will somehow reverberate and strike their imagination in meaningful ways. The companion website—hyperlinked and referenced throughout this book—will hopefully serve as a great source of information for everyone interested in sensuous, multimodal learning and a new way of doing research and of knowing.

Our writing crisscrosses issues related to technology, sense of place, lifestyle, energy, sustainability, and everyday life. These are topics that cross the disciplinary boundaries of geography, cultural studies, sociology, and anthropology. They are subjects of interest to those keen on teaching and learning about material culture, skills, slow living, and much more. We also hope that our book will stimulate the sociological and geographic imagination of students enrolled in introductory courses and in qualitative research methods, especially ethnography, as well as courses on sustainability and the environment. Though each chapter focuses on a key concept and a particular topic, both the book and the website are organized by province/territory. There are ten provinces and three territories in Canada, and therefore there are thirteen chapters to this book and thirteen main pages on the book's website. Each of the chapters narrates our travels, describes our encounters with off-gridders, and reflects on and analyzes the significance of various aspects of their practices and experiences. All the photos are shared to evoke a sense of what we witnessed, not as objective documentation. We chose photos that we liked: pictures that Jonathan took to animate our recollections and enliven your vicarious experience. The videos were produced with the same purpose as the photography and the writing: to tell a story and to allow viewers to "meet" characters and see their homes, as well as to listen to their narratives. Each medium seems to "speak" differently, and we hope you will enjoy the cacophony.

ACKNOWLEDGMENTS

Our fieldwork, this book, and its accompanying photography, audio, video, and website could not have been carried out without the generous assistance of three separate grants by the Social Sciences and Humanities Research Council of Canada. Additional funding was provided by Royal Roads University. Steve Rutter and Samantha Barbaro at Routledge also deserve our gratitude for trusting our vision for the project and seeing the book through. We are similarly grateful to the four peer reviewers who took the time to read our work and give us advice:

Paul Stoller   West Chester University
Tim Edensor   Manchester Metropolitan University
Christopher J. Schneider   University of British Columbia
Nick Osbaldiston   Monash University

During the time Jon and I conducted fieldwork, Lindsay Vogan first and then Kate O'Rourke worked tirelessly to establish and maintain rapport with several media outlets that granted us interviews and coverage to make our work public. Lindsay was also responsible for the production of two short audio documentaries on off-grid living, while Kate took the lead in designing the book's website. We are also grateful to Lindsay Marie Stewart, who oversaw the extensive knowledge mobilization plan after the book, video, and photography were completed. Finally, a big thank you goes to Matt Clarke, who contributed his focus, dedication, and film editing skills to our team.

Several of the chapters comprising this book have appeared before in different (often more technical) versions in a variety of academic journals and books. For their permission to reproduce, we thank the publishers of

Transfers; Environment & Planning A; Body & Society, Food, Culture & Society; Environment & Planning D; Cultural Geographies; Journal of Consumer Culture; as well as Ashgate and Palgrave MacMillan. We are also indebted to all the journal and book editors and reviewers who gave us feedback on these early articles and chapters along the way.

However, most importantly of all, our book could not have happened without the kindness of the nearly 200 off-gridders who gave us their time, opened their homes, fed us, gave us shelter, shared their experiences, showed us their places, trusted us with their stories and images, and taught us so much. Many of them also went out of their way to introduce us to off-grid acquaintances, friends, and neighbors. This book is dedicated to them.

OFF THE GRID

Dave's House.[i]

1

GRIDS

I stepped off the small boat mystified, with my eyes fixated on a blue heron conspicuously pretending to be ignoring us—in the way herons are wont to do—from a safe distance behind Alistair and Eleanor's home. The 40-minute glide on the waters of the shadowy inlet had been swift but smooth, punctuated by the predictable sights, smells, and tones of Clayoquot Sound: cedars overcrowding next of kin in search of gleams of sunshine, docks covered in a slimy sheen of freshly spilt sockeye blood mixed with seagull shit, and stunted swells meeting the impassable resistance of rambling channels and coves. No element of the postcard-perfect but thoroughly familiar waterscape seemed to stand out the way the house did though, as if hovering weightlessly upon the glassy ocean surface. Feeling awestruck at the incongruous architectural sight, I wondered for a moment whether the crane-like bird wasn't indeed as baffled.

"He's our neighbor," said Alistair laconically.

"Must be nice to have discreet neighbors like that," I joked.

"Better than the otters! They're cute, but when you live in a floating home, otters are like 30-pound rats swimming under your house and chewing away your foundations."

I plodded unevenly on the walking path while Alistair tied up the skiff on his own. A long but narrow—three and a half feet at most—wooden plank rendered slippery by the morning's moisture separated the front door from the mooring area. As Eleanor opened the door, I cast a glance straight across the living room and out through the large window on the opposite side of the house. And saw water. Cold Pacific Ocean water drifted east, west, north, and south of every wall and every window. No driveway. No fence. No adjacent buildings. No hanging phone or cable or power lines. There it was: a rancher on pontoons, right in middle of the wilderness. Shadowed by massive red cedars and Western hemlocks, with its image perfectly mirrored in the still, shallow, crystalline water surrounding it, dwarfed by the vertical walls of Vancouver Island's Bedingfield Range, Eleanor and Alistair's solar- and wind-powered float-house only conceded ingress to the rest of the noisy world in the form of a radio, cell phone, and internet airwaves. Aside from the ropes anchoring it on terra firma it was wholly cut off—the epitome of off-grid.

Eleanor welcomed me inside with a smile and a cup of hot coffee and invited me to tour the place. Lush indoor plants and musical gear adorned the unpretentiously snug living room. The kitchen window artfully framed distant cone-shaped mountainous islands and lazy tidal currents. A small garden patch yielded a few precious veggies in plastic pots. A motley crew of barrels and buckets collected rainwater. Despite the infrequent ripples caus- ing the floor underneath the couch to undulate gently, the domesticity of this gently drifting abode oozed an air of serene normality, feeling surprisingly cozy, comfortable, and safe. We could have been in any "normal" house, really.

"Off-grid" is an abused expression. I have heard people say they're "off- grid" if they switch off their cell phone for a day. Others think that any- one living far from the city is "off-the-grid." Some use "off-the-grid" to label people who wish to run and hide, to go incommunicado. Off-grid, in actuality, is a technical expression with a precise meaning. Engineers and architects—to whom the expression can be attributed—call "off-grid" those dwellings that are disconnected from the electricity and natural gas infra- structure servicing a particular region. In this sense we cannot even say that someone is more off-grid than someone else. By this definition, a home (not a person) is either off-grid or on the grid, period. Administrative bod- ies, such as the government of Canada, abide by that definition too. And so does this book.

Off-grid people unduly suffer from a mixed reputation. Some people lionize them as our civilization's last homesteading pioneers. Others prefer to stereotype them as oddballs, loners, hermits, bush hippies, and paranoid survivalists. But Eleanor and Alistair were nothing of the kind. Friendly, warm, and open about their unusual but seemingly idyllic life, neither of them thought of themselves as particularly eccentric. Born in the UK, Alistair explained he had learned not to take for granted the unimaginable beauty of the West Coast. "It never gets old," he told me, "it really puts you in touch with nature's rhythms." The ecology of the place—illustrated with countless stories—was fraught with its own needs, its own cycles, and its own unique expressions. Living off-the-grid puts you in touch with a place in a way that people in the city never could understand, they explained. Eleanor had even lived in a float-house before. She found the untied-up feeling allowed her to live **freely**.[ii] "All I wanted was to look out the window from my kitchen and see water everywhere," she revealed with a glimmer of pride in her achievement.

No real-world home is a land of milk and honey, of course. Alistair's ingenious desalination system—the kind of technological marvel that you'd expect Wiley the Coyote could assemble from one of those legendary ACME kits—had been out of order for some time. And that very morning one of their boat engines failed—hardly a novel event when your entire way of life revolves around saltwater vessels. "And we could do without pesky, nosey summer kayakers," Alistair complained. Not to say that more human contact would be unwelcomed; "I go to town once a week or so," Eleanor admitted, "but it's not enough to maintain strong rapport with people." No one can ever be an island unto themselves; not even on an island home.

I returned to my home the following day wondering whether I too could live like that. I am no stranger to island life, to maintaining my own water supply, growing veggies, living life slower, filtering out unwanted television, social media, or cell phone signals, but I questioned whether I could go the extra mile and sever my ties to the power grid too. I puzzled over whether I had what it takes: the ability to do with less, to rely on myself more, to embrace a little inconvenience. I agonized over my lack of handy skills and my tendency to tackle domestic projects with stress and panic, rather than the required "I-can-fix-it" attitude that I admired in so many tool-box-endowed friends. I tossed and turned, debating ad nauseam whether as a good ethnographer I should indeed "go native" and practice firsthand the life I chose to write about.

The prospect of going off-grid, for most people, rightly feels like taking a leap into the dark. Most of us have become accustomed to flicking on a switch and, in virtue of the technological miracle called electric light, stretching daylight deep into nighttime. Those of us living in the Western Hemisphere, and fortunate enough to pay the monthly bills, are spoiled with the historically unique privilege of being able to microwave our food in seconds, tumble-dry our machine-washed clothes in minutes, and power up dozens of digital gadgets all day long. Our homes can be warmed at the twisting of a thermostat and cooled during the muggiest of summer days. Our store-bought foods can be preserved effortlessly for months in capacious freezers. Our bodily business can be flushed away in an instant, out of sight and out of mind. So, how can we, and why would we, cut off these lifelines? Some might say because our lives may have gotten just a tad too boring, too disconnected from the natural world, too comfortable, too

---

[ii] https://soundcloud.com/innovativeethnographies/eleanor-tofino

lazy, too irresponsible, too crowded, too expensive, too confined, too satu-
rated, too superficial, too fast, too incompetent, and too dependent. There
be may some truth in these critiques, but I didn't know if these arguments
would really compel me and my family to make the leap. Still, I felt the
urge to understand them better, to experience and practice them vicariously
through the everyday lives of full-time off-gridders.

An Ocean for a Fence

Many residents of the Western world have become accustomed to the
simple convenience of the automobile "trunk," or "boot," as they might say
across the Pond. In fact, vehicle manufacturers understand that the larger
and easier to access these compartments are, the happier most drivers will
be. So when sedans and even hatchbacks suffice no more, drivers move on
to the larger trunks of station wagons, SUVs, mini-vans, and pick-up trucks.
Aware of the carrying capacity of these tools, retailers have learned to sell
larger products, to build larger box stores, and to move their operations farther away to the peripheries of our communities.

In fact, the trunk is an ingenious mechanism around which many technologies have evolved. Trunks, for example, rely on the common domestic driveway for their operation. After being used to load up objects at a
store, the trunk is opened by a driver at the end of this short but incredibly
convenient stretch of road connecting the residential street with the front
door—and *voila:* the goods are delivered to shelves, cabinets, and closets
quickly and free of back pain. It doesn't end there, of course. With the additional help of shopping carts, loading dollies, and at times even elevators,
trunks and driveways make shopping and re-supplying our homes a relatively hassle-free job.

But not on Lasqueti Island, British Columbia.

To reach Lasqueti your car must first be marooned on another island,
Vancouver Island. Lasquetians lock up their cars in the French Creek Marina
parking lot, north of Parksville. There, they begin the short trek across the
harbor, down the pier, onto the dock, and finally onto the stern of **M/V
Centurion VII**[iii]—the island's small, passenger-only ferry boat. Surely this
ambulation is nothing compared to a Himalayan expedition, but do imagine
the complexities of their routines. Like many other islanders, Lasquetians
try to minimize their shopping trips to the "big island" to save time, money,
and hassle. Most average about one trip a month. There are virtually no
stores on Lasqueti—save for a seasonal farmers' market and a couple of

---

[iii] http://lifeoffgrid.ca/wp-content/uploads/2014/02/Life-Off-Grid_British-Columbia_
01-1024x682.jpg

shelves' worth of basic goods at the coffee shop—so whenever Lasquetians go "to the other side" they have to carry a lot of stuff.

I arrived at the pier for my first trip to Lasqueti on an early summer morning. Jerry[1] was busy shuttling back and forth at a hurried pace. He had 14 more minutes before the ferry would leave. Besides carrying his own stuff he was also helping Betty, a fellow islander whose gait was much slower. An unseasonably cold summer drizzle was making the dock slippery, so I put aside my field journal and offered Betty a hand. She accepted graciously and asked me to help her carry the remaining large plastic bins as we hurried back toward her Toyota. It was low tide and the dock rested on the pier at a very sharp angle, making the climb to the parking lot steeper and troublesome for her sore hips.

Coolers, boxes, bins, and large cloth bags like Jerry's and Betty's told the stories of islanders who had become used to getting home without the convenience of a trunk connected to a driveway connected to a highway. Hardware, wood panels, bikes, pets, and everything else a trunk could accommodate found space on the small boat for the 45-minute (on a calm day) crossing, waiting to be carried off at False Bay, on the Lasqueti side. "This is it," remarked Jerry, "this is the real first big grid that we're off of: the highway."

A few days before, knowing I wouldn't have the privilege of driving around on the island, I had bought a $99 mountain bike at precisely one of those big box stores and driven it home in my car trunk. I hadn't biked in a few years, and though you don't really forget how to do it, it's actually quite easy to consign to oblivion just how hard it is, especially on hilly, unpaved roads. About an hour after getting dropped off at False Bay, I arrived at Tracey and Grant's place for our scheduled interview, utterly exhausted and drenched in sweat.

Of all aspects of off-grid life on Lasqueti, none seemed more important than what Lasquetians simply called "space"—as the nearly three-hour-long chat with Tracey and Grant revealed. A population density of 4.8 people per square km^2 made it possible to do many off-grid things on the island. It allowed for potentially sustainable groundwater extraction; for many hillside properties to be blessed with creeks and streams, which were exploited for micro-hydroelectricity; for small food crops to be grown; for waste to be disposed of cleanly and unobtrusively; and for firewood to be collected at a renewable rate. Tracey and Grant's place was a case in point. Situated on a 35-acre property, adjacent to a beautiful cove facing southwest, their small cabin made the best possible use of passive solar heating, photovoltaic energy, and all the resources available on their land. For example, in order to collect rainwater for their micro-hydro turbine, they had dug up a pond uphill from the house and channeled outflow with a plastic hose linked to a simple waterwheel spinning and generating electricity 24/7.

Availability of space and the privacy it afforded also allowed them to shower outside, year-round. Fed by gravity from another nearby pond, shower water ran through a coil of black pipe sitting atop a plywood board facing the afternoon sun. "From 3 o'clock to 5 o'clock, in the summer, the sun beats down on that thing," Grant explained, and "heats up the water inside the pipe very hot." That's the time of the day when they would have a shower, using the nearby apple tree branches to hang a few toiletries. So, as the clock inched closer to the mid-afternoon hours I thought I'd leave them alone to their habitual cleansing and slogged back to False Bay in time for the ferry ride home.

"Space," or availability of land, was not a problematic issue on Lasqueti Island. Despite the broader coastal region's inflated real estate market, the utter lack of basic "amenities" such as electricity, natural gas, paved roads, and car access filtered out demand and made it relatively affordable to buy land on the island. As Karl, another islander, put it in a later interview: "You don't have to be nuts to move here, but it sure helps!" Space, however, was bound to play a key role elsewhere. Even though Canada is the second-largest country on the planet and has one of the world's lowest population densities, most of its population is concentrated on a rather narrow strip hugging the US border. Density is quite high in places, and so are the prices of land. To boot, Canada's climate is very diverse. The West Coast's wealth of lumber, its copious water flowing free of ice year-round, its mild climate, and the richness of its soil enabled lifestyles like Tracey and Grant's, and Eleanor and Alistair's—this much was obvious. But where do you find fire-wood in the tundra? How can you buy large pieces of land in urban areas? How do you deal with frozen water in the rest of the country?

As the *M/V Centurion VII* sailed back to Vancouver Island, I crunched some numbers and came to the realization that to truly understand whether the off-grid quest for a better way of life could work everywhere else I had to stretch the grant budget and weave a vast journey across the whole nation in order to meet as many off-gridders as possible. It wouldn't be easy, but I could check a few places off my bucket list for sure.

Tangles of Lines

Myriad lines exit and enter our homes. Wires connect to electricity posts that power our outlets. Cables hook us up to telephone and internet net-works. Other lines reel the world closer to us and our homes closer to the world: paved driveways link us with roads and highways, pipelines tap into common water reserves and flow into municipal sewers, satellite beams reach into the atmosphere to download television signals into our living rooms, and natural gas conduits allow us to stay warm and cook our food.

Together these lines constitute extensive and powerful webs of material cultural significance in which our lives are suspended.

Our homes are not as immobile as they seem. From the phone calls we make to the electricity and fuels that power our cars, from the daily commute to special holiday trips, from the foods we transport to the supermarket to the water we drink and bathe with, and from the materials we use to build our houses to the forms of entertainment and social networking we allow inside our homes, flows of energy constantly pulse and radiate within our mundane existence.[3] These flows have very recently become a concern of social scientists who view their circulation and the operation of the infrastructures on which they rely as part and parcel of complex *assemblages*.[4] We can understand these assemblages as mobile "moorings": "rhyzomatic attachments and reterritorializations" that "configure and enable mobilities," or, in other words, "transmitters through which mobilization of locality are performed and re-arrangements of place and scale materialized."[5]

Though historically all societies have relied on various forms of energy and fuels, what is arguably unique to our current society is how deeply we depend on the operation of the vast assemblages that make energy and fuel easily available and their myriad applications possible.[6] Made up of human and non-human, mineral and vegetable, raw and manufactured materials, these assemblages function as human history's largest-ever networks of flows. In common talk we refer to these assemblages as "grids." Grids can be viewed as socio-technical networks affording us with economies of "flows of energy that irradiate, condense, intersect, build, and ripple."[7] These "meshworks"[8] are "developing bundle[s] of institutions and technologies, understood as non-exclusive and diverse organizations of knowledge-discipline-perception circulating in a constantly shifting 'parliament of things': embodied subjects, machines, texts and metaphors and the like."[9]

Grids of light, speed, and power can make life comfortable and convenient,[10] but they are also troublesome companions.[11] One key source of such trouble resides in the concentration of politico-economic power that grids rely upon, with consequences for the costs and control of their utilization. Another source of trouble lies in the over-dependence patterns in which they hook their users, resulting in the global exploitation of natural—often non-renewable—resources. These and related troubles are the forces that have pushed some people to go "off-grid."

Off-grid means being disconnected from electricity and natural gas networks, but the reality on the ground is a bit more complex. Off-grid households capable of generating their own heat and electricity are often also intent on harvesting water, growing food, and disposing of their own sewage and waste without the aid of municipal infrastructures. These homes typically also have a cautious attitude toward communication links, and may therefore be cut off from telephone landlines or television cables. At times they may be in remote places, even off the road. All these are interesting lifestyle choices that no student can neglect, so while throughout this book we maintain the technical definition as a necessary and sufficient condition for being off the grid, we also remain interested in how the total or partial absence of these other "grids" shapes these households' everyday life.

In light of this, we view off-grid dwelling as a "tactic"[12]: an often opposi-tional (but also often negotiated, necessary, and contradictory) everyday life practice. Off-grid dwelling tactics are "infinitesimal transformations," "errant trajectories" constantly "jostling for position[ing]"[13] and repositioning, which wind up "weaving"[14] new assemblages of light, speed, and power. By delink-ing one's home from one or more grids, a household makes a more or less explicit "technological choice"[15] for a different type of social relations, a dif-ferent way of life, and a different collective "synchronicity"[16] with the rest of society. Why and how this lifestyle takes place is the focus of this book.

*　*　*

All I knew about off-grid living after the first couple of outings in the field was that it was a radically unique existential quest: a simple search—through many different means—for a better way of life. The importance of such a quest is something I understood quite clearly from both personal and work experience. I had spent years, during a previous fieldwork project, try-ing to grasp why and how people sought a better way of life on small islands off the West Coast of Canada[17]—and ended up moving to one of them in the process. Though I lived in a BC Hydro-connected home, the off-grid lifestyle resonated with me at an impulsive and intuitive level. But at the same time it seemed so strange that a better way of life could be pursued in the face of so many challenges that potentially impaired the comfort, effi-ciency, and convenience of our modern homes.

Unabashedly ignorant about wattage, amperage, passive solar design, and inverters—to name only a few mind-boggling details of these homes—the first interviews had yielded the feeling that I was in it up to my eyeballs. I quickly realized not only that the learning curve was steep, but also that the sights and sounds of off-grid homes presented serious challenges to the imagination. From lavishly decorated outhouses and **gorgeous barns**[iv] to hand-cranked clothes wringers and **warm greenhouses**,[v] the technologies

---

[iv] http://lifeoffgrid.ca/wp-content/uploads/2014/02/Life-Off-Grid_British-Columbia_09-682x1024.jpg

[v] http://lifeoffgrid.ca/wp-content/uploads/2014/02/Life-Off-Grid_British-Columbia_03-1024x682.jpg

and the architectural details of off-grid homes had to be seen and heard to be believed and appreciated. And their dwellers—often bold and unique characters—had to be "met," however vicariously, through a camera. So I posted a want ad for a research assistant job on the university's website. A few days later I phoned one of the applicants—Jon, an MA student in communication and a professional photographer—and asked him whether he was interested in coming along with me to all of Canada's 13 provinces and territories to film and photograph the fieldwork over the next two years. "Yes, I think I can fit that in my schedule," he coolly answered from his part-time tug-boat job, summoning every single ounce of his English aplomb in order to keep calm and carry on the interview.

An avid camper, fisherman, nature-lover, and all-around outdoors enthusiast, Jon showed up for the first day of the most unusual student-job in the world with bicycle panniers full of cameras, lenses, batteries, mini tripods, and an iPhone with an alarm setting that sounded like a submarine. He also brought a toothbrush, toothpaste, ear plugs, and underarm deodorant—incidentally the very same four toiletries I had harvested from my home bathroom. I, on the other hand, had been in charge of stocking the pantry of our rented off-grid cabin on Lasqueti. My backpack contained Clif bars, Kashi bars, dried pineapple rings, trail mix, instant noodles, beef jerky, and juice. Jon took the Clif bars and I the Kashi, and we divvied up the rest, hoping the trip's budget would allow for a couple of burgers at the only local pub. Once quickly settled, we headed off for the road.

Inhabiting Place, Incorporating Materials

There were only three lines stretching out of Daniel's home. First, there were two invisible but very important communication lines comprised of electro-magnetic waves that transmitted a cellular phone and a radio-based internet signal. Then, there was a steep, unpaved, rocky lane linking his backyard to Lasqueti's main road (so steep that I broke my cheap plastic bike pedal trying to climb it, which, thankfully, Daniel replaced later with one of his many spares). But absent from Daniel's house were other lines typically found in conventional homes—such as wires conducting grid-supplied electricity, and mains channeling fresh water in and taking human waste out to municipal sewers.

The building itself—an absolute marvel of vernacular architecture and ingenuity—resembled a tall, wooden tower evocative of a Nordic medieval style. Because he had ample access to cheap lumber at work, but limited access to roofing material, he had found it more convenient to create space vertically and thus minimize roof-related expenses—the result being a building of five stories, each measuring roughly 20 feet by 20 feet. Over the next two years of our travels it would remain unchallenged as Canada's only off-grid skyscraper.

Daniel was born and raised on the island and still lived there with his wife and baby daughter. Until recently he "used to *really* live off-the-grid," he told us as we walked around his front yard under the lukewarm rays of a shy June sun. He used to have no phone of any kind, no internet, and no electricity. Compared to living with candles as he used to do, his current home—powered by solar, with no backup generator—was nothing special, he found. "Back then, that was something else altogether." "Living off-grid is not for everybody," he added pensively. "If you want to understand if you can pull it off, you should try it and go for a week or two without electricity of any kind. No appliances, no phone, no internet, nothing at all. If you can make it, and if you enjoy it, then you can be off-the-grid, I mean, *really* off-the-grid," once again emphasizing the word "really" as if infrastructural disconnection was the stuff of competitions.

The coast of British Columbia bursts with small islands and remote coastal villages disconnected from the BC Hydro grid. Lasqueti is only one of many such islands that have never seen power lines. However, and uniquely, several years ago Lasquetians were offered a chance to hook up. They rejected it. Living without power bills, enjoying a strong sense of privacy, maintaining self-reliance and resilience in the face of the frequent storms that bring power lines down on the Georgia Strait, and avoiding the need to upgrade homes to the utility-mandated standards of advanced building codes, was precisely what they desired—much to the chagrin and surprise of the large monopolistic corporation. For a long time Lasquetians had simply lived without provincially supplied electricity and all the thrills and frills that come with it. And most of them **liked it**[vi] just fine that way.

As Daniel told his version of this story, Jon and I silently began to wonder where in the world we had landed. Gentle, exurban Gabriola Island, my home, was only a few slivers of water down the Salish Sea. Busy Vancouver, Jon's birthplace, was also close enough from Squitty Bay to be reached in a single day's worth of paddling. Yet both places felt a whole galaxy away. It was as if we had reached the Annapurna Range of Nepal. As in the Himalayas, life on Lasqueti felt unpretentious yet not unexamined, laborious and yet simple, busy and yet not hectic, involved and yet not stressful. It felt as if Lasquetians were in their own time zone, operating a hand-wound clock that marked the rhythms of a life pace of their very setting. An islander had captured this feeling with a few carefully chosen words the day before: "If you want everything to happen quickly, you are in the wrong place."

---

vi. http://vimeo.com/30635900

But besides a keen appreciation of slowness, Lasquetians also seemed to cultivate an aesthetic of quiet and darkness. Tall, **lush vegetation**[vii] dimmed sunlight and hampered the movement of sound waves effortlessly. The foot-passenger-only ferry muffled car traffic noise. Limited power curtailed commerce and annihilated neon lights. The sheer absence of public street lighting rendered the place pitch-dark—indeed so uniformly tenebrous that suppliers of the only vending machine at the pub had even found it profitable to sell flashlights and batteries. The dark evenings at our cabin moved slowly. We read books, often seated on a log on the beach below, until dusk gave way to night and our minds and eyes gave up on the day.

Both Jon and I felt it would have been easy to fall irreparably in love with Lasqueti, had it not been for the biking. Or maybe the problem was just with cheap, heavy mountain bikes. Jon's crossover road/mountain bike seemed to handle the terrain slightly better than mine, though both of us were constantly preoccupied with double-checking our tires for flats and making **minor repairs**[viii] with improvised tools and parts. Continuously having to dodge feral goats and puddles of mud did not exactly put our minds at ease on the road either. To boot, our lovely cabin, the **Driftwood Cove Beach House**,[ix] was situated at the very southern end of the island and our interview plan—and I use the word "plan" sardonically—every single day seemed to call for morning interviews in the north end, followed by early afternoon ones in the south end, and late afternoon visits back on the northern tip of the island. I had no one to blame for that but myself, which made logging 50 km all those days even more aggravating.

Our northern end visit with Dave was planned, unsurprisingly, for the late afternoon: a brilliantly conceived time to master an incredibly precipitous hill that not even our lowest gears could conquer. Once the road ceased being useful the walking trail to Dave's house—carved out of low-hanging conifers overgrown over basaltic bedrock—proved to be barely wide enough for our backpacks, leading us to wonder how anyone could have shipped here the material necessary to build a house.

Tall, lean, confident Dave was a committed, intelligent, well-informed environmentalist who divided his time between Vancouver and Lasqueti. He had lived on Lasqueti for nine years at the time, and spent most of his days there building his dream eco-friendly home. For the first six years he had lived in a tent pegged toward the bottom of his property, and for the last three years

---

[vii.] http://lifeoffgrid.ca/wp-content/uploads/2014/02/Life-Off-Grid_British-Columbia_08-1024x682.jpg

[viii.] http://lifeoffgrid.ca/wp-content/uploads/2014/02/Life-Off-Grid_British-Columbia_04-1024x682.jpg

[ix.] http://beachhouse.driftwoodcove.ca/

he had upgraded to a **cob shed**,[x] to which he was now adding a greenhouse. In the meantime he was also working toward building the final home just down the path. As we sat down around the outdoor table to discuss off-grid living, Dave offered us a plate of greens from his garden, a snack that—given our rapidly dwindling supply of Clif and Kashi bars—was truly life-saving.

But there was little time for munchies, as we soon began to scuttle around the 11 1/3-acre property to understand the functionality of his strategically scattered operations. Dave told us he wanted to rely on renewable resources and to pass on his skills, values, and technologies to his six-year-old daughter. For her the future would be much different—he predicted as we walked—because life on the planet won't be the same as we've known. Dave's argument wasn't driven by paranoia. It was hard to disagree with him: read any newspaper or watch any newscast and you won't help feeling the same way. Dwindling supplies of energy and food resources, a fast-growing worldwide population, and an increasing appetite for a consumerist way of life that could be sustained only by exploiting several planets, seem to make for a perfectly volatile and explosive mix, striking fear and anxiety for our collective future. Off-grid living was just a simple response to all this. If there was any core political component to the off-grid quest for a better life it was the sense that, by living somewhat more independently from this world run amok, at least you could feel you were *doing* something about it.

We began our tour from the highest and sunniest point atop the rocky hill, where Dave had placed—right on the ground, resting on the bare rock—two small metal- and glass-sided containers. Inside each of the containers was a steaming pot that had formed a great deal of condensation on the glass cover. As Jon and I stared, looking as if we had caught sight of two steaming gremlins, Dave excused himself, interrupting the conversation as he bent down to pick up each of the two quixotic containers. He lifted them gingerly and moved them a few feet. He didn't have to be extra perceptive to sense that our jaws had dropped.

"Guys, you've seen these before, right?"

"Yeah, kind of . . ." I mumbled, ". . . actually, no."

"They're solar ovens. They work like a normal oven. I'm just cooking dinner in them. You see, the water is going to be boiling soon for the pasta in this one, and I'm making tomato sauce in the other one." The trick, he explained, was to move them around throughout the day as the sun played peak-a-boo with the trees as it moved east to west. Depending on cloud cover and temperature it could take anywhere from an hour to a full day to cook a "normal" meal. I wish I had inquired about the preparation of a Thanksgiving dinner.

---

[x] http://lifeoffgrid.ca/wp-content/uploads/2014/02/Life-Off-Grid_British-Columbia_05-682x1024.jpg

Sun ovens were not the only off-grid tools that required being moved around in different ways throughout the day and the seasons in order to maintain harmony with the movement of the sun, the temperatures, and the winds. The angle of solar panels had to be adjusted for maximum efficiency, especially at northern latitudes, for example. And for those who owned them, solar shower-bags needed to be shifted around, among many other tasks. "I plan every movement very carefully," Dave confided as we started walking toward the bottom of the hill, "whenever I go up or down the path I want to make sure I pick up or drop off whatever I need to while I'm on my way to doing something else." And we could see why: the trail down to his cob oven was narrow and steep, and even steeper was the one up to his **micro-hydro**[xi] station and 3,000-gallon water tank—which, we learned, he "rolled" down to its current location through the bushes from the upper road.

Indeed, living in an off-grid homestead was an exercise in geographical choreography. From making the most of a stream for micro-hydro power, to integrating passive solar into a house's active heating system, and from exploiting gravity to feed water into domestic pipes, to maximizing the fertility of a garden, designing and maintaining an efficient off-grid homestead was like line-dancing with nature and technology.

But of all these movements nothing impressed me more than Dave's bicycle-powered transport. Few, very few, off-gridders across Canada were able or willing to surrender their automobile. Indeed we would only meet less than half a dozen carless ones over the next two years. In part this is because not all off-gridders practiced their lifestyle in order to reduce their carbon footprint; in larger part it is because off-grid life was generally practiced in rural locations that had no public transport. Unfazed by the latter challenge, Dave relied on a recumbent bike to commute the 4 km to "downtown" Lasqueti, where he boarded the bike on the ferry, and then from French Creek to Departure Bay in Nanaimo—for a treacherous 39.7 km in the emergency lane of busy Highway 19. At Departure Bay he would then catch the ferry to Horseshoe Bay, on the mainland. There he pedaled up and down the even busier Upper Levels Highway for the remaining 20 km to downtown Vancouver, as busy urban drivers whizzed by him at speeds of over 100 km/h. "A recumbent bike is great for your upper body," Dave remarked, "it's so comfortable that at times I almost fall asleep on it." If it had come equipped with a GPS detecting feral goats and mud puddles, I would have bought it from him and napped my way back to the cabin.

* * *

[xi] http://lifeoffgrid.ca/wp-content/uploads/2014/02/Life-Off-Grid_British-Columbia_06-1024x682.jpg

A place "owes its character to the experiences it affords to those who spend time there—to the sights, sounds, and indeed smells that constitute its specific ambience. And these in turn depend on the kinds of activities in which its inhabitants engage," anthropologist Tim Ingold[18] has observed. The experiences and activities in which off-grid home inhabitants engaged were undoubtedly different from those we, dwellers of grid-tied environments, are accustomed to. And as a result, so are our respective places. It is this simple observation that has guided our entire interpretation of the cultural, geographical, and socio-anthropological significance of the off-grid lifestyle.

The different experiences and activities shaping our different domestic lifestyles begin with the everyday movements of the fuels and energy resources employed to operate our homes. Off-gridders, it was obvious, needed to engage in unique movements and activities in order to procure, channel, generate, store, and utilize those fuels and energy. It is those practices that ended up lending their dwellings their particular ambience. Whether it was wheel-barrowing propane tanks through bushy trails, channeling creeks into waterwheels, directing urine at rhubarb plants instead of flushing it down toilet bowls, or carrying groceries down a floating dock, living off-grid meant moving around and inside one's home differently. Off-grid living was therefore a unique set of *material practices* through which domestic lives were woven together in original ways. This required, on our part as interpreters, a different, material understanding of lifestyle: an understanding informed by relational and non-representational theoretical ideas.

Materials are not synonymous with materiality, according to one of the chief proponents of these ideas, Tim Ingold[19]: materiality is an abstract property, symbolically extracted from objects, conceptualized, and rendered inert through analytical thought. Materials, on the other hand, act and move without the mediation of our ideas and metaphors, he has argued. For Ingold, materials are the media, substances, and surfaces that "partake in the very process of the world's ongoing generation and regeneration."[20] Though they vary greatly in their properties (like viscosity, mass, density, etc.), fuels such as oil, natural gases, and biomass are obvious examples of *substances*. Water, a quintessential source of energy, is also a substance. The air we breathe and its currents in the sky, as well as the light (and warmth) reflecting upon the *surface* of Earth are different kinds of materials: they comprise the *media* in which we exist, move, and perceive. Though media, substances, and surfaces are different from one another, they all are active agents of a world in constant motion, undergoing continuous transformation. "Wherever life is going on," Ingold has remarked, these materials "are relentlessly on the move—flowing, scraping, mixing, and mutating."[21]

Materials, like energy and fuels, are therefore life forces continuously acting and interacting with one another. Electricity flows, air masses blow, bodies of water stream. These forces aren't abstract; their workings are real and consequential—consisting of their flows, their kinetic doing. Water *is* its flowing, the "wind *is* its blowing," Ingold has observed.[22] Materials of all kinds are "hives of activity"[23] that exercise their agency in virtue of their own spontaneous movements and the movements for which humans co-opt them. Our co-optation of these materials is what our *habitation* of the world consists of.[24] In co-opting them we do not arrest them, however. Rather, we put them to use; we incorporate them into our daily life. Water still continues to flow through a waterwheel, the wind continues to blow past a **wind tower**,[xii] fuels continue to live long after burning in the form of heat and carbon dioxide. In co-opting materials for the sake of generating power, heat, light, speed, and comfort and convenience we become engulfed, encompassed, and at times even swept away in their very movements.[25] In other words, we move together with materials; we become incorporated together with them through a common environment. It is of these specific movements and processes of mutual incorporation that habitation of the world consists of.[26] It is of different ways of incorporation that different forms of habitation consist of.

Different places are different bundles of movement and activities[27]—different meshworks[28] in which people and resources are woven together[29]—incorporated into one another. Different home inhabitants incorporate their different places in many different ways. For instance, by flicking a switch to turn on an electric lamp at my home I am in a way incorporating the kinetic power of water channeled into dams, waterwheels, and turbines by my utility provider. Someone who lives off the electrical grid had to incorporate the same essential resource (e.g., water) and assemble a tool (e.g., a turbine) to generate electricity. But the key difference relies in the way our respective bodily activities unfold. For me, a rather typical consumer of electricity, flicking on a switch is a rather mindless and uninvolved activity. BC Hydro has already taken care of the task of generating electricity, so I just need to get off my chair. For an off-gridder, flicking on a switch required a different orientation: life off-grid generally demanded a much greater *involvement* in the generation and use of energy resources and fuels. Indeed, for someone like Dave, electricity had to be first assembled by way of making use of whatever was at hand in the place where he dwelled and solving concerns as they presented themselves with the passing of the seasons and the movements of the clouds and sun, thus exercising caution, judgment, creativity, skill, and physical effort.

[xii.] http://lifeoffgrid.ca/wp-content/uploads/2014/02/Life-Off-Grid_British-Columbia_02-1024x682.jpg

As Ingold has noted, places are an outcome of the practices of their inhabitants; they in fact "arise within the current of their involved activity, in the specific relational contexts of their practical engagement with their surroundings."[30] Because places are incorporated through these tasks, we can think of a place as a *taskscape*.[31] Everyday living is an ensemble of tasks and goals, carried out in relation to the resources and tools available, as well as our practical orientations and skills. Living off-grid was a very peculiar taskscape, it seemed. Virtually every off-grid living task required choreographing bodily movements and activities with the naturally occurring movements of energy resources and with the technologies available to harness them, channel them, and incorporate them into domestic lives in order to provide heat, light, cleanliness, nutrition, information, or power. Thus, off-grid taskscapes required and enabled unique resources, rhythms, costs, effects, speeds, and lifestyles.

Habitation is the central theoretical idea behind all our arguments in this book. The principle of habitation is based on the idea that every organism, including every person, is immersed into the lifeworld as an inescapable condition of existence.[32] From such immersion and the relations that emerge, "the world continually comes into being around the inhabitant, and its manifold constituents take on significance through their incorporation into a regular pattern of life activity."[33] Therefore, by strategically incorporating the world into their existence, inhabitants of off-grid dwellings became bound together with these materials and with their places, becoming habituated to particular matrixes of movements and practices. Like a mariner wayfaring the seas, the off-grid inhabitant "watches, listens, and feels as he [sic] goes, his entire being alert to the countless cues that, at every moment, prompt the slightest adjustments to his bearing."[34] This involvement is how an off-gridder generated her place and in the end her own way of life.

But off-grid living also allows us to challenge and question what we so routinely take for granted: our ordinary domestic life in the modern, on-grid world. It sensitizes us to a different understanding of domestic assemblages than the one we are used to. It forces us to come to terms with life in a domestic world completely or partially devoid of the presence of large infrastructures. It pushes us to question how else life could be. It invites us to rethink what our future—a future that will require a much greater reliance on renewable resources and a much more intelligent utilization of life-giving materials—might feel like.

Off-grid living allows us to understand how alternative socio-technical assemblages can be produced with the most basic and raw materials of life. Off-grid living, thus even more than on-grid living, epitomizes how life is a form of production—that is, a coming into being together with different materials—and how such production is an ensemble of activities made of blazing trails and following new and old paths. A *way* of life after

all, to conclude with Ingold, is a direction, an orientation, a line of movement along which places are incorporated, "skills developed, observations
made, and understandings grown."[35] Perhaps, then, studying off-grid living
was about revealing the types of understandings, observations, and skills
required of the rest of us if we truly wish to re-establish our relation with our
endangered environments. Perhaps it was about revealing the ways of life of
an alternatively sentient body—a body that is "at once both perceiver and
producer"—a body able to re-trace for the better "the paths of the world's
becoming in the very course of contributing to its ongoing renewal."[36]

Notes

1. Though Jerry and Betty are fictitious names, most of the names used in this book are
   real, as explicitly preferred and consented to by off-gridders.
2. Compare it to London, England's density: 5,285/km².
3. Thrift, 1996.
4. Thrift, 1996, 2008; Urry, 2000, 2008.
5. Hannam, Sheller, and Urry, 2006:3.
6. Thrift, 1996; Urry, 2008. Also see Borgmann, 1987; Heidegger, 1982.
7. Lingis, 1992:3.
8. Ingold, 2007a.
9. Thrift, 1996:263.
10. Thrift, 1996.
11. Bennett, 2005; Bijker and Law, 1991.
12. deCerteau, 1984.
13. deCerteau, 1984:xviii.
14. Ingold, 2000b.
15. Lemonnier, 2002.
16. Edensor, 2006a.
17. Vannini, 2012.
18. Ingold, 2000:192.
19. Ingold, 2011:32.
20. Ingold, 2011:26.
21. Ingold, 2011:28.
22. Ingold, 2011:17.
23. Ingold, 2011:29.
24. Ingold, 2011:115–125.
25. Ingold, 2011:134–135, 138–139.
26. Ingold, 2011:31.
27. Ingold, 2011:14, 29.
28. Ingold, 2011:63–94, 2007: 72–103.
29. Ingold, 2011: 177–207.
30. Ingold, 2000:186.
31. Ingold, 2000:199.
32. Ingold, 2011:111–120, 168.
33. Ingold, 2000:153.
34. Ingold, 2007b:78.
35. Ingold, 2011:12.
36. Ingold, 2011:12.

Brian and Water Pump.[i]

[i.] For more photos, visit lifeoffgrid.ca.

2
THE PULL OF REMOVE

Air Canada Flight 289 touched down on Whitehorse Airport's lone runway on time at 1 p.m. The fuselage door opened to a crisp north-easterly that stung the Yukon's **autumn-infused**,[ii] Alpine-scented air remorselessly. While Jon collected our luggage I secured the keys to a rental Chevy and a couple of road maps. We swiftly stocked up on groceries in town and then headed for the **Alaska/Klondike Highway**[iii] with our compass set for the **Wheaton River Wilderness Resort**[iv]—a 45-minute drive from the pretty and surprisingly cosmopolitan territorial capital. The first outside-of-BC trip had begun, employing a travel format that would remain essentially unchanged for the next two years.

The standard operating procedure was simple. Every trip would last approximately one week; that was the time frame both the budget and our endurance would allow. Each trip would feature about one daily interview—though we ranged anywhere from a weekly minimum of four to a record 22 interviewees. This strategy, we knew very well, would yield first and foremost breadth. Classical ethnographers generally seek depth, rather than breadth, by settling down on one particular site for an extended period of time ranging from a few months to years. As appealing as that longitudinal depth might have been, we dismissed the feasibility of this approach early on. Given the numerous differences at play—off-gridders' varying motives, economic capital, and lifestyles, as well as differing technologies, climate, land availability, and so on—we felt

---

[ii] http://lifeoffgrid.ca/wp-content/uploads/2013/11/Life-Off-Grid_Yukon_03-1024x682.jpg
[iii] http://lifeoffgrid.ca/wp-content/uploads/2013/11/Life-Off-Grid_Yukon_11-1024x682.jpg
[iv] http://wheatonriver.net/

that by concentrating on only one off-grid household, or a limited number
of cases, we would not have been able to paint a sufficiently diverse portrait.
We also doubted whether we would have been able to stay at anyone's home
for more than a few days. Instead, by being mobile and meeting as many off-
gridders as possible, we thought we could achieve depth indirectly through
breadth—that is, by combining multiple fragments of everyday life gleaned
from all our 200 interviews into a coherent but diverse bricolage.

Our standard operating procedure was also quite routinized. We'd schedule every house visit in advance using email and the phone to coordinate
details. At best, every such correspondence would generally yield an address
and colorful directions (e.g., "turn left where the power lines end"); at worst,
it would yield nothing but longitudinal and latitudinal coordinates on a
Google Earth screenshot. Armed with such information we would then
embark onto often long journeys between destinations, equipped with the
hope that the weather would cooperate (traffic was hardly ever a concern)
and that at the end of each long driveway we'd face a rifle-less human being
armed only with an agreeable disposition.

Often, though, at the end of those driveways we'd first run into canine
guards. The salivating Shepherds manning the gate of our Wheaton River
rental cabin looked like they had scared away grizzlies much larger than our
sedan so I slammed on the brakes at the very first growl. As I was behind
the wheel I coaxed Jon into opening the gate while I stayed inside in case
we had to peel off. Luckily, it was an unnecessary precaution.

Robert, Carmen, and their two lovely kids lived off-grid behind that gate
with their several canine companions—equally well meaning, it would turn
out—at the end of a momentously long driveway set amid skinny, **growth-
impaired timbers**.[v] Like a handful of other off-grid families across the
country, they had enough acreage and spare lumber to build not one, but two
off-grid dwellings, so they rented one out to wilderness-seeking tourists and
wayward spirits like us. Carmen—like her husband a Swiss émigré—briskly
showed us around our cabin and taught us how to use propane lights and
the cooking stove, how to deal with the lack of electricity, where to store our
cooler to keep it (and us) safe from bears' pre-hibernation appetite, how to
light the Franklin woodstove, and where to find **the wood**.[vi] Though the
outhouse wasn't far, since we were both boys we could always easily help
ourselves to the bushes for urination. As for running water, there was plenty
of it in the aforementioned **river**.[vii] Saturday would be sauna day, and if we
fancied washing up that would be a good time to do so.

[v] http://lifeoffgrid.ca/wp-content/uploads/2013/11/Life-Off-Grid_Yukon_10-1024x682.jpg
[vi] http://lifeoffgrid.ca/wp-content/uploads/2013/11/Life-Off-Grid_Yukon_02-1024x682.jpg
[vii] http://lifeoffgrid.ca/wp-content/uploads/2013/11/Life-Off-Grid_Yukon_01-1024x682.jpg

As the sun went down Jon and I broiled some char and opened a bottle of spirit-raising Yukon Jack, idly chatting away about why, when Carmen demonstrated how to use pepper spray to fend off ursine attacks, she had stretched her right arm way over her head and pointed the nozzle several feet up in the air. Both Jon and I turned in for the night trying not to dream about how big these formidable beasts could actually be.

The next morning I drove us south to meet Brian and Susan, some 150 km away. As one of our several common character traits would turn out to be a hankering for routine, I got into the habit of piloting while Jon always settled in as navigator—giving me directions while recharging batteries with the preciously useful cigarette lighter and transferring heavy visual files from the cameras onto his Mac.

We had been referred to Brian and Susan by a governmental territorial agency dealing with renewable energy. Though finding off-gridders would seem to be an oxymoronic enterprise, between various organizations, renewable energy retailers, business websites like Robert and Carmen's, personal blogs, or stories in local presses and other media reports—not to mention the number of off-gridders who actually invited us in the first place—the only difficulty would be assembling reasonably paced interview itineraries.

Our interviews would also generally unfold in a ritualistic way. After shaking hands and dealing with informed consent procedures, I would begin with a battery of conversational questions about the "whys" behind the off-grid lifestyle, followed by an extended tour of a house and the rest of the property for a hands-on guide to "how" various technologies worked. I typically worked with my ears, while Jon employed his eyes, mediated by whichever type of recording device (if any) was preferred by the off-gridder du jour.

"Why indeed . . ." Brian repeated my first question pensively. "Well, there is a sense of . . . 'let's see how little I can get by with,' you know?"

"So, that's why you do it?"

"Yeah, it's sort of . . ." Brian replied, "let's see how basic I can make my life, or, how simple I can make my life and still be happy and comfortable." That's the guiding philosophy, he explained, as he took a small bite off the tomato-and-cheese toast Susan had just fixed for lunch in their propane-powered oven. But the word "philosophy" did not seem to suffice. It was something larger, more complex, and yet simple, he indicated.

Brian started "simple, real simple." After he relocated to the Yukon from Vancouver Island in the early 1980s to work for the government, he settled into a rough cabin in the forest. A couple of years later he moved to the shore of Lake Laberge—a widening of the Yukon River surrounded by dry hills and a half dozen homes. Lake Laberge felt like home. He eventually met Susan and dedicated himself to raising goats there. Now in his sixties—though I never asked, that's what his bushy beard and unkempt silver hair led me to assume—Brian had been farming for the last 20 years, growing a few hardy crops and selling cheese at the farmers' market and at the Alpine Bakery in Whitehorse. Because of the distance from the nearest access to the grid, installing all the necessary power poles would have been impossibly expensive. So they decided to make their own electricity with solar panels.

There was a gentle quality about Brian that I couldn't quite grasp as he spoke. Perhaps it was his warm blue eyes—which never seemed to make eye contact, always escaping into the distance, seemingly looking for the right words. Or maybe it was his calm, accepting demeanor, which made me feel unhurried and welcomed. We were bound to find out soon.

The lake served as their **water supply**,[viii] Brian explained. "We used to haul water in buckets," but that method became tiring as he aged, so he upgraded to an electric pump channeling water through a freeze-resistant soft plastic hose. The water was collected inside a large tank under the house and then purified by a UV-ray light system. That was the simple part. The hard part was, and still is, the Yukon climate. During winter the lake freezes, so Brian needs to walk on the icy surface, about 100 meters from the beach, to drill a hole. That is where he inserts the hose, protected by a wooden cover meant to keep snow away. Depending on the temperatures, which regularly dip as low as −30°C (−22°F) or −40°C (−40°F), he needs to drill a fresh hole every few days. "But the shoulder season is really the tough part," Brian added in his unworried speech pattern. "You see," he continued, "that's when the ice isn't frozen solid offshore yet, but it's frozen at the shore, where the hose is." A bit of a standoff: too shallow at the shore to use the pump, and not frozen solid enough offshore to walk too far. Didn't this sound like the perfect epitome of a simple way of life?

But there was another complication. Brian was, and had always been, entirely *blind*—we were stunned to learn half way through the interview. A computer program allowed him to use email, a speaking charge-control display allowed him to monitor how much energy was stored in the house batteries, and all his other senses allowed him to live the simple life he craved. The key part of the simple lifestyle, he explained, is that "this is just a lovely place to live, you're close to nature, totally quiet, if you want something done, **you just do it yourself**."[ix]

Voluntary Simplicity?

When Brian and other off-gridders spoke of living a simple life, they evoked—some explicitly, some without actually naming it—a philosophy of "voluntary simplicity:" a set of values based on frugality, sustainability,

---

viii. http://lifeoffgrid.ca/wp-content/uploads/2013/11/Life-Off-Grid_Yukon_06-1024x682.jpg
ix. http://soundcloud.com/innovativeethnographies/brian-why

self-sufficiency, and resilience. Voluntary simplicity is not a recent invention, as it draws from ascetic influences present in Puritanism, Quakerism, Confucianism, Jainism, Taoism, Hinduism, Islam, and especially Buddhism.[1] Its diffusion and uptake, however, are quite contemporary. Fueled by currently *en vogue* impulses to hamper the reach of consumerism, by the urgency of reducing dependence on non-renewables, and also by the more bourgeois desire for "downshifting," voluntary simplicity has gained many followers in the last three decades. Its popularity is due in no small part to the writings of Duane Elgin, who penned the movement's manifesto in 1981 and followed it up with three successful spinoff books.

The "voluntary" part refers to a deliberate act of choice: an awakening leading to a lifestyle conversion. The awakening consists of gaining the critical awareness that global society has spun out of control. Its voracious addiction to consumption and to the resources necessary for the production and distribution of ostensibly unnecessary goods lies at the basis of what Elgin calls "involuntary complexity." Involuntary complexity is a modern syndrome marked by waste, stress, greed, clutter, pollution, anxiety, lack of personal control, economic inequality, and social fragmentation. Gaining critical consciousness of this condition leads to a revelation that the complexity characterizing global capitalism is not a result of freedom and choice. We are instead "running on automatic," argues Elgin, and we need to wake up and "live more consciously."

"Simplicity," the second cornerstone of the lifestyle, refers to a willed curtailment of the so-called unnecessary complications of everyday life. "To live with simplicity," writes Elgin, "is to unburden our lives—to live more lightly, cleanly, aerodynamically"[2] in the ways we work, consume, dwell, relate, learn, and entertain ourselves. Simplicity is about modesty, but it is not to be confused with poverty. Poverty is "involuntary simplicity"; it is not deliberately chosen and it is repressing, hopeless, passive, helpless, and degrading, whereas simplicity is consciously chosen, liberating, self-empowering, creative, beautiful, and functional.[3] Simplicity consists of voluntary choices, such as to buy less, consume sustainably and ethically, eat more local and natural foods, reduce clutter, recycle and re-use, practice creativity, participate in cooperatives, take a more active role in self-education, use renewable energy resources, prefer smaller-scale forms of living, and develop skills based on the values of self-reliance.

Elgin's ideas were gradually adopted by people worldwide, and these groups and individuals attracted the attention of many researchers. For example, Grigsby[4] found that voluntary simplifiers are not only concerned about the perils of environmental degradation, the vicious logic of consumerism, and the ideology of competitive careerism and its accompanying materialism, but also are preoccupied with the importance of restoring communitarian values intended to make interpersonal relations and collective life more equitable and less self-centered. These values also characterized the homesteaders examined by Kneale-Gould,[5] though she also found that the self-sufficiency ideals inherent in the back-to-the-land movement took on an especially spiritual tone in the US. The voluntary simplicity of homesteaders, she argued, was a response to diffused cultural and personal problems of meaninglessness. Similarly concerned with the sociological significance of voluntary simplicity, Cherrier and Murray[6] found that followers of this social movement underwent a personal identity transformation focused on bringing significance to an otherwise inauthentic and commodified existence.

Many academics portray voluntary simplicity as a rational, instrumental, calculated choice. For example Leonard-Barton[7] viewed it as "the degree to which an individual selects a lifestyle intended to maximize his/her direct control over daily activities and to minimize his/her consumption and dependency [. . .]. This choice is voluntary; this low-consumption and low-energy lifestyle is often selected by individuals who are financially able to afford a more luxurious way of living." The intentionality and voluntarism present in the literature is especially explicit among those who have studied the motives, attitudes, and lifestyle satisfaction of voluntary simplifiers. For instance Etzioni[8] found that voluntary simplicity is an expression of "free will": "a choice a successful corporate lawyer, not a homeless person, faces." For Chhetri and colleagues,[9] the self-empowering simplification of life by "relatively affluent, highly successful, middle-aged people choosing to live a less work-oriented lifestyle" resulted in a broader process of "downshifting"—a trend typical of a broader exurbanization movement that allowed people to take more control over their lives. As well, Zavestovski[10] and Huneke[11] found voluntary simplifiers in the US to live more intrinsically satisfying, authentic, healthier, mindful lives focused on making ethical consumption choices. Similar findings and assumptions are echoed in the social psychological literature on samples from Japan, Western Europe, the UK, and Australia.[12]

The Canadian off-gridders we met were a unique kind of voluntary simplifier. While they were a diverse group, the tendency among them was to embrace most of the voluntary simplicity values. Almost all of the individuals we interviewed, in fact, strove to reduce dependence on nonrenewables and took an intensely active role in practicing smaller-scale living. Like other voluntary simplifiers, off-gridders generally grew some food—some even cultivated, raised, hunted, or fished the majority of their calorie intake. They were often very unconcerned with fashion or the latest "must-have" product. They were masters at the art of re-using—often utilizing discarded wood products to warm their homes or for their building projects. They were remarkably well educated, combining good doses of formal education with copious amounts of critical social consciousness, environmental awareness, and practical know-how. They were also keen on finding their own sources of entertainment—typically preferring community gatherings, outdoor pursuits, and face-to-face interaction to television programming. And most of them were very concerned about limiting their carbon footprint. In short, living off-grid was, undoubtedly, a form of voluntary simplicity.

However, what exactly was so simple about a lifestyle based on, among many other daily activities, drilling through ice for water? And were these lifestyle choices actually voluntary given that—just like Brian—so many Canadians lived off-grid because of the high costs of hooking up their homes?

Showering with Grizzlies

Guarded by a scruffy coyote and a disinterested black bear, the road to Bill and Jenny's felt like an abandoned roller coaster path: twisted, dangerous, and manically craggy, all with a distinctly forgotten feel. We reached the house in the dark, on a chilly evening. Bill and Jenny had been renting their cabin for a year at the cost of $350 per month. Both quite young and from Southern Canada, they had recently come up North after getting married. Bill was tall, slim, and friendly looking. He spoke a mile a minute. Jenny was calmer—introspective, but warm. We sat down for tea. While Jon endeavored to get the lighting right for the video recording, I spotted Heidegger and several anthropology texts on the small bookshelf.

"When we were renting from other landlords it felt like we were making the rich richer," Bill explained, "but then we were inspired to try living off-the-grid. The lifestyle felt adventurous, edgy. But it feels like we've become more philosophical the more we tell the story, as if we've found more political meaning in it than we set out to," he reflected. "The lifestyle shaped who we are now. In the beginning, it was really all about getting ahead and saving some money." Setting up an off-grid power system requires a lot of cash upfront. While it is possible to save money compared to being on-the-grid, the payoffs can be quite slow. Living off-grid made economic sense in their case though, as they could rent a place already set up.

Their home was a small, romantic, cozy, wooden chalet with only one open-concept room downstairs and a bedroom up the narrow ladder. Propane fueled a cooking stove and two lights. Three candles provided additional glow. There was no plumbing so a bucket had to be placed under the sink to capture dishwater. An outhouse served their bodily needs, though they typically planned "BMs" for the workplace. There was no TV, telephone, microwave, washing machine, drier, or dishwasher. No refrigerator either. They used to keep food in a box placed in a hole dug outside, but it was too easy to forget about it and provisions would often go to waste, so they recently acquired a cooler. A woodstove warmed the house. They'd get their wood by Facebooking the wood-delivery guy, as they had, of course, internet access. No need to sacrifice necessities.

As they described their day-to-day routines, their portrait of the minor inconveniences of off-grid life grew humorous, even paradoxical.

"We once found ourselves turning on the generator to recharge our iPod. That really made us think of what consuming energy means. We stopped doing it after that."

"We didn't have a generator at first, so we couldn't plug in our car during winter nights. So when the temperatures would fall below −30°C (−22°F) we'd need to get up in the middle of the night every two hours to start the car and get the engine running for a few minutes. It was like having a newborn."

"It's a lot of work to live like this. You need to plan your day very carefully," Jenny observed. "It'd be nice if things were a bit simpler. Everything needs to be thought-out because we don't want to drive to town too much. Like, every day our bag needs to have clean clothes, shampoo, a towel, fresh underwear because we do our laundry and shower at work," she said with a laugh.

"Yeah, I think my co-workers get annoyed with me sometimes, with how my work and home boundaries blur," Bill observed with a mischievous grin, "the baskets of laundry, the bags of groceries . . ."

"*Groceries?*" I wondered.

"Yeah we can't leave our groceries in the car because of the mice . . ."

"*Mice?!*"

"They seem to have found a way inside the car. Jenny left her coffee mug in the car the other day and they went after her mocha."

"But you wouldn't want to leave your groceries in the car anyway, at least during winter," Bill continued.

"Why is that?"

"Because you'll buy fresh fish and veggies for dinner and when you take it out of your trunk it's all frozen!"

Bill and Jenny's routines seemed to muddle the voluntary simplicity argument even deeper. Our own personal experiences at the cabin further bedeviled it. Our mornings had to start early to accommodate our busy interview schedule, but in order to fire up the woodstove we had to set Jon's submarine alarm for an even earlier time. Having breakfast in a warm space was an absolute necessity as morning temperatures were already reaching −10°C (14°F). Toothbrushing and face-washing were no mindless tasks either. With no plumbing available we had to collect fresh water from the cold-as-hell Wheaton.

Nighttime chores were equally convoluted. Years of camping had prepared us to wash dishes with water warmed up on a propane stove. Camping had also trained us to appreciate the sense of accomplishment inherent in starting a fire quickly. But camping on BC's Southwest Coast hadn't exactly raised our—or at least my—tolerance toward grizzlies. Petrified at the prospect of a dark encounter on my way to the gents', I had resorted to peeing in a milk jug overnight. None of this was a big deal and the raw beauty of it all seemed to compensate for everything, but the simplicity argument wasn't exactly scoring too many points.

The longest drive of the week, about two and one-half hours each way, was reserved for a sunny weekend afternoon. As we sped along the deserted, permafrost-ridden Alaska/Klondike Highway, a bizarre flash-storm spoiled an otherwise memorably scenic ride set between stunning boreal forests, alongside turquoise glacial lakes, and through ample valleys flanked by massive, **snow-capped ridges**.[x] After reaching Haines Junction we turned left at aptly named . . . junction onto Haines Road. Suddenly the road surface changed and the asphalt became as level and smooth as a pool table. Residents of Haines, Alaska, and of the adjacent communities scattered on the US Chilkat Inlet must drive through Haines Road, and therefore through the Western Yukon to reach the rest of the state. As a result, the Americans funded the road's maintenance and the result was impressive. The electricity grid wasn't as advanced, however. Even though a hydropower generating plant was located in the area, its lines whizzed straight to Whitehorse. The bypass left Haines Road in the dark and angered the local residents, left with off-grid living as their only option.

Annette had organized a potluck dinner for our evening visit and invited a dozen of her neighbors to tell us all about their choice *not* to live off-grid on Highway 3. It sounded as if the "voluntary" part of voluntary simplicity was about to get challenged too. "We're not off-the-grid by choice, make no mistake about it, we'd all hook up tomorrow if they gave us the choice," we were told by a harmonious chorus of angry voices, "without power there is no economic development; without access to power there is no democracy."

There were about 50 full-time residents scattered near Kluane National Park, on a stretch of 60 kilometers reaching the Alaska border. Despite

---

[x]. http://lifeoffgrid.ca/w-content/uploads/2013/11/Life-Off-Grid_Yukon_08-1024x682.jpg

concerted efforts to lobby the territorial government, rural electrification was still a pipe dream. Like many others around there, Annette and her husband relied on tourism, and with the increasing costs of diesel for their backup generator and propane heating they found it impossible to avoid passing off the costs to their guests. The **Kathleen Lake Lodge**[xi] wasn't alone. Neighboring businesses and homes had similar systems, which cost them a monthly average of a thousand bucks on diesel alone. "It's not bad enough that the politicians don't give a damn," we were told, "but you also get this attitude from people who have power: 'well it was your choice to move there, now suck it up!'"

The dynamics of that "choice" were very complex. As we devoured generous helpings of delicious grilled Kathleen Lake trout, Annette and friends shared their stories of what pulled them here. Their "choices" to relocate were urged by the irresistible call for a better life. "The Yukon picks its own people," someone said, "you come here one day and you're hooked." "I felt a calling to the North, I felt I belonged here," another voice in the midst of the disorderly dinner chat cried. Intrigued, when I asked for more explanation I was simply told to just take a look **out of the window**.[xii] Dark, impassable, almost perfectly triangular slabs of rock exploded out of the greenery into the sky, reaching 4, 5, and 6,000 meters. At their feet, calmly reflecting their snowy heights, lay placid waters. The ancient wilderness of Kluane National Park had an obvious **haunting power**.[xiii] It was the kind of place you stumbled upon on your quest for Klondike gold and felt compelled to keep as your own treasure before the rest of civilization would discover it and ruin it.

* * *

Over two years of research we met two basic groups of off-gridders. The first group was comprised of people who moved off-the-grid because they were determined to generate their own power. They were the rarest. The second type consisted of people who settled for living off-grid because the nearest power pole was too distant from the land they had purchased—and therefore too expensive to connect to. If we can speak of a clear, free-willed choice for simplicity, we can only do so for the first, small group. For the greatest majority, instead, living off-grid was a compromise. It was a necessity of sorts that—combined with serendipity, vocation, discovery, reflection, and acquired taste—was gradually turned into virtue.

To say that living off-grid was a "necessity" is not the same as saying that it was a financial necessity. Social scientists are often tempted to argue

---

[xi.] http://www.kathleenlakelodge.ca/
[xii.] http://lifeoffgrid.ca/wp-content/uploads/2013/11/Life-Off-Grid_Yukon_12-1024x682.jpg
[xiii.] http://soundcloud.com/innovativeethnographies/the-pull

that people's conduct is explained by financial forces and economic need. Though money does matter, it would be wrong to suggest that it determined off-gridders' actions. Take Brian, for example. The farm he owned with his wife was off-the-grid because it would have cost too much to install 6 kilometers' worth of power poles. But Brian didn't "need" to be off-grid. He settled into his new place after migrating from elsewhere in search of a better way of life. He chose to move, but he did not necessarily choose to live off-grid. So, while the decision to be off-grid was influenced by the exorbitant cost of connection, the decision to relocate in the first place was not determined by capital.

The nature of the "choices" made by the people living along Haines Road wasn't terribly different. For the couple of aboriginal individuals at the dinner table, living off-grid was a cultural tradition they continued to practice out of the spirit of attachment to both place and community. For the others, migration to the area was also explained by the connection with the spirit of place and by the lifestyle they could practice there. But for neither the aboriginal nor the Euro-Canadian off-gridders of Haines Road could free choices or necessities explain why they were off-grid. Clearly theirs was not an exercise of either "free will"[13] or a financial decision. Living off-grid was voluntary only in the sense that all these individuals had realized they could live a pleasant life by moving to, or remaining in, a place they felt compelled to inhabit.

Finances did play a role in Jenny and Bill's choice to rent their cabin, because by living off-grid they saved money. But as renters they were an exception to the norm—off-gridders are typically homeowners who, most often, are also involved in the house-building process. Very few Canadian off-grid homeowners (namely, those for whom the connection cost would have been truly exorbitant) would argue that living off-grid is a clearly superior financial option than living on-grid. To boot, the "financial need" argument had limited purchase even in Bill and Jenny's case, since saving money was not the only factor in their decision. They, in fact, also wanted to "live in a nice place." So, it would be wrong to explain a move off-the-grid as either a clear and free "choice" or a strictly monetary "necessity."

Our fieldwork in BC and the Yukon had also shown that off-grid living was not so simple either. Domestic consumer technologies and the modern assemblages on which these rely have been designed to increase comfort and convenience, and comfort and convenience are now normal expectations in the Western world.[14] Obviously these assemblages are quite complex in both their design and operation—well beyond the capacity of the typical consumer to build or fix, and perhaps to even comprehend. But despite their mechanical complexity, typical domestic technologies are generally designed to be easy, if not downright foolproof, to use. Flicking on a switch to light or warm up a room requires no technical knowledge on the consumer's part. On the other hand, living off-grid relies on a deeper involvement. It demands knowledge about the capacity of one's energy-generating system, awareness about the precise extent of one's needs and wants, an understanding of the architecture and ecology of one's dwelling,[15] and possibly even the ability to repair things or make them last longer.[16]

What appeared to be a voluntary plan, realization, awakening, or deliberate choice, wasn't. And, as even our own experiences at the cabin had shown, enjoying a simple life resulted in several complications and mundane challenges.[17] Though still partially useful, the voluntary simplicity thesis had to be seriously amended if we really wanted to understand why people lived off-the-grid.

In Love with Place

Freed from the habit of vegging out in front of the television, evenings at our cabin became focused on scrutinizing visual material, making notes, and sketching out plans. Among other nighttime considerations, we decided that every province/territory would correspond to a chapter of this book, and that every province/territory would serve as a case study of a different aspect of off-grid living. The cases, we felt, would be driven by whatever we'd stumble upon, as well as the timing of our travel and the most outstanding features of a province/territory. For example, visiting frozen Alberta in January—our next trip—seemed like the perfect time to study heating and the importance of domestic warmth. The architecture of this book, almost entirely as it looks now before your eyes, was outlined under the propane light illuminating the small dining table of our cabin in the Yukon.

One of our most debated topics on those nights was simplicity. The seeming discomforts, sacrifices, and inconveniences of off-grid living were obvious. The lifestyle was apparently not for everyone. Yet, just about any off-gridder we met was adamant about the simplicity of it all. "It's simple!" "It's easy!" "Piece of cake!" "What's the problem?"—we kept hearing. Maybe the problem was with our own disposition.

The next morning we got out of bed even earlier and bee-lined it for the Baked Café, in downtown Whitehorse. As Jon relished his usual Americano and I my gourmet latte we went online and looked up the meaning of *simplicity* in the dictionary. One unusual definition jumped out at us. *Simple* does not just mean "easy," we learned. It's too seductive to equate the two within the context of a consumer society structured to be consumer-friendly, user-friendly, hassle-free, and drive-throughable. Simplicity also means "freedom from guile and pretense" and "genuineness." That was it. Off-gridders were telling us that life is not necessarily as complex as it's made to seem nowadays.

After all, our species has made it thus far without smart phones, microwaves, tumble driers, and the seemingly unrelinquishable convenience of so many domestic technologies. Off-gridders' point about simplicity was obvious: "We do not need to build yet another dam or dig up another mountain of coal to fuel an electrical infrastructure in order to recharge batteries for gadgets we can easily do without!" Life does not need to be that complex, and we need to stop pretending we are unable to take care of it by ourselves.

All caught up with semantics, email, and caffeine, we parted ways with the mid-morning office crowd and hit the unpaved road again, this time to meet **Barrett**.[xiv] Growing up in the San Francisco Bay Area, and globetrotting for work by way of Oxford, Prince Edward Island, and other places in between, Barrett always knew he wanted to be "**in the bush**."[xv] When he and his Alaska-born wife, Carol, visited their son, who had declared the Yukon his new home, they "fell in love" with the place and began planning their quasi-retirement. Standing well over six feet tall, of strong build, and of confident poise, Barrett needed no Florida-style, condo retirement. "We had four mutually exclusive criteria," he recounted while Carol occasionally pitched in off-camera. "We wanted inexpensive acreage, we wanted to be somewhat near to town and the airport, we wanted some kind of water frontage, and we wanted to be in the bush—I was feeling claustrophobic living in a 800-square-foot semi-detached house in an old council neighborhood." They eventually found their dream lot near a bend of the Yukon River, only a few minutes away from central Whitehorse.

There was only one problem; while the grid was almost at gunshot distance, the lines carried only high-tension power. Building a transformer substation and installing poles to connect their house would have cost a quarter of a million. "So you can see how the four variables for moving here did not include being off-grid," he explained, "it was never really our choice." But Barrett viewed that as a fun challenge, not an obstacle. After sketching the design of their would-be house and hiring himself as the general contractor, Barrett installed a wind turbine "out of a kit mailed from Michigan and a 'how to build wind mills for dummies' book." Solar panels, **a heat sink**,[xvi] and a hot water solar collector soon accompanied it. A diesel generator was put in place for backup, though Barrett admitted he never stopped strategizing how to make do without it.

Stepping into Barrett and Carol's exquisitely designed 1,900 square-foot villa, you'd be hard-pressed to tell they are off-grid. "And that's the idea," Barrett remarked with pride as we ate lunch together, "we knew we'd have

---

[xiv.] http://lifeoffgrid.ca/wp-content/uploads/2013/11/Life-Off-Grid_Yukon_09-1024x682.jpg
[xv.] http://soundcloud.com/innovativeethnographies/barrets-values
[xvi.] http://soundcloud.com/innovativeethnographies/barretts-heat-sink

guests, and we didn't want to sacrifice on comfort." So, there was a microwave oven in the house—used cautiously—and a propane-powered clothes drier, which was only employed when uncooperative clouds wouldn't retreat. On their deck, graced by the vista of an ocean of trees, they even had a hot tub.

In spite of the tantalizing Jacuzzi sessions, Barrett and Carol weren't the "sit-around-and-do-nothing-all-day" types, though. Barrett, in particular, seemed to be able to turn every chore into a fun-filled, big-toy-powered activity.

"You guys wanna go on a ride around the property on the Kubota?"

"Sure!" What self-respecting off-grid ethnographer could refuse an RTV ride!?

The Rough Terrain Vehicle—we learned as we bumped and ground along his well-maintained trails—was used regularly to pick up firewood and "fire-smart" the forest. In charge of his own road maintenance, during the long winter Barrett also carried buckets full of ash to improve traction for his truck. "Ash gives you the best grip in the world."

"You always need to be mindful," Barrett explained, as there are a lot of chores. The generator needs filters to be changed. **Batteries**[xvii] occasionally need to be maintained. **Monitors**[xviii] need to be checked. Wood needs to be collected and added to the **wood gasification boiler**.[xix] Water must be picked up in town, driven home, and emptied into the house tank. And of course, sometimes things break. "It's about an hour a day on average," he found. But it was no big deal. It was all good physical activity that kept him from needing to join the gym and from wasting time with lazy pursuits. And it was all worth it to be able to live in paradise.

The 21 off-gridders we met in the Yukon were a diverse bunch. Their homes (and businesses) were quite different from one another, and so were their motives, skills, resources, and day-to-day ways of living. Compare the different comfort of Barrett and Carol's home with the minimalism of Bill and Jenny's, for example. Yet, interestingly enough, both couples had to deal with similar amounts of daily complexities: Barrett and Carol had to look after the idiosyncrasies of their large and expensive system, whereas Bill and Jenny, on the other hand, had to tackle the challenges of "making do" with whatever little they had available. Both of these households faced more complications and inconveniences than the average on-grid home and yet they—as well as other off-gridders—enjoyed living "simply" because they had managed to embrace the challenges that their relative self-reliance demanded.

"How do you cope with all these inconveniences?" I had asked two Lasquetians by the name of Peter and Sue a few months before.

[xvii.] http://soundcloud.com/innovativeethnographies/barretts-batteries
[xviii.] http://soundcloud.com/innovativeethnographies/barretts-monitoring
[xix.] http://soundcloud.com/innovativeethnographies/barretts-wood-boiler

"Cope?" Sue answered authoritatively. "We don't *cope* with *inconveniences*," she corrected me as she looked me straight in the eyes. "We *embrace challenges*."

Studying off-gridders' motives had revealed that life as a whole is not meant to be easy—whether we live on- or off-grid. Off-gridders' experiences showed us that power is best understood as the innate ability to do work,[18] not just the stuff that comes out of an outlet. Off-gridders knew that the assemblages designed to make modern life convenient, comfortable, and downright easy had resulted in making entire generations dependent, lazy, scared to fend for themselves, and unaware of the vast amount of resources we consume and waste.[19] "The chaos caused by even the briefest of power cuts shows just how many institutional interests are involved in the mass production and industrialization of comfort," sociologist Elizabeth Shove has observed, "such events also show how much consumers rely on the technologies of central heating and cooling and on the utilities that supply them."[20] Off-gridders' lifestyle, on the other hand, put them back in touch with the basic complexities of living. It is through these everyday complexities that they learned that it is actually quite normal, undaunting, indeed even expected of a living being to put up with life. "What people take to be normal is immensely malleable . . . there are no fixed measures of comfort," observed Shove[21] or, for that matter, of simplicity.

Though rife with complexities, the off-grid life was not at all unbearably complicated—we were now coming to realize after the initial shock. It was just something off-gridders had gotten used to—much like we have all gotten used to operating complex computers and finding it so easy. The simplicity of off-grid consisted not in foolproof ease but in its minimalist elegance, in the restraints typical of the lifestyle, in its direct relation with place, and in its freedom from the modern pretense that human survival demands distant supplies of resources and expert intervention and authority. Simplicity was just another word for unpretentiousness.

But a full amendment to our understanding of "voluntary simplicity" also required a different understanding of place: a less rational, less calculated, more affective relation with the places we call home. Going off-grid was a way for people to separate themselves from the more undesirable aspects of the world and carve a little safe haven for themselves. It was a way of removing oneself from uniformity, greed, unsustainability, laziness, pollution (material and symbolic), irresponsibility, and everything else that corrupts the world. A few years before, I had coined the concept of "remove" in order to capture this performance of self-distancing.[22] Remove, I had suggested, was a set of practices of a distinct lifestyle that is spatially disconnected from, or at least alternatively connected to, a maligned, powerful counterpart. I had used the idea to describe the lifestyle of exurbanites who left crowded and noisy cities in search of peace and quiet on small, idyllic islands. Acts of remove were many different "practical ways in which the individual handles his or her material surroundings,"[23] and the concept held up well in the off-grid context.

Rather than a calculated option, remove was experienced by off-gridders as a "call" or an affective "pull" they had little control over. It was an unexplainable attraction toward the idylls of the countryside, the wilderness,[24] the "physical quality of the environment,"[25] the "wildscapes," the "adventurescapes," and the "farmscapes"[26] of their places. Off-gridders were in love with place—a love they couldn't help, and a love that led them to seek a better way of life wherever the pull of remove came from.

The pull of idyllic places and the appeal of "the rich intimate ongoing togetherness of beings and things which make up landscapes and places, and which bind together nature and culture over time"[27] played a crucial role in explaining why off-gridders removed themselves into their "spaces of alternate ordering."[28] Indeed, this played even a greater role than political ideologies like voluntary simplicity did. Rather than instrumentally planned utopias, off-grid homes and properties could then be better understood as affective spaces; places with a unique enchanting power of their own.

The practice of remove was a "tactical" move, a move that altered, disrupted, and re-signified relations with an exterior power without really changing it.[29] By disconnecting from a large utility company, an off-grid household closed down certain lifestyle possibilities and opened up different ones. By removing themselves from dominant energy assemblages, off-gridders created a peripheral and alternative space. And there—like back-to-the-landers,[30] smallholders,[31] permaculturists,[32] and politically radical self-sufficient farming groups[33]—they enacted a version of place based on the value and practice of hard work,[34] family and community time, environmental sustainability, skillfulness, the pursuit of physical and moral health, and the romantic mystique of wilderness and nature.

Through their remove, they actively performed a symbolic and material distance from urban consumerism, similar to the widespread trend of counter-urbanization.[35] By practicing remove they also performed a radical rurality that challenged the logic of dependence on light, speed, and power and that aimed to develop an alternative lifeworld less based on ephemerality, careerism, and disposability.[36] An alternative lifeworld less keen on struggling to overtake power and more interested in reassembling it on a local scale in the way it was generated, distributed, and used.[37]

Our search for answers as to why people lived off-the-grid had, in sum, yielded the impression that off-grid living was a modest and unpretentious form of removal from the societal drive toward assimilation into large-scale networks. Off-gridders' quest for de-centralization and self-reliance—though admittedly never complete and at times even contradictory—stood as a contestation against large-scale development, the fetishism of economic growth, distant supply mechanisms, and reliance on professional expertise.

This quest characterized the off-grid lifeworld not as a utopian, separate space of political transformation, but rather as an alternatively connected, relational space. Individuals' motives, we had come to believe, revealed strongly held convictions but also hopes, failures, aspirations, pleasures, complexities, irrational drives, impulses, struggles, ironies, disillusions, compromises, and the negotiations typical of any lifestyle quest.

Notes

1. Daoud, 2011; Kneale-Gould, 2005; Librova, 2008.
2. Elgin, 1981:11.
3. Elgin, 1981:12.
4. Grigsby, 2004.
5. Kneale-Gould, 2005.
6. Cherrier and Murray, 2002.
7. Leonard-Barton, 1981:244.
8. Etzioni, 1998:620, 632.
9. Chhetri, Stimson, and Western, 2009:346. Cheetri, Khan, Stimson, and Western, 2009.
10. Zavestovski, 2002.
11. Huncke, 2005.
12. Craig-Lees and Hill, 2002; Etzioni, 1998; Iwata, 2006; McDonald et al., 2006; Shaw and Newholm, 2002.
13. Etzioni, 1998; McDonald et al., 2006.
14. Shove, 2003.
15. For similar characteristics amongst homesteaders, see Heinz-Housel, 2006.
16. Also see Shaw and Newholm, 2002.
17. See Holloway, 2000; Librova, 2008.
18. Whitehead, 1934. Also see Caygill, 2007.
19. For a similar finding among homesteaders, see Heinz-Housel, 2006.
20. Shove, 2003:45–46.
21. Shove, 2003:199.
22. Vannini, 2011.
23. Crouch, 2003:1945.
24. Bunce, 1994; Cloke, 2003; Thoreau, 2003.
25. Halfacree, 1994.
26. Bell, 2006.
27. Cloke and Jones, 2001:651.
28. Hetherington, 1997:53.
29. deCerteau, 1984.
30. Halfacree, 2001a, 2001b, 2006, 2007a; Holloway, 2000; Jacob, 1997; Meijering et al., 2007.
31. Brinkerhoff and Jacob, 1984; Crouch, 1989, 1997; Holloway, 2002.
32. Schwartz and Schwartz, 1998.
33. Bell and Valentine, 1995.
34. Crouch, 1997.
35. Boyle and Halfacree, 1998; Halfacree, 1992, 2001a, 2001b.
36. Halfacree, 2003, 2006, 2007b, 2009; Mormont, 1987.
37. Holloway, 2010.

Don and Tractor.[i]

i. For more photos, visit lifeoffgrid.ca.

3

INVOLVEMENT

Wood and the City

The thermometer read a stunning 9°C (48°F) when we reached Edmonton. The locals looked beside themselves on the busy streets: jogging, walking cats and dogs, reading on park benches, playing (field) hockey, and having a jolly old time. It was January but it felt like spring break. Edmonton is one of North America's northernmost and coldest cities. Its chilliest month is January, during which its average daily temperature is a brisk −11.7°C (11°F). Its record low, also established in January (back in 1886), is a traffic-stopping −48.3°C (−56.9°F). To make matters worse, Alberta's capital is very windy. There are winter days when Edmonton is colder than Moscow, the planet Mars, and even Winnipeg. But in spite of the heat wave we decided we would stick to our plan to study heating. While the weather wasn't the most propitious, Alberta still retained its status as Canada's most natural-gas-dependent province and, it goes without saying, the world's most controversial oil producer due to its resource-intensive obsession with bitumen extraction. Alberta, in other words, was *the* place to research off-gridders' reliance on fire.

Our interest in domestic warmth was apropos for another reason: a few Google searches had revealed that Edmonton was home to one of the liveliest Net Zero urban scenes on the continent. Net Zero building is a type of design characterized by an equal balance between the energy consumed and the energy generated on-site by a home. Because of Alberta's reliance on coal for electricity generation and natural gas for domestic heating, any form of involvement in independent renewable energy generation—even a partial one—could have a very meaningful effect on the local carbon footprint. So, while Net Zero is not synonymous with off-grid, Jon and I had made plans to begin our trip by visiting three such residences in the city.

Conrad's recently re-designed heritage home, for instance, was still connected to the electricity grid but was off the natural gas network. More notably, his home faced the back alley: due south. This was a seemingly small detail, but one whose importance cannot be emphasized enough. Urban and suburban single-detached houses are typically designed to front the street, regardless of whether the building ends up facing east, west, south, or north. Our houses are oriented to the street because we want them to look their best for the Joneses, but by aiming them the wrong way (as essentially three fourths of them are) energy conservation ends up taking a backseat to curb appeal.

Not only did Conrad's home look south, but angled in that direction were also 32 solar panels and a solar hot-water collector that produced almost as much electricity as Conrad, his wife, and two kids needed to light up and power their home.[ii] The panels, functioning as movable awnings, also provided cool shade during the short but warm summer season, thus circumventing the need for air conditioning. True, Conrad and family weren't off-the-grid, but by utilizing grid electricity mostly as a "plan B" for stretches of dark days, they treated the grid like a genuine off-gridder would use a backup gasoline generator. The difference was only nominal. And given the fact that their home sold excess renewable energy back to the dirty grid, some might even argue that in the end the advantage was theirs.

Unintelligent orientation isn't the only energy-efficiency fault of most typical homes. Poor wall insulation, large leaky windows, glass on all sides, tall building towers casting cold shadows on one another, and many more design and construction obstacles get in the way of saving energy. In contrast, Conrad's double-wall system—comprised of two 2 × 4 walls 16 inches apart, one inside the other, with studs on 24-inch centers—had a true R value of 56. This meant that only about a quarter of the heat that escapes typical homes actually snuck out of this one. Triple-pane, fiberglass frame windows contributed to that goal too—with south-facing windows achieving a compromise between allowing heat in and trapping it, and east- and west-facing windows focusing squarely on preventing heat from oozing out.

Young, highly educated, motivated by voluntary simplicity, and driven by a deep concern for the environment, Conrad and his wife didn't own a car.

[ii] More details available on Conrad's site: http://greenedmonton.ca/MillCreekNetZeroHome

They relied instead on a bicycle trailer to carry goods home, such as fire-wood for their woodstove—strategically scavenged from construction sites' discarded lumber. Besides growing vegetables in the back of their beautiful home in the historic heart of Edmonton, Conrad and his wife gardened on several plots throughout the city, including a community garden site and a friend's backyard. They both worked part-time to accommodate the extra domestic labor their lifestyle demanded and also to make time for home-schooling their two children.

Conrad may not have been as disconnected from the grid as others, but all emissions considered, as an urban resident he had a key advantage over his rural counterparts. "I can walk or bike to work or to most of the stores where I need to shop, and I can take public transit to reach mostly every-thing else," he explained, "whereas in the country you need to get in your car every time you need to go somewhere." He scored a great point, I realized, nodding pensively as the living room woodstove competed silently with the morning sun to warm us up.

Passive solar design, along with burning firewood, allowed Conrad and his wife to minimize the use of their electrical baseboards, whose heat con-stituted only about 10% of the house's warmth making. Their thermostats were turned as far down as you can go, "though there is no zero," Conrad remarked, "the lowest you can go on thermostats is seven, but when it's −30°C (−22°F) outside we turn them on in the kids' room up to 12°C (53.6°F)." Burning firewood in the city isn't always the easiest thing. **Fire**[iii] warms up an urban dwelling the same as it does a rural one, of course, but municipal bylaws can curb smoke emission; some ban woodstoves outright for new home construction or limit their use on days when other anti-pollution measures are stringently enforced due to inclement weather.

Like smoke, heat is often a type of waste. Machines of all kinds—from laptops to automobiles—produce unwanted heat as a by-product of their operation. While it is a natural process—indeed even human bodies gener-ate it as part of physical exertion—waste heat is a quintessentially symbolic expression of late-modern, climate-change-inducing industrialism. Though we like to tell ourselves we live in a post-industrial service and knowledge economy, smoke isn't hard to find. In Edmonton, if you follow the North Saskatchewan River east through the city center you will eventually find compelling visual evidence of this. Near West Sherwood Park, in an area locally known as Refinery Row, gargantuan smokestacks towering over oil refineries belch out puffy, gray plumes of waste heat. Neither oil nor coal converts perfectly to energy. The burning of coal to generate electricity, for example, results in 50% to 65% waste heat.

[iii] http://soundcloud.com/innovativeethnographies/conrad-how-to-make-a-fire

Passive solar design,[iv] on the other hand, concentrates on not wasting anything. The design is intuitive. It all begins by allowing the sun to penetrate large south-facing windows. Most, if not all, of the more frequently inhabited rooms should be designed to face south in order to benefit from this source of free and renewable heat. Ideally, south-facing glass should range from 12% to 18% of the total square footage of a house, whereas west-, east-, and north-facing window surfaces should collectively amount to no more than 6%. Efficient insulation should then keep warm air inside and not let it go to waste. Thermal mass, like concrete floors, can absorb heat during the day and release it slowly at night.

Besides the sun, inhabitants of regions situated far from the tropics have throughout the millennia made use of many different resources and tools to keep warm. Fire has often been at the center of these. Fires have warmed people in their homes and have gathered families and communities together in large communal spaces, allowing us to focus on domestic, celebratory, and work-related tasks. Indeed, no history of our species and its evolution can be told without attention to fire. The importance of keeping the fire burning is even reflected in many symbolic traditions, from the ongoing cultivation of the ever-lasting Olympic flame to the mythological idolization of Prometheus—who stole the gift of fire from Zeus and gave it to the mortals.

Fire has always been a troublesome companion, however, for its history is also the history of resource depletion.[1] Firewood was free for all in England, for example, only until the eighth century. Restrictions began shortly thereafter and records show that a handful of Berkshire villages were fined as early as the twelfth century for excessive logging.[2] Lumber was also a valuable building material, of course, and early in its modern history England began to witness significant deforestation. It was in light of such trends that coal eventually became a valuable alternative to wood.

The burning of coal, however, even more than wood, caused noxious smoke. Coal had been known to humankind since 371 BCE, though burning it within homes had in later years been subject to several bans. But as firewood became less available, cities had to give in and allow coal burning for both domestic and industrial purposes. In order to live with less smoke, people would hire the services of smokehouses and cookhouses for preparing their meals. The popularity of pubs—short for public houses—also grew in part because of the need to keep cooking-emitted smoke away from the home. But it was of little use. Air quality grew so poor in London that the city eventually became known as "the Big Smoke." The air was so bad that for many years burning coal while Parliament was in session was forbidden.

[iv] http://lifeoffgrid.ca/wp-content/uploads/2013/11/Life-Off-Grid_Alberta_01.jpg

In the meantime, technologies were gradually improving. Open fires—such as coal crates, braziers, and fireplaces—have always allowed for ease in cooking and are rewarding to stare at, but it was not until the fire was fully enclosed within masonry or cast-iron stoves that smoke was effectively dealt with. A series of improvements to the hearth succeeded one another until in 1624 Louis Savot reduced the size of the flue above the hearth and the size of the hearth itself. He also fixed iron plates behind and at the sides of the hearth. This created ducts through which warmed air was directed back into the room, heated by way of convection.

A crucial invention in the progress toward domestic smoke control was the invention of the catalytic converter. Catalytic converters increase the efficiency of wood burning by 10% to 25%, thus increasing the heat you get from wood and reducing the need to use more. They also reduce dangerous creosote buildup in the chimney by 80%.[3] They work through the use of a ceramic honeycomb structure coated by a catalyst placed atop the fire. The catalyst, palladium or platinum, completes the combustion of unburned hydrocarbons.

As wood gave way to abundant coal, coal eventually gave way to the popularity of gas. Gas cookstoves began to appear in the 1850s, and in 1854 *The Sunday Times* boldly forecast the end of smoky chimneys. But it was not until the following year that Baron Bunsen, applying previously known principles of radiation, improved domestic gas heating by creating small punctures in gas tubes, which drew air in to mix with gas, thus allowing it to burn hotter.[4] Whereas coal had to be carried in horse-drawn vehicles and hand-delivered to homes, gas could circulate unobtrusively through mains laid underground. Vast networks of urban gas mains were thus laid out throughout the early twentieth century.

Electric heating came onto the scene only later, due to its early high costs. Even today electric heating is quite pricey in some regions, though as fewer and fewer people employ oil furnaces due to rising costs, electric heating continues to gain favor. Though it would seem logical to use electric heating to warm an off-grid home—Canadian off-gridders unanimously utilize wood—with a small minority employing propane as well. It simply takes too much electricity to fire up baseboards or even to operate the air pumps required by geothermal systems.

Wood is not a common heating resource across the general Canadian population, though it is traditionally used in rural areas where it is within easy reach and often even free.[5] Oil burning is also becoming less common. Statistics show that whereas oil was used by 60% of the population in the 1960s, it is now utilized by only 15% of Canadians—still twice as many as those who use wood. About a third of Canadians use electricity for heating, whereas natural gas is employed by about one of every two households. These figures, however, obscure sharply different regional realities.

No statistics on the employment of passive solar are available. Though you might think that a cold country like Canada would have little to gain from the use of passive solar, many of the most densely populated areas of the country receive enough sunshine to warrant serious investments in that design. Even cold cities like Edmonton and Calgary manage to soak up between eight and twelve daily mega joules per square meter on an average autumn day—a fact that somehow made our disappointingly balmy stay in Alberta seem more acceptable.

Affect and Ways of Heating

"What happens when you apply heat and cold to a Peltier junction?"

Long pause. Silence. You could practically hear the crickets chirping.

"Come on guys, haven't you ever heard of a Peltier junction?!" **Don**[v] prodded Jon and me for an answer. It was useless. I bombed high school physics. And I underachieved even more shamelessly at shop. I recall my shop teacher pleading with my parents to keep me away from any job that would require me to use my hands.

"Well, you get electricity!" Don answered, giving up on the both of us.

"I did well in social studies," I replied to save face.

"I concentrated on the visual arts," Jonathan added with a smirk from behind his camera.

Unimpressed, Don soldiered on to explain how a simple (sort of) physics principle, a 24 × 24-inch Peltier junction, wood heat, and a self-assembled geothermal cold-water pump might eventually allow him and his wife Maxine to generate enough electricity to supplement their wind turbine and photovoltaic system.

Don and Maxine lived at the end of the power lines, down an unpaved country lane in Alberta's open sky country. They had camped for years at this site, while gradually building their dream energy-efficient home one piece at a time. To make heat, **Don and Maxine**[vi] collected a yearly average of four and a quarter cords (a cord is a wood stack four feet deep by four feet high and eight feet long) of pine beetle-killed timber from their 320-acre Peace River region property. The climate change-thankful beetle made it easy for them to cull trees, but the firewood still had to be chopped onsite in the bush, transported, cut, brought indoors, lit, and looked after with TLC to maintain a constant ambient temperature. "It's not a lot of work," Don demurred, but it certainly required a greater deal of effort than flicking on a switch.

[v.] http://lifeoffgrid.ca/wp-content/uploads/2013/11/Life-Off-Grid_Alberta_05.jpg
[vi.] http://soundcloud.com/innovativeethnographies/don-max-their-heat

Wood heat is notoriously temperamental, flaring up in bursts of tropical temperatures soon after lighting and causing indoor temps to plummet soon after the fire goes out. To discipline it—as good teachers like Don and Maxine used to be—they applied basic scientific principles. A collection of 5,300 **gallons of water**[vii] had been stacked in the crawl space in motley piles of carefully sealed containers of different shapes and sizes. The containers didn't come from the local hardware store. Formerly used for soap, wax, laundry detergent, and soy sauce, they had been methodically scavenged by Don and Maxine from schools, restaurants, hotels, and recycling depots over a 15-year period. Heated during winter by a woodstove and during autumn and spring by warm air fanned down the solar collector by their old Datsun car heater-blower, the water worked as thermal mass. It absorbed and radiated heat slowly and thus reduced the need for additional wood burning and stabilized temperatures upstairs.

It was only one of myriad inventions and ingenious applications we found in Don and Maxine's home that morning. Among them we noted a briefcase-shaped portable solar panel designed to fulfill electricity needs on the go, and a wind turbine assembled from **oil barrels**[viii] sawed in halves—making it look like it belonged on a foreign planet to assist some kind of NASA mission.

Awestruck by Don and Maxine's display of resourcefulness and creativity, we thought it would be nice to share their inventions with a larger audience, such as that of ***Canadian Geographic***.[ix] This type of collaborative magazine writing—collaborative[6] because our work needed to be checked and corrected by detail-oriented teachers like Don and Maxine—wasn't the only way in which the ethnography became more public as time went on. As we arrived in Calgary a few days later, we learned that a journalist from the *Herald* wanted to speak with us. A brief phone interview yielded a newspaper article that opened the floodgates to nationwide media coverage. By the time we left St. John's, Newfoundland, two years later, we had accumulated over 30 newspaper appearances and two dozen radio interviews, in addition to the many magazine articles and ***Huffington Post***[x] blog pieces we were creating on our own.

Most of the media calls were fielded while we were on the road. That was the most likely place we'd be found, given how the long distances and our busy schedule in provinces like Alberta meant that being on the road (or in mid-air) occupied most of our time. **Highway 43**[xi] northwest of Edmonton

---

vii. http://soundcloud.com/innovativeethnographies/don-max-insulation-and-thermo
viii. http://lifeoffgrid.ca/wp-content/uploads/2013/11/Life-Off-Grid_Alberta_04.jpg
ix. http://www.canadiangeographic.ca/magazine/jun12/inhabitat.asp
x. http://www.huffingtonpost.ca/phillip-vannini-and-jonathan-taggart/
xi. http://lifeoffgrid.ca/wp-content/uploads/2013/11/Life-Off-Grid_Alberta_03.jpg

was one of those endless stretches of driving that connected the pieces of our over-ambitious interview itinerary. When we finally arrived at our destination we learned that Terry was in town running errands, but she had kindly left much-needed coffee and a fresh batch of cookies to keep us focused as we talked and walked with Lorne.

Lorne and Terry had lived off-grid since 1980. They could have hooked up to both electricity and natural gas, as their 160-acre property laid no more than a slingshot's range from the two grids, but they chose not to. Lorne explained he grew up with the dream of the cabin lifestyle, removed from the hustle and bustle of the city, valuing freedom and independence. All but the hermit cabin type he struck me as a very gentle and entrepreneurial soul. Sixty years young, he operated a busy home-based business that kept him connected with many people. He spoke of discovering and utilizing photovoltaic energy, well before most people had ever heard of it, with a grateful sense of enchantment, as if it was a gift he'd be silly to refuse.

We sat around the table to visit while the sun charged the array of solar panels right outside the kitchen window. As I looked away for a moment, furtively licking my fingers from the last cookie, I noticed the presence of a cat sleeping on the floor. The air inside the 1,300-square-foot house was comfortably warm and the furry friend's location clued me in on the hearth's location. Lorne confided that this particular corner was in fact both his and the feline's favorite. Warm air released by the burning of carbon stored within wood circulated in loops inside the cookstove, warming the cooking surface and the air around it. A water jacket wrapped around the flue provided hot water too. There was also another source of heat in the living room, a glass-covered woodstove whose fire they would blissfully **light up and watch**[xii] on cold nights.

Lorne collected wood from his forest. Once his poplar trees would reach the age of 40 or 50 they would die, often still standing up. He would then cut them with his chainsaw and bring them down to size with his hydraulic wood splitter. Other times he would collect fallen trees, either poplar or birch. In Alberta's climate, death cures trees, drying them out of water and sap and allowing them to burn faster, emitting less smoke. During a typical year Terry and Lorne would consume four or five cords. He'd go out and split wood every second week or so, for a couple of hours on a sunny day.

Terry's delicious cookie recipe called for flour, eggs, sugar, and . . . two pieces of birch. Birch was essential to cook with, allowing for the right heat. Birch burned hotter and longer than poplar, Lorne explained, "It's got a nicer aroma too. . . . Poplar is better for spring and summer because

---

[xii.] http://soundcloud.com/innovativeethnographies/lorne-feeling-the-heat

it makes a fast fire" and burns itself out quickly. That's a good thing
when you don't want cooking to turn your house into a sweat lodge. Just
like cooking is an art, so is warming up a house. "You get a feel for it,"
he reflected, "you can almost feel when it's time to add another piece of
wood to the fire to keep it going." It was −4°C (25°F) outside (I did say it
was a heat wave, but this was still northern Alberta after all) and Lorne
decided to act on his instinct and throw in another piece. "Wood heat
feels **different**,[xiii] doesn't it?" he commented. I agreed, and indulged in
another birchy treat.

* * *

Unlike fish, frogs, and reptiles, human beings are warm-blooded animals hardly tolerant of dramatic temperature changes. Our bodies tolerate
internal variations of no more than 3°C (ca. 6°F) and consequently our preferred home temperatures range within a narrow span. *Thermoception* is the
sense through which we perceive temperature. Despite being recognized as
a sense by well-established biological standards, thermoception is not considered one of the common "five senses."
   A few culturally informed studies have helped shed light on how the
temperature sensorium works. For instance, in a recent ethnographic study
conducted within a Chicago public housing project, Fennell[7] found that
central-heating policies were tied with political and economic power, class,
and race dynamics. Access to warmth, in other words, was not an equalitar-
ian or democratic process, and the perception of what constituted a sufficiently warm indoor environment was just as complicated by many variables.
And in New Zealand, Cupples and associates[8] found that indoor heating
was intertwined with national identities and hegemonic notions of masculinity as well. Therefore, bearing the cold there would often become a test
of gender identity and bodily and moral fortitude. These are just a couple of
examples—many other cultural and social factors like these mediate sensory
experiences worldwide and show that thermoception is no neutral physiological affair.
   Everyday experiences and practices of warmth are just as varied. We've
all known people who always seem to be feeling cold, as well as others for
whom no number of open windows will suffice. We've also all experienced
cold days that feel warmer than what the thermometer says, or mild days
that feel colder because of wetness or wind. Similarly, we know that different technologies warm us up in different ways. Thermoception is both
the medium through which these experiences are possible, and the means

[xiii.] http://soundcloud.com/innovativeethnographies/lorne-what-wood-heat-feels

through which these activities unfold. No study of the experience and practice of heating can unfold without a deeper understanding of how thermoception works.

Temperature perception unfolds through the work of thermoreceptors: receptive elements of sensory neurons that register states and changes in temperature. But thermoception is also about bodily movement and physical action, as its operation inevitably implies active regulation and manipulation of temperature. A body's thermal register is in fact not a passive recorder of conditions already laid out, but a productive interface immersed in the world's constant transformation of itself.[9] Sociologist Bruno Latour explains this idea in simple and elegant terms when he writes that the body as a whole "is not a provisional residence of something superior—an immortal soul, the universal, or thought—but what leaves a dynamic trajectory by which we learn to register and become sensitive to what the world is made of."[10]

If we understand thermoception as an interface, and therefore as a skill, a hub of activities, a sensibility, and an orientation to modulate the world, then we essentially treat thermoception as a type of *affect*. Affect is a bodily pull and a push. Affect is the body's capacity to be moved and be affected, and the body's capacity to move and affect other people and other things. Affect is "a transpersonal capacity which a body has to be affected (through an affection) and to affect (as the result of modifications)."[11] Thermoception, therefore, is not like a thermometer. It is instead an atmospheric attunement[12]: an affective force that manifests itself in corporeal involvement in warmth and in the transformation of living environments.

Warmth, heat, thermoception—these are all nouns. But from the perspective of habitation there are no nouns in the typical sense, because things are their relations, their doings, and their movements—with each noun actually describing something that is going on.[13] Warmth making and heating are the doings of sun and fire as well as the mediated and relational doings of sun-collecting and fire-making inhabitants of the planet. Thus, a fire burns not only by the flickering of its flame and the swirling of its smoke, but also by the warmth making of the body.[14]

Individual and collective expectations for thermal comfort and convenience play a crucial role in warmth making. Heating with wood, for example—even after the successive introduction of cleaner, more efficient, and less physically demanding technologies—is more labor intensive and therefore less convenient than other common options. Comfort and convenience are key factors in many domestic technology choices because of an ongoing escalation in consumer demand for comfort and convenience.[15] This is part of a broader historical tendency toward perceiving comfort and convenience as a right belonging to all and not just a privilege of the few.[16] Such normalization of comfort often leads people to forget that indoor thermal conditions are the result of the operation of complex infrastructures, as well as socio-cultural processes of standardization of sensory experiences, needs, and expectations. These "needs have been defined and reproduced in an incredibly precise manner," according to Shove, "and in a manner that takes no account of the historical variability of indoor climates or the range of conditions in which people of different cultures say they are comfortable."[17] Indoor thermal seasonal variation, thus, increasingly seems a thing of the past and the social cycles and individual skills associated with securing thermal comfort become subject to oblivion.[18]

Thermoceptive capacity varies along with such changing expectations, standards, and habits, but also in terms of the skills, techniques, and materials involved in the experience and practice of warmth making. These variations consist of what we might call *ways of heating*. Ways of heating are common parts of our ways of life. They are profoundly social activities in their rhythms, inflections, and propensities, weaving together different relations between humans, resources, and technologies. Ways of heating are individual and collective thermal pursuits and accomplishments shaped by environments, habits, dispositions, and even individual idiosyncrasies.

Off-gridders' bodies have the same thermoceptive potential as the rest of us, obviously, but our fieldwork showed that they practiced different ways of heating than most of us do. Their thermoception, in other words, took place (and *made* place) differently. For example, collecting wood required a good deal of physical activity. Designing a home to benefit from passive solar energy demanded careful foresight. Living in synchrony with diurnal and seasonal solar patterns necessitated planning and forbearance. Maximizing the potential of thermal mass called for abstract knowledge and careful application of principles from material science. Relying on renewables and reducing the use of non-renewable resources demanded that off-gridders relinquish some conveniences. In short, if energy—as its etymology tells us—is the capacity to do work, then off-grid ways of heating required the actualization of great intensities of the capacity to do domestic work.

Through the perspective of habitation, we were able to understand off-grid ways of heating as something that arose within the currents of their "involved activity, in the specific relational contexts of their practical engagement with their surroundings."[19] Through practical engagement with renewable (and non-renewable) resources and technologies, off-gridders

generated heat in the process of working with the materials available to
them, bringing warmth into being through their abilities to remain attentive, improvise solutions, assess failures, and exercise creativity.

* * *

If you don't like the weather in Alberta, just wait five minutes. Temperatures
outside had suddenly plummeted to –25°C (–13°F), while our bedroom at
the Red Deer Holiday Inn roasted at an equally uncomfortable 22°C (72°F).
I'd have loved to get the thermostat to dip even a single notch below 18.5°C
(65°F), but neither it nor the unopenable window would accommodate my
preference for a chilly sleeping environment. Unable to sleep in this carpet-
and-pillow-rich version of the Gobi Desert, I resorted to swimming a few
laps in the heated indoor pool downstairs to tire my body just enough for
the night. The total carbon footprint of our stay was appalling.

Dinner, at least, had been very sustainable: homemade vegetable lasagna
prepared with mostly locally grown ingredients and a zesty carrot salad on
the side, courtesy of **Lynn**[xiv] and Mike. Lynn and Mike not only gathered
their vegetables and chicken eggs from their premises, but also collected
wood from neighboring properties. It is not unusual for people to cut down
trees to make space for something else and then leave the trees to rot on the
ground. Lynn and Mike would simply go around the area and recycle what
otherwise would go to waste.

But wood was only one component of their heating plan. Whereas
dwellings like the Red Deer Holiday Inn got their warmth from supplies of natural gas and then routinely wasted it to allow for breathtaking
north-facing views of the Queen Elizabeth Highway, the key to Lynn and
Mike's warmth could be found in the ground underneath their feet and in
the walls around them. Lynn used a picture-filled storyboard to tell their
design story.

Their house was a small, gray monolithic **dome**.[xv] It sat near the top
of a gently rising, barren hill decorated by sparse snow blotches reflecting the dim, setting sun. Under the house floor were 1,800 cinder blocks
lying on their sides with their cavities lined up north to south. Sunshine
came in through the south-facing windows and heated the concrete floor.
R-60 (measured loss at –30°C or –22°F was two watts per square foot)
insulated walls with three inches of foam insulation on the outside, and
six inches of reinforced concrete, prevented heat from escaping outside. At

---

[xiv] http://lifeoffgrid.ca/wp-content/uploads/2013/11/Life-Off-Grid_Alberta_09.jpg
[xv] http://lifeoffgrid.ca/wp-content/uploads/2013/11/Life-Off-Grid_Alberta_08.jpg

night, thermo-shutters (R-20) were shut to seal windows and doors from the inside.

The semi-spherical shape of their monolithic dome gave them a minimal surface area to heat. As we walked in a clockwise circle around the dome, realizing how pervasive 90° angles are in ordinary homes and how meticulous dome dwellers needed to be in smoothing out their dominance, we noticed how evenly **warm air circulated**[xvi] around the monolithic structure. Re-orienting one's house and changing its surfaces were certainly different ways of heating I was aware of, but re-inventing its very shape was . . . well, very cool.

Hot and Cool Energies

Upon my return home from Alberta I noticed that my mail had quickly stacked up. Amidst credit card bills, advertising leaflets, and newspapers, one item in particular stood out: my BC Hydro bill. As I read it in greater detail than usual, I thought it was odd that I had no clue where the electrons that warmed up my house at a constant 18°C (65°F) came from. Maybe it was a dam somewhere in the coastal region, or maybe up in the north of BC. I was utterly unaware of, and uninvolved with, my way of heating my house. This was in such contrast to how well Mike, Lynn, Conrad, and the other Alberta off-gridders knew so well where to find wood, how to cut it, and how to keep its warmth inside their homes. Without exaggerating the differences between the two ways of heating, I wanted to refer to them with two different concepts. One way to quickly characterize off-grid ways of heating and the intensities of involvement they required might be, I thought, to call them *hot energies*. Their on-grid counterparts could instead be known as *cool energies*.

Hot energy and cool energy have nothing to do with how warm it is. Hot and cool here are adjectives describing intensities of personal *involvement*—that is: how corporeally engaged a person is in the making of domestic heat. Off-gridders appeared to be more involved than on-gridders like me because their heating assemblages were quite demanding. Off-gridders' hot energy heavily depended on a process of education of their attention.[20] Throughout this process, their sense of thermoception became "attuned" to the atmosphere of their homes[21]: becoming more sensitive to the changing temperatures of their domestic surroundings; more aware of their technologies, local climate and weather, locally available resources, and broader global environmental forces; and more sensitive toward their specific needs

---

[xvi.] http://soundcloud.com/innovativeethnographies/mike-lynn-heat-circulation

and preferences. This process showed that off-grid thermoception is a hub of activities:[22] a lively nexus of interrelated practices through which off-gridders became deeply involved in generating warmth throughout their homes with the intervention of their heating technologies.

Warmth stirs our bodies: moving, comforting, and sheltering all of us. A fire's flame may even dazzle and enchant us at times. These are expressions of warmth's vital capacity: its capacity to enable (or in its absence impede) our everyday life; its ability "to make a difference, produce effects, alter the course of events."[23] It is easy to forget that a non-human agent like warmth has this capacity when its generation ceases to be a mundane concern. Most of our workplaces, shops, and homes are kept so evenly warm that warmth invariably loses much of its actual affective intensity, receding in the background of our consciousness. Living off-grid resulted in a reversal of this tendency: off-grid warmth was a dramatically vibrant matter that fully retained its enchantment, calling for care, attentiveness, and respect.[24]

Insulation, thermo-mass, and the efficient windows and woodstoves I had seen in Alberta were *interveners* in these processes: elements of a heating assemblage that made a crucial difference in virtue of their positioning, working as the decisive force catalyzing warmth as an accomplishment and an event.[25] Thick walls, cement floors, windowpanes, and the foamy stuff inside walls were hardly spectacular to look at. And yet these interveners mattered because they operated as intended, enabling bodily involvement to achieve its transformative potential. They drew sunshine, collected warm air, held it within, and released it at the right time. Together they were a "shifting assemblage of practices and practical knowledges" that gave off-grid ways of heating "the quality of a continual motion of relations, scenes, contingencies, and emergences."[26] They were just quiet things that worked—most of the time at least. They were ordinary affects[27] that, through their unique flows, gave off-grid hot energies their unique forms.

Our body's thermoceptive power has the capacity to affect us and—not unlike a catalytic converter—the capacity to affect and transform the temperature of the air we inhabit. Geographer Nigel Thrift[28] has explained that affect is somewhat like the networks of pipes and cables that provide the basic conveniences and comforts of everyday life. Well, of on-grid life, at least. Intensities of comfort and convenience worked differently when a body was disconnected from those networks, without access to pipes and cables. Hot energies required a different "artful use of a vast sensorium of bodily resources,"[29] or, in short: a greater bodily involvement. Hot energies demanded a re-engineering of affect: a "skillful comportment"[30] through which off-gridders became intensely sensitive to changing thermal dynamics and intensely involved in manipulating their homes through their ways of heating.

Every home, like other types of buildings, affects its inhabitants. Yet, different architectural designs operate in different ways to "channel, preclude, and evoke particular affects."[31] Ordinary, on-grid homes, for example, are often intended to create a feeling of relative separation from nature, relegating it to the alienated and foreign outside.[32] Off-grid homes instead were designed to maximize participation within natural processes—such as solar radiation and its absorption and release—pulling the outdoors indoors and pushing the inside outside. This relation was not marked by separation from the surrounding environment but by architectural involvement: an ensemble of building and everyday domestic activities unfolding in contiguous relation to other ecological processes.

Off-gridders' involvement was a form of habitation intended not as occupation of, but as connection with, place: an emergent participatory openness to multiple goings-on. Off-grid homes were characterized by involvement because their inhabitants' hot energies were immersions in the world's own ways of heating, ongoing acts of adaptive participation "in the currents of a world-in-formation."[33] Involvement, like affect, is a noun, but it is a noun that captures a swirl of activities, a hub of movements and sensations. To be involved, to involve, to be affected, to affect, are verbs: bindings of people and of non-human inhabitants of the life-world through which substances, intelligences, feelings, and intensities are wrought together.

Involvement had a key transformative property in off-grid spaces: it was catalytic. Catalysis is a chemical process: an increase in the rate of a chemical reaction provoked by the participation of a catalyst within the process. A catalyst does not "burn out" after one single act of participation; it retains its capacity to affect the process again and again. A catalyst is something that has ongoing transformative power on an assemblage within which it operates. A catalyst works as an intervener with the capacity to affect a process by either increasing or decreasing its intensity. Passive solar technologies were an obvious example of how catalysts could work, by either inhibiting the escape of warm air from the interior of a house (through insulation) or by augmenting a building's exposure to solar radiation through appropriate positioning and warmth capture.

By attending to Albertan off-gridders' domestic "spaces of practice,"[34] we also realized something very important about the broader off-grid quest for a better way of life. Whereas we on-grid dwellers have become very much uninvolved in the process of making warmth within our homes, off-gridders' involvement in the heating process allowed them to be more mindful of their impact. This was a very important realization. It began to show that a possible way of reducing environmental harm was by increasing our capacity to become involved with the working of our homes.

Our interest in the off-grid ways of heating, therefore, revealed to us that the senses and the human body were important lenses through which to understand grave social problems, such as the changes in climate caused by the domestic burning of fossil fuels. By taking a greater interest in the mundane, "embodied, affective details of habitation,"[35] we could learn a great deal about how energy is channeled, generated, used, manipulated, invested, stored, and re-directed through unique lifestyles and unique ways of heating, cooling, powering, refrigerating, etc. These embodied geographies of domestic architecture provided us with important evidence on the many ways in which habitation skills may radiate out to the rest of the world and therefore on the large potential to "re-engineer" affect[36] and thus enact a more sustainable way of living.

Notes

1. Wright, 1964.
2. Wright, 1964.
3. Chiras, 2011.
4. Wright, 1964.
5. Snider, 2006.
6. All the off-gridders featured in all our writings and visual documentations were given an opportunity to review our work before publication, as well as to suggest edits and request modifications.
7. Fennell, 2011.
8. Cupples, Guyatt, and Pearce, 2007.
9. Ingold, 2000, 2011.
10. Latour, 2004:206.
11. Anderson, 2006:735.
12. Stewart, 2011.
13. Ingold, 2011:168.
14. Ingold, 2011:117.
15. Crowley, 2001.
16. Shove, 2003.
17. Shove, 2003:41.
18. Flandrin, 1979.
19. Ingold, 2011:10.
20. Ingold, 2000.
21. After Stewart, 2011.
22. Ingold, 2000, 2011.
23. Bennett, 2010:ix.
24. Bennett, 2010:ix.
25. Bennett, 2010:9.

26. Stewart, 2007:1–2.
27. Stewart, 2007.
28. Thrift, 2004.
29. Thrift, 2004:60.
30. Thrift, 2004:70.
31. Kraftl and Adey, 2008:226.
32. Kaika, 2004.
33. Ingold, 2011:129.
34. McCormack, 2003:490.
35. Kraftl and Adey, 2008:214.
36. Latham and McCormack, 2004; Thrift, 2004.

View From Above.[i]

4

(Off)Roads

The short and narrow slope descended sharply down the bank of the Mackenzie River. Deep, compact snow rested heavily upon its many layers of suffocated ice. Upon all this whiteness a few pallid tracks—marked by the sparse vehicles that had ventured down before us—faintly showed the way. The lane then bent gently to the right, leading to the hardened icy surface of the Mackenzie. It is there that it met one of the continent's longest rivers and one of the Northwest Territories' most important roadways. Born from the waters of Great Slave Lake, the Mackenzie travelled for 1,738 kilometers to form a massive labyrinthine delta and disorderly disperse in the Beaufort Sea. The river had been cast under the spell of seasonal ice for almost 100 days by then. Congealment had given birth to an ice-road network that sinuously contorted its way through the meandering delta, reaching the otherwise–isolated communities of Aklavik and Tuktoyaktuk. It was toward Aklavik that we were driving.

I was behind the wheel. The mid-morning fog lingered in the air, wrapped in a mantle of anemic clouds and frozen mist. The feeble sky folded itself onto the blanched path. **White, white, and white**[ii]—it looked as if white was everything the world had to give, its shallow atonality the only chromatic expression of life. What happened next took a mere second. Blinded by the pervasive mist, my aimless eyes failed to inform my steering hands of the impending turn. The unchained tires of our Dodge

---

[ii.] http://lifeoffgrid.ca/wp-content/uploads/2013/11/Life-Off-Grid_Northwest-Territories_12.jpg

Durango grunted as I mistook the starboard-side powdery riverbank for the actual road. The hood lurched forward, as if punched violently. Then all that could be felt was the disturbed ground giving way underneath us with a sinister thump. Before I could take stock of what had happened, for a brief moment, optimism overtook me and I thrust my foot on the gas, only to sink more hopelessly. We were now stuck even deeper. With the forbidding air hovering around –15°C (5°F), all I could do was turn off the engine to save fuel, drop my head, and mumble "sorry." What had to happen next, I was afraid, was beyond me.

Tank Farms and Utilidors

Jon and I had left for the Northwest Territories six days before. Our Air North plane, a throwback Hawker-Siddeley 748, had puddle-jumped its way north from Whitehorse—connecting the dots between castaway places like Old Crow, Dawson City, and Inuvik and leaving behind crates of peanut butter, chips, soda, and other long-shelf-life comestibles. We had sat in the small cabin impatiently, amidst thrill-seekers, government salarymen, modern-day explorers, and locals returning from distant Costco stores, as the Rolls-Royce Dart turbo prop engine droned on. The flight had been unsettling from the very get-go. A large "CUT HERE IN CASE OF EMERGENCY" sign painted above a segmented square frame on the fuselage had rattled my nerves as I climbed aboard. Jon, who was still working on acquiring a taste for adventure airliners, had felt his heart stop after a barely perceptible but unforgettable stall-like vibration during takeoff. Neither of us was in a serene enough mood to appreciate the stunning beauty of the tundra unfolding underneath us, yet Jon's field notes had managed at least to capture its appearance:

> From the air the Mackenzie River Delta—at least the extent of its massive area **visible**[iii] through my limited porthole—is an expanse of white and grey. It's a monochrome echo of a pattern I've seen before: the splatterings of bacon fat, water, and soap left in a frying pan after breakfast, irregular bubbles of oil-like dark polka dots in an orange sheen. In the summer I can imagine how the scene below me would be reversed: the menisci of myriad islands pushing back in the water of the Mackenzie, light land amid a dark stilt stream, but today the scheme is much more

[iii.] http://lifeoffgrid.ca/wp-content/uploads/2013/11/Life-Off-Grid_Northwest-Territories_01.jpg

subtle. Today, in the middle of winter, stunted trees poke about the snow, the halftone pattern created by their tops the only hint amongst a sea of ice and snow.

We landed safe and sound.

Inuvik, the regional capital, was the port o' call for about 4,000 people. Many of them had come from away, either to exploit the riches of what had yet to become Northern Canada's longest natural gas pipeline, or to settle the busy government affairs that all frontier towns spun. Others, ethnic Inuvialuit and Gwich'in, had been there not from time immemorial, but at least since the late 1960s. It was then that the territorial and federal governments had built Inuvik almost overnight to compensate for the unreliability of the former designated hub, flood-prone Aklavik, and citizens had begun migrating there.

We were part of a different, ongoing migration. Throngs of academics—mostly of the hard-nosed variety—regularly invaded Inuvik and the surrounding area in order to study anything the Western Arctic allowed. With more and more federal grant money cast upon the many units of analysis of the Great White North—in a politico-economic attempt to fuel local business and flex the muscles of national sovereignty—Inuvik rightly cast itself as a mecca of scientific fieldwork. In light of that, we had figured we'd blend in easily for our first Arctic venture. To make matters even easier, the Aurora Research Institute—a sort of one-stop shop for all gatekeeping and data collection and storage needs—had flung its arms wide open to us as we were just about the only ivory-tower dwellers brave (or foolish) enough to come up in February and the first they'd ever met who were interested in the sheer mundanity of the local **utilidor**.[iv]

Together with the tank farm (more on that shortly), the utilidor was in fact the most glaring manifestation of Inuvik's status as an off-grid town. That's right: an off-grid town. North of the 54th parallel, Canada is laden with villages, towns, and even cities disconnected from region-wide natural gas and electricity networks. As a matter of fact, there are hardly any region-wide networks to speak of up there. The population density is simply too low and the distances dramatically too prohibitive to build grids of any significance. As a result most of these minute conurbations operate independently of one another—typically fueled by massive generators burning diesel shipped from the South (here via the Mackenzie during summer)—hence being technically "off-grid."

[iv] http://lifeoffgrid.ca/wp-content/uploads/2013/11/Life-Off-Grid_Northwest-Territories_05 .jpg

The utilidor had nothing to do with fuel. Power lines drooping from electricity poles webbed Inuvik's curiously colorful, LEGO-like homes not unlike they did elsewhere, rendering each dwelling responsible not for generating power but rather, and more simply, just enough pecuniary matter to pay monthly bills. The utilidor, instead, was a network of large pipes, about three feet in diameter, propped up on stilts two- to four-feet high above ground. Dull in its metallic gray color, robotic in its clumsy cubic shell, and fully unassuming but entirely unmissable, the utilidor snaked its way around Inuvik, **connecting**[v] every house with every apartment complex and every store with every school and government building. All those, in the end, were linked by the utilidor to Septic Lagoon (more conveniently known as Shit Lake) on one business end and with the two sources of fresh water on the other end—the Mackenzie River in the winter and a nearby lake in the warm(er) season.

The utilidor, make no mistake, was not an extravagant form of vernacular architecture. This was no Lasqueti: the utilidor hadn't been dreamed up by a resourceful guy with excess plumbing. Indeed it was serious business, free of any improvisation, adornment, and intended aesthetic value. Its instrumental raison d'être was to be found in the permafrost, or, better yet, out of it; Inuvik's Arctic climate was such that burying common mains and sewers in the permafrost would have been a foolhardy enterprise. Really, all it did to stand out was be visible—in contrast to the usually arcane, sheltered, introverted nature of city infrastructures worldwide; a big deal for easily amused cultural scientists of our ilk.

But the utilidor had no semiotic monopoly over Inuvik's off-grid identity. The **tank farm**[vi] located right downtown, steps away from the Mackenzie, was an equally powerful landmark. There, monumentally large tanks of the size and type found in large oil refineries stored enough fuel to generate electricity for the whole town until the next cargo ship would arrive. Together with a natural gas plant, located not too far from town, the tank farm yielded all the comfort and convenience that the off-gridders we had met in BC, Alberta, and the Yukon would scavenge, assemble, and harvest all on their own. Power, light, and heat: all courtesy of humongous turbines, machinery, and experts. And this, incidentally, was a serious problem for us.

House visit after house visit, Inuvik's off-gridness had become buried under a bewildered chorus of "What do you mean we're off-grid?" In a way,

---

[v.] http://lifeoffgrid.ca/wp-content/uploads/2013/11/Life-Off-Grid_Northwest-Territories_06.jpg

[vi.] http://lifeoffgrid.ca/wp-content/uploads/2013/11/Life-Off-Grid_Northwest-Territories_07.jpg

the residents' confusion was justified: they weren't truly off-grid in spirit. Solar panels and wind turbines were unheard of. Light bulbs, TV sets, and toasters went on anytime a switch was flicked. Central heating kicked in regardless of personal involvement. Shit Lake was out of sight and out of smell's reach. True, the costs of electricity and heat were a real issue here—despite subsidies—but the depth of insightful and original observations we could produce about the subject wasn't enough to justify the **lunchtime expenditure**[vii] on the $15 package of expired frozen tortellini from North Mart, let alone that of the flight up here.

As Jon and I listlessly waited in traffic at the only stop light in town, it occurred to us that we might have very little to go on. The visuals had been remarkable but the interview data were lacking the usual fervor and depth. A micro-grid, after all, was nothing but a grid, and a grid was something much too easily confined to the background of daily consciousness. Though Inuvik, Aklavik, Tuktoyaktuk, and many other Arctic towns were actually off-grid, there were no "off-gridders" here. There were no "errant trajectories," no "infinitesimal transformations," no "tactics," no independently woven assemblages of light and power, no technological choices for an alternate synchronicity, no re-inventions of everyday life.[1] From now on, we decided, the word "off-gridders" would only be dispensed when referring to self-sufficient households, and not to residents of off-grid towns. Tank farms and locally owned and managed micro-grids were simply no good for us, other than for confirming—interestingly enough by serving as a perfect contradiction—our arguments on habitation and involvement.

"I have an idea!" I exclaimed as the light turned green.

* * *

"Is everyone ok?"

"Yeah. But what do we do now?"

I got out of the driver's seat and quickly went to inspect the damage. Nothing was bent or broken or displaced, save for a pile of fresh snow. While Jon and William—a "fixer" sent from the Aurora Research Institute to guide us—pushed from the front, I pushed on the accelerator in reverse gear. It didn't work. Going forward was no option either. I apologized again for getting us stuck in this mess. "I swear I drove to Tuk yesterday and I didn't make one single mistake," I pleaded my case with William. He was silent, unruffled. Jon seemed equally unperturbed, so much so that he unlatched his satchel bag and looked for the right lens to start recording the moment.

[vii] http://lifeoffgrid.ca/wp-content/uploads/2013/11/Life-Off-Grid_Northwest-Territories_04.jpg

My big idea, two days before, was to start focusing our attention
on the one type of assemblage that made Arctic towns feel, somehow,
off-grid: their roads. A **160 km ice road**[viii]—one of the longest in the
world—connected Inuvik with Tuk(toyaktuk), to the north. A slightly
shorter one led west to Aklavik. Collecting road stories and driving the
roads ourselves, I thought, would yield interesting information about the
diffused sense of remove as well as about the likely inconveniences of
living in such distant locales.

"Well, at least," I surmised as William started dialing for help, "this
should turn out to be an interesting bit of participant observation, eh?"

Jon twitched.

"No one's answering," William announced, poker-faced.

Roads, Access, and Insulation

Mobility is a key aspect of life both on- and off-grid. Accessibility of places
of employment, supply stores, schools, medical centers, and administrative
institutions is essential to individual survival and collective well-being. Social
justice, democratic inclusion, political participation, community integration,
employment, education, health, and leisure are nearly impossible without
physical mobility, even as people learn to rely more on distance-bridging
cellular, satellite, and computer-mediated communication.

Geographer Tim Cresswell has conceptualized mobilities as varying
constellations of practices, experiences, and representations of movement.[2]
Different places afford local inhabitants with different patterns of mobility.
These patterns, or constellations, are comprised of things like the different
speeds of mobility, its costs, motives, frictions, rhythms, sensations, routes,
and degrees of remove from other places. Take the concept of "route," for
example. "Mobility is channeled"[3] along conduits such as trails, dirt roads,
town arteries, highways, freeways, shipping routes, airways, and railroads.
Depending on the kind of existing routes and how these are used, places
have a different feel. From the busy and lively streets of Covent Garden to
the festive moods of Las Vegas's main strip, and from the frenzied pace of
Kowloon to the serene atmosphere of the Camino de Santiago de Com-
postela in Spain, different mobility constellations constitute different places
and ways of life.

Canadian off-gridders had more distinct mobility patterns than most of
us. Over two years of fieldwork, Jon and I had to resort to 4 × 4 vehicles,

---

[viii.] http://lifeoffgrid.ca/wp-content/uploads/2013/11/Life-Off-Grid_Northwest-
Territories_03.jpg

passenger boats, float planes, bush planes, canoes, kayaks, bikes, RTVs, snowmobiles, and snowshoes to reach off-gridders' homes across the country. This is because typically off-gridders' homes were linked to the rest of the world by record-setting long driveways, dirt roads, bushy trails, steep paths, un-bridged bodies of water, and other elbow-scratching conduits that most people would find difficult or inconvenient to access on a regular basis. These routes connected off-grid homes to distant cities or nearby towns, but also simultaneously kept them somewhat separate from those places. Such careful balance of connection and disconnection lent off-gridders' places an aura of relative isolation characterized by slower rhythms of life, distinct soundscapes, cleaner air, closeness with wildlife, a diffuse sense of stillness and peace, and a pervasive feeling of being insulated from the dangers, annoyances, and noxious forces of the rest of the world. Inconvenient access routes were quintessential to filtering out unwanted presences. Relatively inconvenient routes, in other words, deeply shaped the feel of off-grid mobility constellations nationwide.

As an off-grid region, the Mackenzie Delta was no different in this regard. Besides airways, Inuvik was accessible by only one road. The Dempster Highway started off in Dawson City, Yukon, 736 km south. One of North America's most famous roads, the mostly unpaved Dempster traversed vast wilderness areas and offered extremely few vital services, making it difficult for drivers to refuel, rest, or make repairs. Isolation, darkness, tire- and window-shredding shrapnel, and wolves weren't enough. While one could drive the Dempster Highway to Inuvik in either winter (weather permitting) or summer, it was impossible to do so during parts of spring and fall. During spring the ice that formed natural bridges over the Peel and the Mackenzie rivers would break up, but not yet in small enough chunks to allow for ferry navigation across the river. Throughout the short autumn season ice—only beginning to take form at that time—impaired boat access while not being consistent enough to allow for driving. During these times, respectively referred to as "break-up" and "freeze-up," Inuvik was only accessible via expensive[4] air links.

Other communities in the Mackenzie Delta—like Aklavik and Tuk— were only accessible via Inuvik. However, during the warm months, car access to these towns from Inuvik was impossible due to the permafrost. At that time of the year only small boats could wind their way through the maze-like delta waters, which incidentally revolutionized their directional patterns year after year, further complicating travel. During the cold months, on the other hand, ice roads made access possible, though wintry weather could hamper travel at a moment's notice and make simply being outside extremely dangerous. The day before our unfortunate Aklavik-bound outing, Jon, Jamie—an Ontario transplant working at our lodge, whose Arctic-acclimatized eyes generously guided our ice road introduction—and I had experienced precisely a taste of that thrill.

We had departed from Inuvik at the crack of dawn (roughly 10 a.m. at that time of year) and had driven our Durango at a 70 km/h clip on the Mackenzie River for 160 km (100 miles). Then, suddenly, the route had disappeared before our eyes. The road up to that point had been rather **ordinary**.[ix] As wide as a three-lane highway, with no stop signs, marking lanes, or advertising billboards, trafficked by about one vehicle every ten minutes or so, and policed by no one but moose and low-flying ravens, on a clear day like that the Mackenzie River route stood out only for its eerie polar landscape.

But as we abandoned the Mackenzie and gradually curved right to drive on the frozen Arctic Ocean for the last 40 kilometers to Tuk, the visibility had begun to drop steadily. The ice road had been easy to follow until then: the track had a distinct azure hue and was clearly marked by grooves created by maintenance vehicles and kept visible by other cars, whose passing accidentally swept wind-drifted snow off the icy surface. But as the morning sun had given way to a low overcast ceiling, a faint but effectual wind had gradually begun swirling fresh heaps of powdery snow and depositing them on the road surface. The drifting snow had rendered the ocean-carved path nearly indistinguishable from the milky horizon and utterly featureless landscape. (After all, what land features can one expect while driving on the sea?) Though the likelihood of hitting something was low, the prospect of unknowingly driving for miles in the wrong direction en route to the North Pole was mildly unnerving to say the least. Fortunately, we got out unscathed.

* * *

Luckily, we hadn't had to wait too long for help. A half-sunken slab of blue metal stood out in the field of white snow like a sore hitchhiking thumb begging for a ride. The very first vehicle to stop was a muscular Ford truck on whose bed I spotted a bloody, still steaming-hot moose carcass loosely wrapped up in old pieces of cloth and tarpaulin.

"Moses?" William puzzled, as the truck driver rolled down his window.

"If it isn't my big brother stuck in the ditch!" Moses noted with a teasing chuckle at the sight of William.

"It's all my fault," I remarked, trying to help William save face.

[ix] http://lifeoffgrid.ca/wp-content/uploads/2013/11/Life-Off-Grid_Northwest-Territories_13.jpg

Moses glanced at me from his driver seat, his engine still running: "No native eyes, eh? What's the matter? Southerners can't tell white from white?" We all exploded in laughter.

Over the next 10 minutes I became the happy recipient of a few more teasing one-liners while Moses made good use of the ropes that everyone habitually carried in their vehicles in the North. Though we were close enough to Inuvik that we could have trekked back in search of help, there was no need for an embarrassing walk of shame. After just a few tugs and skids, we were mobile again and free to go.

"Just make sure you keep the road signs to your right next time!" Moses winked as he sped off.

"What signs?"

* * *

As Conrad had observed back in Edmonton, most Canadian off-gridders were simply hooked on gasoline. Gasoline was regularly needed to power the cars and trucks necessary to travel from rural locations to town- and city-based services and supplies. Petrol was also burned whenever off-gridders flew on airplanes or sailed away on boats for chores, work, or leisure (as many did). And diesel—as our visits to Inuvik, Aklavik, and Tuk had revealed—was also the lifeline that remote off-grid communities depended on to survive. It was a dire situation but as things were, very limited alternatives existed. Off-gridders' personal routes, and the access routes to off-grid towns, simply could not help relying on carbon-based infrastructures. As several individuals had remarked, "cars, planes, fuel, and roads are the toughest grid to get off of."

The burning of gasoline was costly and dirty—and often the source of guilt among environmentally minded off-gridders—but it was also an indispensable tool for individuals, families, and communities hell-bent on insulating themselves from the rest of the world through the mixed blessings of remoteness and difficult access. To be sure, there was a good degree of inconvenience involved in limiting access to off-grid places—as our road stories had personally taught us—but the sense of remove that inconvenience begot seemed to make it all worth it. Even we—once we learned to keep "signs" on the right—had begun to appreciate the peacefulness and beauty of the tundra. That feeling of remove was precisely why the Mackenzie Delta felt so off-grid, so much like the places we had visited and enjoyed before.

Access issues, in other words, shaped the mobility constellations of off-grid towns and off-grid homes similarly. Whether we looked at Inuvik, Lasqueti, Haines Junction, or the back-roads of the Alberta prairies, the routes, remove, and costs of off-grid mobilities affected the atmospheres of these places the same way. And how could they not? After all, the value of everyday life on our continent is so often measured by variables, such as easy access to shopping and entertainment or to a central location, and proximity to popular getaway destinations. In this geo-cultural context, for anyone to challenge the importance of these amenities and learn to enjoy the pleasure, rather than the tyranny of distances, was tantamount to re-inventing a whole new way of life.

But remove wasn't everything. The differences between off-grid homes and the residences we visited in the off-grid towns of the Mackenzie Delta were greater than their similarities. The way remove from the grid was practiced just did not explain enough. Our very understanding of what off-grid meant was under serious challenge. How could remove from a regional infrastructure be a necessary and sufficient condition for being off-grid? Was the definition perhaps in need of updating? Should we have amended it to exclude connections from any kind of infrastructure, no matter how big or small? That would have made sense and yet, had we done so, we would have ended up excluding households like Conrad's—households that were connected to the mother of all grids but in many other ways so much more independent than other gasoline-reliant off-gridders. It was clear that we needed to rethink what off-grid meant, or, at the very least, better specify and qualify it.

A possible way out of this conundrum would have been to create categories. A category for this type of off-grid home, that type of off-grid home, this type of off-grid town, and so forth. But categories are often unsatisfactory. It actually seemed ironic, if not downright offensive, to place individuals who had dedicated their lives to "living outside the box" back into tidy taxonomies. It would also have done a great disservice to our relational and non-representational approach to the subject, which was meant to focus on relations, processes, and connections, rather than static individuations, ideal types, and separations. With no intention to update a widely accepted technical definition that didn't belong to us in the first place, and with even less interest in drawing a grid to order and rank off-gridders, we turned our attention to the sky.

The sky had been in constant movement throughout our journey through the Northwest Territories. Air turbulence, ice pellets, coalescing particles of fog, shifting weather fronts, and even an unforgettable display of **Northern Lights**[x] had kept us lively company throughout the trip—the sky was just awash with multiple movements and coalescings of different kinds. So it

---

[x] http://lifeoffgrid.ca/wp-content/uploads/2013/11/Life-Off-Grid_Northwest-Territories_08.jpg

was in the sky, and more precisely in the idea of constellations, that we found the answer. We just needed to assemble a constellation of not so much mobilities—because Cresswell's idea was born out of the desire to understand that particular phenomenon—but of power. With that in place we could better understand the meanings of comfort, convenience, efficiency, and all the other facets of the off-grid quest for a better life.

Notes

1. See chapter 1 for more context on these terms and for references.
2. Cresswell, 2010.
3. Cresswell, 2010:24.
4. A round-trip flight from Vancouver typically costs around $2,400.

Johanna at Work.[i]

―――――――――

[i] For more photos, visit lifeoffgrid.ca.

5
POWER CONSTELLATIONS

The opportunity to flesh out the fledgling power constellation idea soon presented itself. While surfing the web in search of Saskatchewan-based off-gridders, I stumbled across Ron and Johanna's **"For Sale" sign**.[ii] Without as much as a second thought, I fired them an email. Ron replied promptly, "Do you know how far we live? We're 100 kilometers away from the nearest road. You can't possibly come all the way here and stay only for a few *hours*! You and Jon can be our guests for a few *days*—so you can really see what we do." Now I just needed to figure out a way to get there.

Power is an interesting word. Power stands for authority, control, sovereignty, economic capital, military-industrial hegemony, social stratification, and all that. But power—especially in everyday usage—is synonymous with something seemingly more immediate, proximate, and concrete. Thus, we may talk of "engine power" that allows us to drive faster, of "body power" that enables us to jump higher, or of "domestic power" that permits us to live comfortable, connected, and convenient lives.[1] What is truly interesting is that the dictionary definition of *power*—that is, the ability or capacity to act—refers to *all* of the above. But power is mostly studied by social scientists as a political force. Power in the other, more physical, sense is instead routinely confined into a "black box" hidden from consciousness,[2] relegated to the back rooms of domestic stages,[3] and outright ignored by most social scientists.[4] So, in coining our simple concept of power constellations, we wanted to try and make our understanding of physical power more concrete, systematic, and simple.

[ii.] http://inthewilderness.net/

Taking inspiration from the idea of mobility constellations, we defined a power constellation as a historically and geographically specific pattern of power generation, distribution, and application. Similar to Cresswell,[5] we viewed a constellation as an assemblage—that is, an ensemble of objects, practices, experiences, and representations that made sense together. All objects, practices, experiences, and representations of, and about, power are entangled in "meshworks"[6] of organic and inorganic materials and technologies, landscapes, and multiple other entities and forces. These meshworks—like our homes, for example—are the sites where power is lived. To make the concept even more useful, we then proceeded to identify 10 components of it: motive-force, friction, route, sensibility, interconnectivity, availability, cost, externality, pace, and efficiency. Equipped with this list, we flew to Saskatchewan.

Have Cessna, Will Travel

The bad news shot at us like an arrow out of the sky. The crackling voice on the other end of the cell line dryly announced that no Cessna 185 was currently equipped with landing skis, despite our earlier arrangement with the airline. If we wanted to, we could still charter a twin-engine deHavilland Otter, but at the cost of $3,000: double the earlier agreed-upon price. I hung up the phone and sank my face into my hands. Jon and I had designed our Saskatchewan itinerary around this flight into the Boreal Forest and we knew we couldn't afford for this to go wrong. We had already flown to Saskatoon and driven a rental 4 × 4 halfway to our destination in the far north of the province. Now the plan was falling apart at the worst possible time.

I pushed aside my mocha, scattered our travel receipts on the small coffee shop table, and crunched a few numbers on a napkin. I mumbled unconvincing "plan B's" to Jon, then asked to borrow his iPhone again. I soon learned that a different company had a Cessna on skis. Because the new pick-up point was nearer to us, the flight to Ron and Johanna's would be longer and costlier than the original plan: $2,700 for the round trip. But it was still cheaper than three grand and it required less driving on snow-choked backcountry highways. We had no alternative.

We drove for a couple of hours and checked into a motel. It snowed all night. We reached the air terminal the following morning, where we finally shook hands with our pilot: a soft-spoken, friendly young man with boyish good looks. Kyle looked 21 or maybe 22. As I loaded my backpack behind the back seat, I ached to pry into how many flying hours Kyle had accumulated over his career. Instead—as I figured I should be gentle with the feelings of someone entrusted with my life—I inquired whether he knew where Johanna and Ron's place was. He said he knew **the lake**.[iii]

There are thousands of lakes in northern Saskatchewan. Some are overgrown ponds, some are big enough to swallow cities, but all have one thing in common: during the winter they are frozen deep and fully covered in snow—a characteristic that renders their features from the air as indistinct as holes on a piece of Gruyere cheese. Though Kyle exuded a laid-back sense of confidence, right before departure I secretly marked the landing strip's coordinates on my hand-held GPS. Just in case. Though this all seemed surreal to me, the trip was all but routine for Ron and Johanna.

There were no roads to Johanna and Ron's house. None. No walking paths, no snowmobile trails, no logging roads, no cross-country ski tracks. A chartered flight was their only way home. Floatplanes could land on snow during winter and on water during summer. About twice a year—generally before break-up and right after freeze-up—the two homesteaders would go to town to stock up. The flight would cost the same whether the cargo space was empty or full, so they'd plan their trips strategically. They'd fly in a whole pig or a side of beef on the pick-up leg, for instance, unload it and stick it in the freezer, then fly to town carrying along something like machinery needing repair. Then three or four days later, on their way back home, they'd charter a Cessna 185 or a deHavilland Beaver—depending on how much stuff they had accumulated on their resupply spree.

Air mile-collecting jet-setters would no doubt be chagrined to learn that the 50-minute flight featured no upgrade eligibility, in-flight entertainment, or snack service. However, Kyle was kind enough to provide an old cloth that Jon and I used to wipe the ice condensation from the **plastic windows**[iv] every five minutes or so. Kyle was even kind enough to fly an extra circle over the house to let Jon record some quality footage. Kyle was a very good pilot too: the landing on the frozen lake turned out to be an absolute greaser.

Standing in the snow, Ron and Johanna, both in their fifties, of tall stature and self-assured but unpretentious poise, wore season-appropriate clothing for the –20°C (–4°F) weather. As we received their warm welcome, I kept recalling Ron's words in an email we had exchanged: "save for forest firefighters a few years ago," he wrote, "we've rarely had any visitors." But as we stood by the frozen lake's edge exchanging mutual first impressions, I began to attribute the paucity of guests to the hefty airfare alone, rather than to any antisocial disposition on our hosts' part. Though "no social butterflies"—in their own words—Ron and Johanna gave off the vibe of being

iii. http://lifeoffgrid.ca/wp-content/uploads/2013/11/Life-Off-Grid_Saskatchewan_02.jpg
iv. http://lifeoffgrid.ca/wp-content/uploads/2013/11/Life-Off-Grid_Saskatchewan_01.jpg

genuinely delighted to meet two perfect strangers who would live with them for three days.

As Kyle had no time for tea, Ron and Johanna quickly traded him an envelope to mail off and three bags full of garbage in exchange for a small parcel delivery—a foot valve for the water line, shipped from the hardware store. Soon enough he was back in the cockpit.

"Do you mind if we wait a minute to see him take off?" Ron asked as I flung my backpack on my shoulders. "It's always a pretty good show."

"Well, do you mind if I film the whole thing?" Jon opportunistically inquired.

As the Cessna skidded away, its engine noise whispered lower and lower from farther afield—its echo reverberating across the surrounding hills and growing more buzz-like as it went, sounding as if powered by a swarm of bumble bees. Once out of sight and sound, the rest of society suddenly became but a faint notion.

The Farthest Home

At 1,536 square feet, Ron and Johanna's two-story house wasn't lavish by North American standards, but it had plenty of room for them to spend time together or to enjoy on their own whenever they needed a break from each other. Johanna liked **sewing**,[v] cooking, canning, and working in the garden. Ron took delight in **building**[vi] wood furniture and smaller decorative objects. These hobbies and skills played key functional roles too. Johanna—with a formal educational background in nutrition and dietetics—managed to fill the shelves of both a walk-in pantry and a secondary food storage area with preserves. Ron—a self-described "Jack of all trades and master of none" with training in industrial electronics—kept in stock tools, nuts, bolts, nails, lumber, and mechanical parts to fix almost anything.

Save for the long winter—when life slowed down considerably—they both kept quite busy, without ever being in a rush. The rhythms of late spring and summer were largely synchronized with those of the vegetables and fruits growing in both the greenhouse and outside: tomatoes, asparagus, zucchini, peppers, melons, celery, different kinds of lettuce, corn, green beans, wax beans, carrots, beets, cabbage, broccoli, cauliflower, Brussels sprouts, potatoes, strawberries, raspberries, Saskatoon berries, rhubarb, currants, and apples. To grow anything above 56°N, they explained, **was not easy.**[vii]

[v.] http://lifeoffgrid.ca/wp-content/uploads/2013/11/Life-Off-Grid_Saskatchewan_03.jpg
[vi.] http://lifeoffgrid.ca/wp-content/uploads/2013/11/Life-Off-Grid_Saskatchewan_04.jpg
[vii.] https://soundcloud.com/innovativeethnographies/ron-and-johanna-growing-food

Underlying all their domestic efforts was an uncompromising commitment to "self-sufficiency."

"It's a lot of satisfaction," Johanna explained when I asked her what self-sufficient meant to her.

"Where does the satisfaction come from?"

"It's something I've always dreamed of doing since I was a teenager and I've been lucky enough to be able to do it. To sit down at the table and know that 90% of what's on the table is stuff that you grew or made yourself is a very satisfying thing."

Self-sufficiency, Ron added, is "the feeling that we're providing for ourselves . . ."

"And," Johanna interjected, "that we're not dependent on the grocery store, or some farmer in California, and the whole distribution system."

Self-sufficiency was obviously impossible. It if were possible, Ron and Johanna should have been able to manufacture solar panels out of their sandy soil, squeeze ethanol from their own corn, and do without flying to town for occasional shopping. However, the ideal of at least *approaching* self-sufficiency and enjoying a better life was what inspired them to move here 14 years ago.

Ron and Johanna had been off-grid altogether since 1979. In 1999 they left the state of Maine, after they had homesteaded there for about 20 years. Seeking more space and more "adventure," they decided to look for land in Saskatchewan, where they knew they could petition the provincial government to lease affordable land north of 56°. They bought a few topographic maps and chartered a floatplane to explore the region from the air, until they **discovered**,[viii] and fell in love with at first sight, their place.

Everything had to be brought in by floatplane and thus minutely allotted in advance. All the construction material, for example, was flown in by a twin-engine Otter over 10 trips made throughout a weekend. But first the site had to be cleared of snow and trees, a waterline had to be hand-dug, a leach field prepared, and foundations laid. And of course, a temporary shelter—an expedition tent serving as their home for three months—had to be assembled. Their photo album told the details of the building process: from Johanna's sketch of the floor plan to the placement of every stud, every triple-pane window, and every insulating vapor barrier. Ron's brother—the only "stranger" in the pictures—provided muscle help, but otherwise this was very much an exercise in self-sufficiency.

As we sat in the living room overlooking the lake and the hills to the south, the stories illustrated their life quest. "This is the land of milk and

---

[viii.] https://soundcloud.com/innovativeethnographies/ron-and-johanna-exploring

honey," Ron reflected. "We've got the best of both worlds here. We have the peace and quiet of the wilderness. And we have modern comforts and conveniences: satellite TV and internet, radio, refrigeration. You'd never know you're a hundred miles out in the bush. There is the feeling of accomplishment of being off-the-grid, the sense of satisfaction that we're providing for ourselves, that we're not dependent on the power grid to keep supplied. We've got everything we want." But as they grew older and slowly reached the age when access to medical facilities became more important, they felt it necessary to inch closer to town. Their plan was still to remain off-grid, but this time at a more accessible location on the Nova Scotia coast.

As the February sun plowed through the morning clouds, the questions and answers of the first interview dissipated. As I scribbled a few notes and Jon changed batteries, a loudly ticking solar-powered plastic toy plant and a cantankerous wall clock sanctioned the passage of each second—sounding a domestic melody that over the next three days would become as habitual as Johanna's **clanking**[ix] in the kitchen and the **fire popping**[x] and hissing inside the woodstove. After a hearty lunch, we resumed our conversation outdoors.

A loop about three kilometers long stretched north of their homestead, hugging low-rising ground and weaving its way through a sparse forest of conifers. Though Ron and Johanna maintained their trail with the footsteps of one daily walk, we latched on snowshoes and grabbed ski poles to conquer the slushier stretches. Once the wind turbine's innocuous but detectable hum was past, the southerly breeze's whispers and the soft tune of snow powder twirling in the air met no sound other than our own weighty strides. In the midst of this soundscape, Ron had no difficulty explaining the comforts of the peace and quiet they enjoyed here. There were inconveniences and worries too, of course. Wildfires, importunate black bears, and oh, not having a dishwasher.

Despite the lack of a dishwasher there were a few amenities, besides the stillness of silence, which made life enjoyable so deep in the wilderness. To provide electricity there was an 800-watt photovoltaic array, a 2-kW wind turbine, and a 6-kW diesel generator needed to maintain the longevity of a near-one tonne worth of 2-volt deep-cycle batteries capable of storing over 1,500 amps. To provide heat, two woodstoves consumed pine and spruce— and one of the woodstoves heated water and served as the cooker and oven as well. But there was more.

Passive solar floor design and thick wall insulation allowed for savings on firewood. Water flowed from the well to the shower and the sinks channeled

---

by an electric pump. Solid human waste first corralled in the indoor com-posting toilet through a simple bucket-like container aged slowly and even-tually fed fruit trees. Compact fluorescent bulbs gave light. The absence of blow driers, a microwave oven, and toaster spared their batteries a heavy blow. Chest freezers—all placed facing east outdoors and sheltered under the porch from the direct sun—remained unplugged during the colder months. Thick walls made the indoor refrigerator extra efficient. An Irid-ium satellite phone could reach help in no time. And chess and Scrabble provided timeless unplugged entertainment.

Not to say that entertainment or information of the plugged-in variety wasn't available. Every afternoon, while Johanna knitted or read a book, Ron would find a seat on his squeaking rocking chair and punctually tune in to the four o'clock financial newscast on MSNBC. Then, using the same satellite signal feeding the TV dish, he would log on to the internet, check further news, and occasionally make a mysterious transaction. Ron and Johanna were essentially retired (though occasional seasonal work setting up expedition outpost camps would occupy Ron), and their savings, as it turned out, grew from Ron's stock transactions. Even here, 100 miles from the nearest shop, amidst flying pigs, roaming hungry wolves, and real ursine ups and downs, the stock exchange's bull and bear seemed to leave consequential traces.

Complete self-sufficiency wasn't truly what was going on in Ron and Johanna's little paradise. It was perhaps more a quest for a fleeting glimpse of sovereign power—a power wrestled from utilities, crowded stores, busy intersections, happening urban scenes, and countryside communities. A power wrestled only partially, true, but no less meaningfully. After all, no constellation appears alone in the sky, does it?

Costs, Efficiencies, Externalities, and More

The study of power constellations aims to describe and understand why, how, and by whom power is generated, distributed, and utilized. Power, like mobility, "is a resource that is differentially accessed"[7] either by virtue of limited opportunity or personal choice. Different places, for example, are characterized by different power constellations. Power constellations have also varied across history, as resource configurations, social expectations, and different technologies have changed.[8] As of late, for instance, power constellations worldwide have "splintered," giving rise to multiple cross-national, sub-regional, and even micro-local entanglements differentiated and stratified along social, economic, political, and technological fault lines.[9] These fractures show us that power is no longer the exclusive domain of uniform and monopolistic structures, as it often was in the past. As power now flows in multiple ways, coalesces in myriad assemblages, and connects and bypasses various groups of people, it becomes more important than ever to examine how disparate power constellations operate in the day-to-day lives of different individuals living in distinct places. The 10 elements below should make the job of disentangling power constellations a bit easier.

First, people need power for different reasons. To some degree we are all compelled to use power to survive, but in most instances our use is informed by degrees of choice and desire. The concept of *motive-force*[10] captures these dynamics of need and want and the degree of their imperativeness. Ron and Johanna, for example, required power to light up their home, keep warm, refrigerate their food, extract water, and operate a few appliances. This was unsurprising—as they, like others, took pleasure in domestic comfort, cleanliness, and convenience.[11] But the real question here is why did they, as opposed to the rest of the Western world, seek to do it on their own, off-the-grid? In other words, how were the motive-forces of off-grid households like theirs different?

As seen in earlier chapters, like most other off-gridders Johanna and Ron lived off-grid for the feeling of independence. Their independence was relative, of course, but the heightened sense of self-reliance and self-sufficiency gave them great satisfaction. This sense of sovereignty over their power—that is, over their capacity to act to take care of their needs and wants—was at the very core of the off-grid quest for a better life across the country.[12]

The concept of motive-force prompts us to ask not only why people need and want power as well as what they need it and want it for, but also what people are willing to do to obtain power; what type of power assemblages people prefer and why; what kinds of power applications people are willing to sacrifice if necessary; what reasons, values, and ideologies inform people's choices for power; and what lifestyle philosophies inform the choices behind different groups' motives to do with or without certain kinds of power and certain power applications—to name only a few possible questions.

Second, where does power come from? What *routes* does power take to flow from its points of extraction, generation, and transformation to its points of utilization? What are the consequences of such routes? Whom do such routes exclude, and why? Like other forms of mobility, power is channeled. Its infrastructures—pipes, cables, wires, mains, pipelines, etc.—are its channels, its routes. As part of their "tunneling effect,"[13] such routes draw some places in intense interaction, while marginalizing and excluding others. For example, most off-gridders in Canada were in no position to connect to the electricity grid given the prohibitive distance of their homes from the nearest pole, or given the unequal political economy of rural electrification. For some, like Ron and Johanna, this remove was a highly desired condition, but for others—like entire communities in the northern regions of the country—this differential access translated into opportunity-debilitating power poverty.[14]

The routes taken by power greatly matter in other respects as well. Because many routes are out of direct view (e.g., buried underground, hidden in back alleys, etc.), most people feel distanced from energy dynamics and for the most part carry on their lives in complete ignorance of, and separation from, power channels.[15] But something interesting happens when power becomes more visible. Whenever crises occur—such as blackouts[16] or droughts[17]—power and its routes suddenly take center stage, changing practices of consumption[18] and at times even stimulating resilient and creative conduct.[19] It is in this sense that we can understand off-grid constellations as hubs of imaginative, re-territorializing practices that—through visible and reflective routings and the consequent creativity and self-reliance these originate—aim to bring order and control[20] in places bypassed by the routes of large-scale assemblages.

The third element is a monetary one. How much does it *cost* to utilize power in all its various applications? How much wattage, and therefore money, does it cost to dry a load of clothes, to toast a slice of bread, to heat a poorly insulated bedroom, to keep a laptop plugged in at night? And how much do competing power utilizing technologies cost to purchase? For example, how much does it cost to install a geothermal system? And is that system more affordable in the long run than an old-fashioned woodstove? Few of us think regularly about the ordinary costs of domestic power. For some people struggling with fuel poverty, energy costs are a growing concern,[21] but for many homeowners and renters alike, the comforts and convenience of electricity and heat seem natural and taken for granted, and their costs feel hidden and distant.[22]

Off-gridders' power constellations were characterized instead by very tangible, very visible cost configurations. To save power, Johanna and Ron had consciously chosen not to have a hair drier or a microwave oven for example, and so had most other off-gridders. Heat-emitting electric appliances can consume well over 1,000 watts/hour—a draw that can put a serious strain on batteries and require the installation of larger photovoltaic arrays. Cost awareness characterized Ron and Johanna's domestic power constellation in other ways. For them, reaching the grocery store was enormously expensive. Their trips to town therefore had to be strategic, carefully planned, and tightly budgeted. It made no sense for them, for example, to fly in the spring to the butcher's to spend thousands of dollars on meats that would cost them a great deal of wattage to keep frozen throughout the summer. Other off-gridders had to tackle similarly complex plans. While most of us have come to take for granted the convenience of nearby supermarkets selling frozen goods that we can store in our freezers,[23] during our visits to the north we learned that residents of off-grid Arctic communities commonly divided up the spoils of their hunting and fishing among extended families, friends, and neighbors—thus reducing the need to buy expensive meat and fish imported from the south, as well as reducing the need to keep large kills frozen for long periods of time.

Fourth, the bills we pay are not the only costs of power. The socio-environmental consequences caused by extracting energy resources, channeling their flows, and applying power to tackle ordinary tasks give rise to short- and long-term ecological costs that are often hidden, but no less meaningful than their financial counterparts. Such costs are known as *externalities*.[24] Externalities occur because we are somewhat mindless of the indirect impacts of our high-carbon lives. As sociologist John Urry[25] has pointed out: "these consequences threaten the basic elements of life for people around the world, and especially future generations: through melting glaciers, declining crop yields, ocean acidification, rising sea levels, deaths from malnutrition and heat stress, displacements of people, ecosystem destruction, reduced diversity, shifts in weather patterns and collapsing ice sheets, and so on."

Externalities are typically the subject of distant global policies (or lack thereof). In contrast, off-gridders treated externalities as meaningful ongoing concerns of their power constellations. Off-gridders engaged in local generation of renewable power, reduced their consumption of non-renewables, and took part in many activities informed by principles of sustainability. To be fair, off-grid living was not always so green. At times, life in remote locations required great expenditures in fuel to reach the workplace or the nearest store, and in some homes backup generators were definitely employed more than they should have been. However, for the most part, off-gridders were infinitely more aware than most other power consumers about their carbon footprint. While no self-styled environmentalists, Ron and Johanna, for example, heated their house with renewable resources harvested locally, and through insulation and passive solar design they made sure to use as little wood as possible. And while flying to town was not exactly as green as, say, bicycling, the distance and cost were key motivators for reducing their travel frequency, as well as for reusing objects of all kinds, thus reducing the need to go shopping.

Power constellations differ from one another not only in terms of how impactful externalities are, but also in terms of how involved individuals are in limiting the negative environmental consequences of their choices. Being self-sufficient for power (at least relatively) in a utility-scarce domain always carried a certain risk—a certain "energy insecurity" as it were.[26] Such insecurity drove off-gridders to develop practical skills and everyday knowledge about energy resources and to cultivate constant awareness of both economic costs and externalities. Thus, people like Ron and Johanna had learned that simple domestic practices like canning, pickling, and dehydrating locally grown foods were both financially and environmentally wise.

Fifth, power constellations are shaped by rhythm and speed. Power moves in different ways than, say, a train does, but it too is characterized by important temporal dynamics. Electricity's flow, for example, is measured in amps. Electricity's potential, or in a water flow analogy, pressure, is measured in volts. The product of voltage times current equals watts. A watt is a rate of work: more precisely the rate at which work is done when an amp of current flows through an electrical potential difference of one volt. Now, I feel bewildered just writing this stuff, but as it turns out power shapes the *pace* of your life in very immediate, intuitive, and practical ways when you live off-grid.

For example, like many other off-gridders, Ron and Johanna lived in great synchrony with the weather's seasonal and diurnal patterns because of the changing rhythms of light and heat. So a load of laundry might have had to wait for a sunny day, when batteries could be quickly recharged from the drain imposed by a washing machine. By synchronizing power generation and utilization with weather patterns, off-gridders engaged in a unique form of slow living[27]—investing their everyday life with a temporal attentiveness and care that challenged the relation between power and speed typical of modern life.[28]

Off-gridders' practices sensitize us to the importance of power's temporal dynamics and teach us to ask questions such as: how fast can energy resources drain, and how quickly can they be replenished? How synchronized must processes of power utilization and generation be? At what type of rhythms do different power resources and technologies work? Do these rhythms work independently or interdependently from our own everyday routines? How long does it take to transform a certain energy resource into usable power?

The sixth element is *availability*. *Availability* is a matter of how suitable and readily obtainable something is. Of course stuff is not always ready for our taking, so the availability of something may depend on an individual's skills, knowledge, creativity, resourcefulness, planning ability, and physical and technical capacities. Even from a collective standpoint the energy resources that we have available as a global society are related to our ability and willingness to generate, distribute, transform, utilize, dispose of, and even re-utilize different resources. Availability is therefore a relational entity.

Resource availability shapes people's skills in distinct, place-sensitive ways. Such skills profoundly characterize the features of different power constellations. Take the availability of land to grow food and generate calories to fuel the body, for example. Johanna and Ron knew that because of the distance to the nearest grocery store they had to make the best possible use of the short growing season. This condition pushed them to localize most of their food consumption, reducing the journey from plot to fork.[29] The gardening tricks they employed to cope with local weather and climate manifested their knowledge of local resources, their creativity, and their ability to improvise[30] and to cope with the demands of their challenging "taskscape."[31]

Availability of resources also shapes issues such as the propensity to conserve. Ron and Johanna did not have unlimited water provided to them by a municipality. To conserve the water they did have, they used a composting toilet system that required no flushing. Billions of gallons of clean, fresh water are flushed away annually in homes and public places, despite rising global concerns over water scarcity. In contrast, just like Ron and Johanna, off-gridders across Canada tended to be very mindful of the limited availability of groundwater and harvested rainwater and/or carefully maintained groundwater wells.

Seventh, there is *efficiency:* a ratio of work done on the basis of energy supplied. Efficiency is a return on investment—a measure of the usefulness of an input. By asking good questions about power constellations we can learn to appreciate the nuances of different efficiencies. Questions such as: how productive are different energy resources and forms of power generation, distribution, and application? How adaptable are power resources to different demands and working conditions? How easy are they to use? How environmentally efficient and sustainable are they?

Researchers interested in energy in everyday life have remarked on efficiency with regard to many different technologies, such as showers,[32] patio heaters,[33] air conditioners,[34] and compact fluorescent light bulbs,[35] to name only a few. Efficiency matters greatly in the context of renewable technology as well. Take for example the efficiency of wind as a resource for power generation. Ron and Johanna had a wind turbine capable of generating 2,000 watts, but that generating capacity was dependent on the availability of constantly useful wind—that is, wind that was neither too strong nor too weak. At high speeds, wind turbines automatically lock to prevent damage and cease to generate electricity, and at low speeds little or no power is produced. However, where they lived wind typically occurred in strong gusts or was otherwise too moderate to be useful. Wind turbines generally present other disadvantages too: they are laborious to install, can be noisy, and can create problems in icy conditions. Because of all these problems a monetary investment in wind turbines tended to be an uncertain one for many off-gridders. Indeed it was not uncommon to meet off-gridders who, like Johanna and Ron, found their investment in wind to be a relatively inefficient one.

Efficiency is subject to varying personal experiences, preferences, and practices. Of course in many power constellations, efficiency is not always subject to reflexive, individual decision making.[36] Many of us living on the grid, for example, may install efficient compact fluorescent lights to save energy but then may mindlessly over-illuminate a room or even leave lights on when not needed. Efficiency was instead monitored assiduously by off-gridders, who had to exercise special caution with their available power and regularly checked charge displays, current usage gauges, and so on.

Or take for example the many appliances that today are sold with an Energy Star® rating, which symbolizes high efficiency. Though comparatively efficient, these technologies are often used in inefficient ways—for example, by users who keep them on "stand-by" mode even when not needed for long periods of time. Off-gridders across the country, on the other hand, were on constant patrol to make appliances more efficient by taking the time to turn them off or to even rig them so they wouldn't cause ghost loads (a ghost load is the electrical draw of a standby technology, such as a TV plugged in but not turned on, or a microwave oven "on" only to display the time of the day). Efficiency too—as these practices showed—is then a relational quality.

Eighth: when, where, and how does power stop flowing? And what happens during these *frictions?* Why do these stoppages occur, and how are they dealt with? "Friction," Cresswell[37] observes, "is a social and cultural phenomenon . . . sufficient to prevent motion" or to significantly slow it down. Traffic gridlock and border-crossing lines are good examples of mobility frictions. In the context of power, frictions generally occur in three ways: interruptions in energy generation, distribution breakdowns, and utilization glitches.

Interruptions in the generation of power can occur, for example, when energy resources become temporarily or permanently unavailable. Because "we build our social relationships and cultural understandings to coalesce around the continued flow of energy of familiar qualities in expected quantities,"[38] interruptions can have dramatic consequences. During unusually long stretches of unpropitious weather, off-gridders felt compelled to cut down on power usage and cope with the consequences. An alternative course of action (for those who owned them) was to fire up their diesel or gasoline generators. Generator use, however, was often extremely problematic. Generators burned non-renewable resources, were loud, smelled bad, were costly to refuel, broke down easily, and required painstaking maintenance. Generators also symbolized a painful defeat in the off-grid quest for self-sufficiency.

Distribution breakdowns are frictions occurring between the sites of power generation and utilization. In the grid-connected world these frictions are known as blackouts. Blackouts are "breaks in the flow of social time"[39] that manifest the vitality and agency of power constellations.[40] In the off-grid world, blackouts do not occur, but distribution frictions are no less significant. Solar, wind, and micro-hydropower sources generate direct current (DC) electricity, as opposed to the alternate current (AC) that flows in common power lines. DC electricity must be inverted from its source to AC electricity in order to operate most household appliances, which work on the latter. Alternatively, off-gridders must endeavor to convert these appliances to work on DC. Either option can be the source of numerous problems.[41]

Finally, utilization glitches occur at the moment of power consumption. For example, light bulbs may burn out, blenders may stop working, and so on. To some degree off-gridders experienced these problems as much as the rest of us do in our everyday lives, but at other times these problems occurred because of the idiosyncrasies of their systems, such as the needed inversion from DC to AC. For example, older and less-expensive inverters were unable to invert to pure sine wave current, and anything but a pure conversion caused appliances to malfunction and even break down. The preventive maintenance and routine repair occasioned by such frictions was no insignificant matter in the off-grid lifeworld: maintenance and repair "illustrate the importance of human labour and ingenuity,"[42] and reveal the different skills and bodies of knowledge[43] existing within specific power constellations.

Electricity, of all forms of power, is "the central symbol of globalizing modernity and its associated urban consumption styles."[44] Electricity's arrival in rural, remote, and developing places throughout the world continues to have dramatic infrastructural, socio-cultural, and political repercussions.[45] Indeed a great deal of our day-to-day lives revolves around electricity's functioning, including the continued flow of other resources. Take gasoline, for example. Refueling a car with a credit card at a gas station relies on complex systems like the construction and maintenance of roads and highways, the global network of oil extraction and distribution, the international finance organization that allows credit cards to work, and the communication networks that send monetary information around the globe,[46] but also on the very mundane operation of the electrical infrastructure that allows for fuel to be pumped into a tank and the payment to be made through a credit card reader. The point here is simple: power sources are interconnected with one another. Power constellations, it follows, are also interconnected with other power constellations.

The ninth question then is: how do these interconnections work, and how deeply? The off-grid power constellations we visited were characterized by a more limited *interconnectivity* than we might expect from a modern, Western home. Off-grid households, in fact, greatly emphasized the value of independence, much more so than typical on-grid homes. Johanna and Ron's distance to the nearest town forced them to be more self-reliant than most of us—something that was a source of satisfaction as well as some inconvenience. But their distance from "society"—as Ron enjoyed referring to the rest of the world—was not synonymous with isolation. So, while the generation of electricity was a relatively independent pursuit for them (save, of course, for "society's" involvement in manufacturing wind turbines and solar panels), the uses to which electricity was put were not. By powering up their TV set and computer, and by generating electricity to download a satellite internet signal, Ron and Johanna's home was enmeshed within global information and entertainment networks. Not to mention that by advertising the sale of their home on the web, and by investing in the stock market, even their family finances were interconnected with the rest of society. Off-gridders—as our two years of travel would reveal in the end—were never truly "off." Their power constellations were, though always in different ways, deeply interconnected with many other assemblages.

Finally, there is the tenth element: *sensibility.* Sensibility is the propensity and ability to feel. It is the capacity to affect one's environment and be affected by it. Different power constellations feel different from one another. To ask about the atmospheres of different power constellations and the sensibilities of people living within them is therefore to ask about the different senses of place, and how these different senses of place arise as a result of various assemblages of power generation, distribution, and utilization.

Off-grid places like Ron and Johanna's felt dramatically different from on-grid domestic environments. From the quiet and the darkness of their environments, to the unique sounds and textures of their abodes, off-grid power constellations gave rise to different sensations to both full-time inhabitants and occasional visitors like us. Different power constellations are characterized by sharply unique atmospheres, and such different atmospheres draw different people with different inclinations, skills, and values—and different ideas of what constitutes a good life.

To ask about the different sensibilities of power constellations and of their dwellers is therefore to ask questions about the geographies and sociology of power and of lifestyle. It requires being sensitive to the sights, sounds, aromas, flavors, textures, temperatures, and fluctuations of a place. It demands thinking carefully about the many ways in which power affects an atmosphere: from the presence of a candle lighting a room or a ringing phone, to the availability of heat and clean water.

And, of course, different sensibilities exist in different environments. Whereas some off-gridders, for example, felt adamant about not using stinky and noisy generators, others were less offended by their operation. Even within a relatively coherent power constellation, such as the off-grid one, many differences existed along the elements we have described in these pages.

* * *

Kyle deposited us back onto terra firma safely once again, three days after we had departed. We de-iced our truck's windshield and set our sights for Prince Albert, where we consumed a hurried deli sandwich lunch in the Real Canadian Superstore's parking lot. We then slogged on to Saskatoon through nearly whiteout conditions and waited in the city for our flight back home. Eerily, Saskatoon felt like a glitzy megalopolis with all its traffic lights, cars, people, and KFC franchises. The shock of coming back to the "real world" after only even a few days off-grid was always a destabilizing—and yet strangely re-energizing—one.

But this one was notably less invigorating. Besides Ron and Johanna, we had interviewed four other off-gridders in the province and had braved more sub-zero temperature days in one week than we had experienced in the last five years on our warm and cozy coast. We were homesick, fed up with snow, and exhausted. And our budget had taken a sizeable hit. There was no doubt we'd have to make a few cuts on the road ahead. Skipping provinces was no option, of course. We had our minds and hearts set on proudly reaching Newfoundland as the thirteenth and last trip, and nothing would change that, even if that meant no cuisine other than "parking lot specials" and no accommodations other than camping for the rest of the way.

"Actually," I quipped as we rushed to return our truck earlier than scheduled to save on car rental money, "maybe we could camp somewhere and save. Like, in Newfoundland. Summers are warm there, right?"

"Yeah, why not?" Jon replied. "Maybe we can camp in Nunavut too. Global warming has probably already turned Baffin Island into a tropical paradise anyway."

"Camping in Nunavut, that's an idea . . ."

Notes

1. Hornborg, 2001.
2. Star, 1999.
3. Kaika, 2004.
4. Graham and Marvin, 2001.
5. Cresswell, 2010.

6. Ingold, 2011.
7. Cresswell, 2010:21.
8. Nye, 1999.
9. Graham and Marvin, 2001.
10. Cresswell, 2010.
11. Shove, 2003.
12. And in the US as well, according to journalist Nick Rosen, 2010.
13. Graham and Marvin, 2001.
14. Compare to Harrison and Popke, 2011.
15. Luna, 2008.
16. Bennett, 2010; Nye, 2010.
17. Chappells and Medd, 2008; Chappells, Medd, and Shove, 2011.
18. Chappells and Medd, 2008.
19. Allon and Sofoulis, 2006.
20. deLanda, 2006.
21. See Hitchings and Day, 2011; O'Neill, Jinks, and Squire, 2006.
22. Fennell, 2011.
23. See Hand and Shove, 2007.
24. See Urry, 2011.
25. Urry, 2011:9.
26. Palen, 2010.
27. See Parkins and Craig, 2006. Read more on this in chapter 9.
28. See Thrift, 1996.
29. For more on this, see Blake, Mellor, and Crane, 2010.
30. Hallam and Ingold, 2007.
31. Ingold, 2000.
32. Hand, Shove, and Southerton, 2004.
33. Hitchings, 2007.
34. Hitchings, 2011; Hitchings and Lee, 2008.
35. Hobson, 2006.
36. Hitchings, 2007, 2011; Hitchings and Lee, 2008.
37. Cresswell, 2014:forthcoming.
38. Strauss et al., 2012:15.
39. Nye, 2010:3.
40. Bennett, 2010.
41. More on this in chapter 6.
42. Graham and Thrift, 2007:4.
43. Dant, 2009.
44. Love and Garwood, 2012:147.
45. Winther, 2012.
46. Urry, 2011.

Naan and Murray.[i]

[i.] For more photos, visit lifeoffgrid.ca.

6
COMFORT

"I would rather sit on a pumpkin and have it all to myself, than be crowded on a velvet cushion."

"To affect the quality of the day, that is the highest of arts."

Henry David Thoreau, in Walden

Groovy Yurts

The Canadian Shield looks nothing like the Mongolian tundra except, curiously, for one common feature: the presence of yurts. A yurt is a portable quasi-conical dwelling framed in wood, covered by layers of fabric and other insulating material, and held together by ropes. Traditionally used by nomadic peoples of Central Asia, authentic yurts are now widely distributed in Canada by an enterprising Quebec company, **Groovy Yurts**,[ii] which markets them as a cool alternative to small cottages, annex buildings, art and yoga studios, and even standard homes.

Now, if you've never lived in a yurt and decide to move into one, you'll find that two of its most distinctive architectural characteristics will require a good deal of adaptation. The first is lack of privacy—a result of the absence of doors and rooms inside them. The second is limited light—a consequence of the absence of windows. There is generally only one **skylight**[iii]

[ii.] http://www.groovyyurts.com/en/
[iii.] http://lifeoffgrid.ca/wp-content/uploads/2013/11/Life-Off-Grid_Ontario_06.jpg

in these structures—an opening that casts natural luminosity straight down from the ceiling.

Stuart[iv] stood up from his bed, tossed on his winter coat, and laced up his boots. As he did so, I took another glance at the glow and shadows cast by his off-grid yurt's skylight. It was a radiant spring morning and the snowy meadow around us reflected the glare from the sun brightly into the air. Even on an overcast day there would have been enough natural light inside—at least during the daytime—to read, cook, or do domestic chores, but the comparative contrast with the amount and type of artificial lighting ideal for a Martha Stewart-like home was still sharp. Many houses nowadays tend to be furnished with task-specific lighting so that different areas feature tools for differing brightness (e.g., neon, iridescent bulbs, compact fluorescent bulbs, windows), different illumination angles (e.g., ceiling-mounted, wall-mounted, table-top), and different intensities and textures of brilliance (e.g., bright, dim, cold, warm).[1] Here there was only one source of weather-dependent natural light, and one artificial source of light powered by a gasoline generator.

"I'll get solar panels soon, maybe next year," Stuart observed wistfully as he led the way outside, "they're pretty expensive." But in the meantime he was perfectly snug—comfort was something he did not seem to lack at all. Comfort, in fact, is not a uniform or objective experience. It is something that can be achieved differently: in variable intensities and with different technologies.

We had met Stuart the night before at a nice house dinner kindly organized by our hosts at **Nature's Harmony off-grid Eco-lodge**,[v] three hours northeast of Ottawa. The province of Ontario is separated from Saskatchewan by a 649,950 km² land mass called Manitoba, a province which should have rightly occupied the sixth chapter slot in this book. We did not forget about Manitoba. But as it happened we badly needed to save money, and when I received an invitation to fly to Ottawa on someone else's dime, I thought of taking advantage of the airfare savings and decided to extend the trip afterward to try and get back on track with the budget. So, after my downtown meeting wrapped up, I rented a rugged Subaru Outback, swung by the airport to pick up Jon, and set the GPS for where the power lines ended. Over the next seven days we would interview a record 22 off-gridders at 14 different sites over a 2,000 km insanely long, triangle-shaped itinerary roughly connecting the North Bay area, Orangeville to the southwest, and our nation's capital to the east.

Though Nature's Harmony's choice of accommodations also included a yurt, we had elected to stay at a secluded wooden cabin that could only be reached via a 15-minute snowshoe trek through the forest. There was no

---

[iv.] http://lifeoffgrid.ca/wp-content/uploads/2013/11/Life-Off-Grid_Ontario_07.jpg
[v.] http://naturesharmony.ca/

running water but, more usefully, two solar panels sitting on the cabin's roof-powered sockets (always a necessity when doing battery-powered fieldwork), and a handful of interior lights. However, the weather had been sour lately and our charge display indicated we were critically low on stored amperage. Without a generator, Jon and I respected priorities and directed the little electricity available to refueling our laptops, recorders, and cameras. Our eyes would just have to manage with fewer lumens of artificial light. Back home it would have been common for either of us to turn on multiple lights in a room, but here there was no possibility for a visual splurge at this time. A 25-watt kitchen light bulb had to be enough for illuminating an improvised meal, and another incandescent bulb provided sufficient luminosity for reading our respective books in the living room.

The limited availability of light turned out to teach me something remarkable. For the first few minutes reading required a bit of squinting, but then my sense of sight learned to ease into the dimmer conditions. In a darker room it was actually easier to read because my eyes were less distracted by other things, and because the slower pace of my reading allowed me to concentrate better. It seemed like my eyes simply managed to do with whatever little light they had. Comfort, it dawned on me, is something we can work on, something we can practice and get used to. All it takes is a little effort to find contentment in whatever little we have.

Though short stays at idyllic cabins like the one at Nature's Harmony were ideal to learn a few hands-on lessons like these, such accommodations did not always make the most logistical sense. This is because they required us to drive off to each interview site in the morning and then retrace our steps to our cabin at night. An easier alternative would have entailed threading a more continuous forward-pushing path between interviews and sleeping at more conveniently located hotels along the way. But since at cabins we could also cook for ourselves and thus save money on restaurant bills, there was really no choice. Though the participant observation was infinitesimally more rewarding, the added domestic responsibilities and road driving (not to mention the additional stretches of snowshoeing, canoeing, snowmobiling, or simply digging ourselves out from the bushes surrounding our rental cabins) was taking an obvious toll on us.

Case in point: on the eve of our departure from Nature's Harmony, temperatures suddenly rose and proceeded to turn snow into ponds of slush and cold water. Then overnight the winds picked up and dragged in snowy clouds from the north, which swiftly dumped 10 centimeters of fresh white stuff as we slept. When we went to pack our car in the morning in −15°C (5°F) weather we noticed that the tires had frozen into the ground—or more precisely in what had been deep slush when we parked, and what had then unexpectedly turned into solid ice. We eventually succeeded in chiseling the wheels out of the ice with well-aimed kicks and stomps but afterward we had to endure driving on semi-square tires, rendered partly flat-sided by the protracted contact with the ground.

Fortunately the rubber warmed up and evened out, as temperatures reached 15°C (59°F) in a matter of a few hours and a few hundred kilometers. By the time we reached Glen and Joanne's home we were in our **T-shirts**.[vi] Joanne and Glen used to live in the city but had eventually grown to hate it. So, a few years before, they had decided to seek the comfort of a rural acreage. The decision to live off-grid came after they found out their ideal property was too far from the nearest power pole. They determined that investing in self-sufficiency rather than monthly bills made sense and resolved to build the house on their own in such a way as to take maximum advantage of passive solar energy. The building was long on its east-to-west axis and very narrow south-to-north. Large south-facing windows let in copious amounts of heat and light.

It took Glen and Joanne and their two young boys some time to become accustomed to the darkness after they left downtown Toronto and moved to their stylish 2,500 ft² straw bale home. Neither of them had ever lived without the light pollution of the city. "We couldn't believe how black it was in the house," Glen remembered about the first winter. "If it was a cloudy night, you couldn't see in front of your face."

One of the solutions they decided to implement in order to increase their visual comfort was installing self-assembled 1-watt LEDs (Light-Emitting Diodes). "You couldn't buy lights like these anywhere at the time," Glen recounted, "so I bought the acrylic plastic parts and made them myself." The idea worked so well and consumed so little energy that Glen also put together another three over the dining table for a hip-looking 3-watt fixture. A few other lights around the house, all compact fluorescents, served as task lighting (e.g., for closets, bathroom, control room), but they were turned on infrequently because the most lived-in areas were bathed in ample natural light. "In the summer time we don't turn lights on, at all," Glen revealed. "With this massive bank of glass here we get all the light we need during the day, and even after the sun goes down at 9:30 you can still walk around the house till 10 or 10:30," he explained, "and we're generally in bed by then anyway."

Lighting the Way, on a Bike

There are at least two different kinds of comfort: emotional and physical. Physical comfort is what interests us here. We can understand it as an evaluative judgment of the ease, enjoyableness, or pleasantness of one's sensual

---

[vi.] http://lifeoffgrid.ca/wp-content/uploads/2013/11/Life-Off-Grid_Ontario_11.jpg

experience of something. The word *comfortable,* however, can also be attributed to insensitive things, like furniture or train seats. In that sense, *comfortable* is a quality attributed to material objects in regard to whether they can
provide that pleasant sensory experience to us. This is why it is correct to
say, "I feel comfortable in this house," as well as, "this house is comfortable."

Certain minimum "standards" of comfort are necessary for human survival, as extreme discomfort can cause unbearable suffering. It would be
impossible, for example, to live exposed in temperatures that cause hypo-
thermia. Dwelling in constant impenetrable darkness would also be very
uncomfortable and would eventually lead to physical pain and death (as
one would be unable to find the resources needed for survival). Just like air,
light is a primary medium of human existence.[2] Yet, the range of conditions
within which humans can achieve comfort is extremely wide. As Wilhite
and colleagues[3] have shown in the context of the different lighting techniques used in Norwegian and Japanese homes, deeply set cultural characteristics shape different notions of domestic comfort.

Comfort is in fact not a universally objective condition. Historically
and culturally variable definitions of comfort,[4] as well as changing architectural and scientific practices that engineer it and even medicalize it,[5]
reflect directly on what people will consider comfortable. As a result, in
our consumer culture comfort is a prized feature used to market anything
from couches to air conditioning systems. Comfort is especially important
within the modern, Western home.[6] Together with ideals of cleanliness and
convenience, notions of comfort inform how we value our dwellings and
relate to them.[7]

Comfort enters the domestic experience in many different ways. We
could talk of thermal comfort, the comfort provided by furniture, and much
more. What we want to do now is focus on visual comfort: the comfort provided by light. Domestic visual comfort—that is, the evaluative judgment
of the experience of lighting within a home—has been subject to a growing
amount of research lately.[8] Our intent is to understand how visual comfort
can be achieved—through what tools and strategies—and to reflect on the
significance of different practices of achieving it. Though we focus on visual
comfort, it is easy to extrapolate our ideas to other kinds of comfort.

We can understand visual comfort as an *embodied affective sensibility*:[9] a
susceptibility to be affected by, or the capacity to affect, the visual characteristics of one's environment. Visual comfort can further be understood
as a three-dimensional set of bodily capacities and intensities of feeling.[10]
The first dimension is an "aesthetic sensibility"[11]: a judgment that unfolds
through the sensing eyes. The second dimension is an "objective capacity"[12]:
the quality imputed to an object, such as a light source, to provide visual
comfort. Third, visual comfort is an "anticipatory affective resonance"[13]:

something that is not felt as the outcome of an immediate interaction with an object, but rather anticipated, predicted, estimated. Intended this way, comfort "clearly depends on the capabilities and capacities of individual bodies themselves"[14] and is therefore contingent on people's manipulative and transformative activities.

Visual comfort is an achievement in the sense that it is something people seek in order to feel good about the amount, source, and type of light in which they live. Visual comfort is therefore an affective register,[15] that is, as a bodily capacity to affect lighting and be affected by it. This capacity varies along with differing power constellations, obviously, but also in relation to different cultural and lifestyle-specific notions of what constitutes comfort. These variations give rise to what we might call *ways of lighting*.

Like the ways of heating we talked about in chapter 3, different ways of lighting weave together relations between humans and non-humans (e.g., resources, technologies), thus comprising different assemblages of knowledge, skills, materials, features of places, and so on. Ways of lighting are individual and collective visual accomplishments shaped by habits, dispositions, and lifestyles. Differently lit environments therefore exist as different "taskscapes"[16] in which people become differently involved in search of varying intensities of visual comfort afforded by different means and required for different ends.

Historically, the arrival of light and power into the modern home had a revolutionary effect on notions of domesticity and comfort.[17] Because current mainstream ideas of domestic comfort are so deeply imbricated with the consumer ideologies that the arrival of electricity brought on, it would seem logical to expect that homeowners who do not rely on large-scale assemblages like grid-transmitted electricity are somehow at a disadvantage in their capacity to configure the comfort of their homes. Off-gridders showed us instead that it was possible to create comfortable spaces through alternative assemblages. The key to achieving various intensities and different kinds of visual comfort resided in off-gridders' capacity to re-assemble the socio-technical system by which comfort was affected.

Take for instance the issue of wiring a house with 12-volt DC electricity. For those of us living on the grid this would be inconvenient and inefficient because power lines carry higher-voltage AC electricity, which travels better over long distances. DC electricity—such as that generated by solar panels and stored in batteries—instead works better when it doesn't need to travel far. Off-gridders who had chosen to stick with 12-volt wiring without the use of an AC inverter enjoyed several energy efficiencies. But their choice also required some adjustments. In the context of lighting, for example, 12-volt systems typically worked better with low-wattage lighting such as

LEDs. LED lights are sources of illumination that not everyone finds visually comfortable, as they are often perceived to feel "cold" and to cast light too narrowly. The point of this example, however, is poignant: the fact that some off-gridders did find this type of lighting comfortable, and the fact that this type of lighting saved considerable amounts of energy in those homes, tells us that by actively working on what we perceive to be comfortable we can change what comfort means and what it can cost.

* * *

Throughout the two years of fieldwork we never bothered to record demographic data because we knew that our sample could never be representative of the broader off-grid population for one simple reason: no one could find out who *all* the off-gridders out there were. Too many of them simply couldn't—and didn't want to—be found, so why even bother guessing about their composition? This didn't stop us from noticing common characteristics of the roughly 200 we met, though. Most of them lived together with a partner, for example, and sometimes had children in the house too. Fewer lived alone. And even fewer of those who lived alone were women. So, when Susan invited us to visit her place we were particularly enthusiastic. Men often took a conventionally masculine role within off-grid households, as the division of labor found in households like Ron and Johanna's back in Saskatchewan revealed. This is not to say that women were disinterested in wiring, plumbing, carpentry, and all that. Actually, many of them took an active role in house design, building, and maintenance. Susan was one of those women.

"Check it out," she announced proudly as she led the way upstairs to show us what she had led us to anticipate in an email. "Isn't that cool? And it's really simple. You just plug it in and start biking."

I had never seen a generator bike, except in cartoons.

"Do you want to see a demo?"

As Susan began to pedal, the small display mounted on the handlebar lit up and indicated how much power she produced with each push. Susan smiled as she pedaled on to the tune of the wheels' soft whir, knowing that her physical exercise was ingeniously good for her body and her house.

"It's the beauty of 12-volt electricity," Susan remarked, sensing my amazement. "You can use it to get power out or put it in." By "in" she referred to her batteries, which thanks to her short stationary jaunt were now a tad closer to being topped off. During the cold weeks of the Ontario fall and winter— when going out for a walk was as pleasant as a freezing-cold shower—Susan would occasionally take a break from writing and generate a few amps.

Her batteries could use the extra juice too. Compared to other off-grid set-ups, her system was miniscule, just enough for her basic needs as the sole inhabitant of her home. The small solar panel array—with no wind turbine or micro-hydro waterwheel to supplement the photovoltaic energy output—was pretty much all she needed to generate enough electricity for her domestic comfort. A diesel generator stood by in case of additional need, but Susan limited its use as much as she could. This may sound like an uncomfortable way of living, but "it's easier and cheaper," she explained in a gentle, assured tone as we calmly drank a cup of tea in her kitchen. "It makes perfect sense for me to live like this," she reflected. With little money to her name just a few years before, she had managed to secure a no-interest mortgage and bought the 7 1/2-acre property from an old friend. She began settling in by clearing space for the driveway, and then bit by bit cleared the rest of the site and assembled her home.

Susan had limited material desires, but one of those was to not sacrifice on visual comfort. "I did not want to live in darkness," she said with a smile. As a result, a great deal of attention went into making space for windows and other smaller fixed openings to let light in. Log homes can be quite dark, as the color of the wood reflects light more poorly than the white-painted drywall typical of most homes. On the other hand, it's easy to cut window frames in log homes. So, Susan patiently managed to find and then fit a mix-and-match set of windows. These included an especially nice and large one that gave her a serene, pastoral view over the surrounding hills. Initially "I was really concerned about light," Susan confided, but she was quite content with her solutions now.

These solutions included another technology likely to startle the urban dweller: propane lights. Propane lights are turned on by striking a match and turning open an adjustable gas shutter, not unlike one would do to light up a barbeque grill. A light-colored coating called a mantle—a socket-like ceramic mesh that encases the flame—is fitted over the gas-line opening. The flame actually escapes the mantle when the light is ignited, but then the trick is to turn the shutter down a bit to reduce the flame. After that phase propane light works just like electric light and is similar in color and brightness. The only difference is in its sound; while low in volume there is a definite hiss that is typical of propane lights. Also different, of course, is their portability. Typically, propane lights need to be part of fixtures and cannot be moved around the home like lamps. Kerosene lamps or candles can achieve that mobility, but they are vastly inferior in efficiency, cost, externality, and comfort value compared to portable LED lights.

Comfort, according to historian John Crowley,[18] took on its modern meaning of sensual satisfaction with commercial "domestic enhancements that provided more privacy, cleanliness, warmth, and light" only in recent times. Previously, the idea of comfort only denoted the emotional, spiritual, and moral worth of personal support. It was only later, after consumerism took hold, that the modern denotation of comfort as material contentment displaced its original reference. Comfort, in the words of Shove,[19] was thus progressively "normalized" within consumer society and "represented as a normal . . . and even natural state of affairs."

The normalization of comfort is the result of an assemblage of objects, representations, practices, and experiences championed by manufacturers and marketers of domestic goods and by affiliated technical experts. With regard to lighting, biological and physiological research has combined with the technical applications of engineers and architects to "determine optimal conditions in order to produce and provide what people need."[20] As sociologist Wiebe Bijker[21] has documented through his study of the evolution of the light bulb, these assemblages of actors, stakeholders, consumers, technologies, resources, ideals, norms, values, and practices have resulted in shaping "combinations of lighting intensity and color that are experienced as comfortable"[22] and seemingly normal and natural. Visual comfort, in a nutshell, is malleable, yet it is often perceived by most of us as natural and fixed, as if an optimal standard could be positively measured, assessed, and uniformly agreed upon.

Off-gridders' ways of lighting illustrated in vivid detail the malleability of domestic visual comfort and how it could be achieved differently. The distinguishing characteristic of their quest for comfort resided in how profoundly they participated in making their own domestic comfort possible through their relative independence from utility providers. By becoming involved in the design and building of their homes and in the generation of power and light, they meaningfully re-assembled the ways in which comfort, technology, domestic environments, consumer objects, and notions of modern lifestyle were entangled.

Off-grid lighting tactics were bricolages through which off-gridders derived great "pleasure in getting around the rules"[23] of the mainstream—the rules that constrained ways of designing homes and generating, distributing, and consuming power (like building and electrical codes). By incorporating comfort into their everyday life on their own terms, by "press[ing] into service" objects and resources around them "to suit [their] current purposes, [they] proceed[ed] to modify those things to [their] own design so that they better serve[d] those purposes"[24] rather than those assembled "by the law of a foreign power."[25]

When comfort is re-assembled in this fashion and taken away from the sovereign domain of automated, centralized, mechanical control, its experience radically changes. When *inhabitants* of buildings (rather than mere *occupants*) take an active role in controlling the performance of their dwellings, their experience of comfort becomes more dynamic, adaptive, and sensitive to the unique features of their interaction with the local environment and material world.[26]

The Thoreau Effect

Off-gridders' visual comfort emerged not only from their involvement in the generation of indoor lighting, but also from their *orientation* toward light itself. We thought we'd call this phenomenon the *Thoreau Effect*. By the Thoreau Effect we refer to a transformation in a person's orientation toward his/her capacity to affect comfort and be affected by material objects' capacity for comfort. In few and simple words, the Thoreau Effect captures a basic adaptive process: the process of learning to enjoy the comfort of something that requires a great deal of personal effort. It is inspired by the concept of the Diderot Effect.

The Diderot Effect is a well-known phenomenon in the study of consumption. Simply put, it refers to a process of upward-spiraling consumption sparked by the dissatisfaction with old possessions generated by acquisition of new goods.[27] The expression comes from a story related by the philosopher Denis Diderot, who detailed how the purchase of a new and beautiful scarlet dressing gown made it increasingly difficult and eventually impossible for him to appreciate his old clothes, which in contrast to the new item began to feel inelegant.

The Diderot Effect can explain the collective historical escalation of the quest for visual comfort as well.[28] This escalation is characterized by a quest for "better" and brighter light: that is, lighting that is more sensitive to the specificities of various domestic needs and wants. This escalation is marked by a series of dissatisfactions with older lighting tools and techniques that were made suddenly obsolete by newly introduced technologies. In virtue of this effect we can understand visual comfort as something that changes with new anticipatory affective resonances made possible by innovations in lighting technologies. In other words, within a consumer culture, increases in the capacity of objects to produce comfort tend to generate higher and higher thresholds for people's experience of comfort. Or, to put it in even simpler terms: the more technologies "improve," the more we seem to become dissatisfied with what we used to find perfectly adequate before.

Take indoor light, for example. Domestic lighting has witnessed a remarkable ratcheting up of expectations over the last two centuries. In ancient times fire, besides natural sunlight, was the main source of domestic light. But the light coming from the fire burning in open hearths was also a source of discomfort. Hearth fires caused indoor smoke, which required ventilation. Ventilation invited in moisture and cold air, as doors and uncovered wall openings were the only options for air circulation. Newer domestic lighting solutions were then sought and soon the invention of glazed glass windows introduced a new level of domestic comfort. This seemed perfectly fine until candles were introduced and eventually made fire inadequate as a lighting technology.

The quest for visual comfort continued to escalate as candle technology was continuously refined. Newer self-burning wicks made earlier candle-wicks—which needed to be manually trimmed every few minutes—seem inconvenient and obsolete. Then, newer, lighter, portable oil lamps pushed away older, cumbersome candlesticks. Candlesticks were originally made of solid iron and brass and felt heavy in comparison to oil lamps.[29] But when gas lighting was developed, portable oil lamps quickly fell out of favor.

After the wonderful comforts afforded by gas lighting were introduced, people felt that earlier domestic lighting options paled in comparison. Gas lighting seemed so good that earlier technologies—such as oil lamps and tallow candles—suddenly started to feel sooty and smell bad in comparison. Moreover, oil lamps required constant refilling and tallow candles congealed easily in cold environments and melted quickly in warm ones; whereas gas flowed automatically and worked well in all conditions. But it didn't end there. Electric light soon arrived.

The successive domestication of electric lighting did to gas what gas had done to candles. Electric light made gas lighting appear to be rife with prob-lems, as gas lighting was—amongst other troubles—recognized to make breathing difficult and to cause headaches and various respiratory ailments. Escalation did not end there either as, later on, the light bulb itself became subject to a great deal of troubleshooting. Interior electric lighting became the domain of experts who made it their goal to improve visual comfort by optimizing task-specific and room-specific illumination, while seeking energy-conservation solutions and fashionable elegance at the same time.[30] Greater and greater intensities of visual comfort, in sum, became progres-sively normalized[31] as the threshold of consumer expectations got higher and higher.

If the Diderot Effect works somewhat like an addictive search for greater doses of comfort obtained through decreasing effort and inconvenience, the Thoreau Effect works by way of reversing that trend. It is a phenomenon marked by contentment, rather than perennial dissatisfaction, with the affective capacity for comfort from whatever one already has. It is also a sensibility to appreciate what you can accomplish by yourself: a sensibility to find greater value in whatever you are able to assemble on your own rather than in whatever the market can provide.

The Thoreau Effect gets its name from the experiences of the most renowned "off-gridder" of all time, Henry David Thoreau. In *On Walden*

Pond, Thoreau described how he spent two years in a small cabin in the woods not too far from Concord, Massachusetts, where he deprived himself of many of the comforts of the city. Instead of being painful, the Spartan lifestyle taught Thoreau to draw contentment from the few "simple things" he had. Thoreau also learned to draw great comfort and pride from the fruits of his own labor. It is the combination of these two processes that makes up the Thoreau Effect. First: a heightened sensibility to find great comfort in objects that many other people would find inadequate, obsolete, cumbersome, inferior, inconvenient, and uncomfortable. Second: a higher appreciation for comfort obtained through hard work and direct physical involvement, especially when practiced in relative autonomy from others.

Domestic visual comfort—which we might now better define as the sense of contentment with the source, amount, intensity, color, and feel of light available in a home—sounds like a pretty superficial thing to worry about. Yet, variations in levels of visual comfort teach us important lessons about comfort in general. To affect the quality of the day by becoming involved in something as important as light generation is one of the "highest arts" of contemporary everyday life, to borrow from Thoreau. That sense of self-reliance and involvement into the provision of the resources needed for their lifestyle deeply infused off-gridders' orientation to domestic comfort and allowed them to find contentment in the lighting systems they assembled, as well as in the many other technologies they employed to make their lives comfortable and convenient.

The Thoreau Effect is the process whereby comfort is felt, anticipated, and imbued into technologies that—like propane lights, low-wattage bulbs, dim environments, or DC electricity—are not the latest, most advanced, and most fashionable. It is a process by which comfort is felt, anticipated, and imbued into objects not by virtue of these objects' market value, inno-vativeness, or contemporariness, but rather by virtue of one's ability to affect the immediate environment through active participation,[32] through relative independence from others, and the capacity to do with less.[33]

The Thoreau Effect does not describe a state of disinterest in greater intensities of comfort. After all there was hardly any asceticism going on among off-gridders—quite the opposite indeed. Rather, the Thoreau Effect describes how the anticipation of future intensities and future kinds of comfort does not necessarily have to come at the expense of the current experience of comfort. Knowing that you can have a more comfortable home tomorrow, in other words, does not have to make you unhappy with what you have today. This orientation runs contrary to the typical feeling of "lack" on which consumerist desire for greater comfort hinges. The Thoreau Effect, in fact, describes how comfort becomes less subject to escalation whenever great personal effort is required for its generation. After all, it makes sense to find comfort in what you already have if you are aware of the personal costs and consequences of alternative kinds and intensities of comfort. The off-grid lifestyle constantly taught its practitioners this simple but important lesson: be happy with what you have, because getting more brings complications, toil, and all sorts of trouble.

* * *

Driving thousands of kilometers had some advantages. Methodologically, it gave us a chance to discuss interviews and reflect on new lessons and experiences as they presented themselves and while they were still raw and fresh. And from a more personal perspective it gave us both a chance to see the country, which was constantly proving to be larger than we had ever imagined. Ontario's size and beauty were especially surprising. As a West Coaster I had always thought of Ontario in the form of busy eight-lane highways, industrial complexes, and bustling cities, but once away from urban and suburban cement the land continuously shone with verdant evergreens, shapely ridges, and myriad lakes that begged to be paddled on. Much of our triangular itinerary paralleled access points into the wilderness of Algonquin Park, whose logo prominently appeared on Murray's green T-shirt.

Murray and Naan's[vii] bookshelves were filled with books on canoeing, camping, outdoor travel, and wilderness skills as well as with socially conscious contemporary non-fiction. While Murray sat on the couch for a moment—posing under the light with a book for Jon to record some additional video—Naan told me how lighting worked in their reading room. Besides basic reduction—they each had one light near a favorite armchair—their secret to reducing wattage was twofold.

First, they cast light only where needed, without wasting it elsewhere. Their portable and adjustable "Air Canada" tabletop lights—that's the nickname they had given their 3 1/2-watt LED lights—worked just like the reading lights found on Boeing and Airbus cabins. The spread of their luminosity was limited, but their rays were perfect when aimed directly where needed.

Their second secret was to utilize DC lighting instead of AC. Naan and Murray had both AC and DC lights, but the former had been a significant source of trouble and were being gradually phased out from their house. "The DC LEDs are much more efficient," Naan observed. "AC LEDs are also available on the market but the sine wave on our inverter is too irregular for AC lighting. We almost started a fire once." And while they felt "colder" because of their blue brightness, DC LED lights were also easier on their ageing eyes, Naan found.

[vii] http://lifeoffgrid.ca/wp-content/uploads/2013/11/Life-Off-Grid_Ontario_03.jpg

As mentioned before, solar panels produce DC (Direct Current) electricity. Direct current electricity consists of electrons flowing in a single direction. However, the type of electricity provided to grid-connected homes is AC (Alternating Current), which flows back and forth at 60 cycles per second (60 hertz), thus much more rapidly than DC. As a result, lighting, appliances, and almost everything else runs on AC on the basis of 120 or 240 volts. Off-grid homes therefore need inverters that convert DC electricity into AC and change voltage from 12 to the needed 120 or 240 volts. This conversion can be more or less pure. The purer output is known as sine wave, whereas modified sine wave is a less pure and more irregular form.

Not all modern appliances and lights are capable of running on modified sine wave, and attempting to operate them—if they can start at all—can cause damage. As well, inverters need energy to operate. Most off-grid systems are sizeable enough to afford feeding energy to an inverter, but some are so small that any amount of saving can make a great difference. Murray and Naan's system, solely dependent on solar and producing only up to one kilowatt, was one such small system. By using DC instead of AC lights, they could bypass their inverter and save about 10% of their power.

Naan and Murray were off-the-grid for environmental reasons. While they recognized that off-grid living was not a solution to global energy security, they believed that relative self-sufficiency and reduced reliance on non-renewables could teach us all a lot about conservation. Their philosophy also went a long way toward explaining their extremely thrifty use of their backup propane generator. "The game is to use it as little as possible," observed **Murray**,[viii] "some years we manage to never turn it on at all." That was one impressive feat with a one-kilowatt solar system.

Off-grid living was not easy, definitely not as easy as plugging in a toaster and letting a distant dam generate enough electricity for our breakfast. But through active involvement in renewable energy utilization, through the feeling of satisfaction obtained by reducing personal needs, and through the sense of fulfillment inherent in making do with self-provision, Naan and Murray—as well as many other off-gridders—were able to find great comfort in their home.

We thanked Murray and Naan for their time, feeding us lunch, opening their home to us, and the inspiring conversation, then once again drove on. "The visuals from **this interview**[ix] are going to be great," Jon cheered as we merged onto the main country road. Given his self-critical and perfectionist tendencies, it was always a good thing when he said that. Producing an

---

[viii] http://lifeoffgrid.ca/wp-content/uploads/2013/11/Life-Off-Grid_Ontario_05.jpg
[ix] https://vimeo.com/46380901

ethnographic documentary is such a complex undertaking. Besides ensuring that all the important conceptual themes are covered by the editing, the selection of empirical material for visual presentation has to take into account light, sound, and a host of other aesthetic variables. And you can never have enough action shots and B-roll. Making a film for the first time was teaching me more about fieldwork than I had learned in years. Writing, for example, allows an author to *create* scenes, but the medium of film isn't so flexible. With film you can only tell a story you actually have footage for—because you can't re-create it like you can with written words. So, as I steered the wheel of every one of our rentals, Jon would be constantly on the lookout for interesting details of the landscapes passing by.

In addition to the B-roll of pretty bucolic scenes, Ontario gave us views of acres of solar panel arrays everywhere we turned: the outcome of a provincial energy policy that had intelligently subsidized household power generation. Selling solar electricity to the grid was a smart investment that many on-grid farmers, especially, had taken up to supplement their income.

"What do you make of all these solar panels?" Jon asked me as he put the camera down for a moment.

I had been ruminating about this for a while, but always in rather incoherent and incomplete patterns until, somehow, the glib answer my instincts spoke precipitated a deeper sense of clarity.

"Seems a bit less selfish than the off-grid way, doesn't it?"

"What do you mean?" Jon replied.

"I don't know for sure, but I've had a nagging question bugging me for a while. Isn't it a bit selfish to live off-the-grid?"

"You mean, like how every off-gridder looks after their own little world?"

"Yeah," I mumbled as I re-adjusted my body on the driver's seat, suddenly feeling uncomfortable in my own skin. "I mean, generating clean power and selling it back to the grid would be a very good thing in places where grid electricity is still generated with coal, nuclear, and all that."

"But off-gridders normally can't do that because they're too far from the grid," Jon observed.

"I know but . . . ," I hesitated to say what I thought.

"What?"

"I mean, I shouldn't even say this because I live pretty far too, but do you think it's right, from an environmental angle, to live so far from the rest of society? Wouldn't it make more sense to concentrate populations in highly dense areas like so many geographers suggest[34] and then pool together our resources, without living in these separate, polarized little enclaves of our own?"

Jon had no immediate answer, and neither did I. But I had just poked a hole the size of Algonquin Park in my entire perspective on the off-grid lifestyle. Until then I had never really entertained these issues at a level higher than rumblings, but venting out like that had instantly scarred my enthusiasm for off-grid living. Maybe that was the reason why I didn't live off-grid in the first place. Or maybe I was just rationalizing—making up glamorous excuses for my obvious inability to take care of myself and my own house. Or maybe I was just tired and cranky. Actually, I knew for a fact I was. We had stopped for a lukewarm, sub-par coffee in Huntsville, and the unrewarding caffeine shot, the uncooperative Wi-Fi signal, the endless calls and emails to return, and a few awful local drivers had profoundly exacerbated the fatigue from the interview marathon we were racing.

We peeled off quickly, but once again the snow started to make our travel miserable. I needed to get off the road. I needed a warm shower too—it had been days since the last one and I confessed to Jon I was starting to look forward to staying at a hotel in Orangeville. I asked him if he could Google a Best Western or a Holiday Inn or some "no surprises" hotel chain where we could get a choice in pillow firmness. He found one right away and made a reservation with his phone. "Not the most off-grid stay," he noted wryly, "but I could use a non-weather-dependent hot shower too. Maybe there's also a sushi place in town; let me look that up."

"Nice, I really need that," I sighed, and sped up west toward Highway 9 and Orangeville.

Notes

1. Wilhite et al., 1996.
2. Ingold, 2005, 2011.
3. Wilhite et al., 1996.
4. Crowley, 2001.
5. Shove, 2003; Shove et al., 2009.
6. Crowley, 2001; Shove, 2003; Shove et al., 2009.
7. Shove, 2003; Shove et al., 2008.
8. Crowley, 2001; Dillon, 2006; Kline, 2000; Nye, 2010; Schivelbusch, 1995; Shove, 2003.
9. Bissell, 2008.
10. Bissell, 2008.
11. Bissell, 2008:1700.
12. Bissell, 2008:1700.
13. Bissell, 2008:1701.
14. Bissell, 2008:1702.
15. Anderson and Harrison, 2006; Kraftl and Adey, 2008.
16. Ingold, 2000.
17. Shove, 2003.
18. Crowley, 2001:10.
19. Shove, 2003:41.
20. Shove, 2003:57.
21. Bijker, 1997.

22. Bijker, 1997:243.
23. deCerteau, 1984:18.
24. Ingold, 2000:176.
25. deCerteau, 1984:37.
26. Ingold, 2011.
27. MacCracken, 1988.
28. For a parallel argument, see Shove, 2003.
29. Dillon, 2006.
30. Dillon, 2006; Shove, 2003.
31. Shove, 2003.
32. Cole et al., 2008; Ingold, 2011; Shove et al., 2008.
33. See Grigsby, 2004; Kneale-Gould, 2005.
34. For a review of the debate, see Steyn and Geyer, 2011.

Gijs and Gadget.

7
CONVENIENCE

"Geographical center of Canada," read a momentous sign posted alongside the Trans-Canada Highway near the town of Landmark, 30 clicks southeast of Winnipeg.[i] "It's official," I exclaimed, "we've made it to the half-way point!" As the summer sun shone assuredly in the still prairie sky, icy roads, budget crunches, and manic interview schedules quickly receded in the rearview mirror, and for all that I caught myself breathing a sigh of relief.

"Wanna stop somewhere really quickly to celebrate?" I asked Jon.

"Sure. But do you really think you can find an iced latte worthy of the occasion around here?"

I didn't. We pulled over a long while later, surrendering to the half-hearted enticement of a non-descript gas station mart.

Manitoba was pleasant. Though it was inimical toward gradients—as popular lore rightly had it—its landscape was **calm and serene**.[ii] The people acted as friendly as their license plate motto ("Friendly Manitoba") promised them to be. And the fauna was amicable too: fireflies flew endearingly in the moonless night, red foxes popped up curiously amidst sparse bushes, and timid mosquitos drew far less blood than their homicidal reputation had us fear. Gourmet coffee was just about the only shortcoming. As a result, the Starbuck's Mocha Frappuccino found in the convenience store fridge had to suffice for an improvised parking lot celebration. With it, we toasted to the remaining half of the country. It was the end of June 2012: one full year before our scheduled arrival in Newfoundland.

[ii] http://lifeoffgrid.ca/wp-content/uploads/2013/11/Life-Off-Grid_Manitoba_02.jpg

Ever since that cranky springtime moment on the way to Orangeville, Ontario, I had obsessed over the societal value of off-grid living. Disconnection had always attracted me. It was a bold act that stood for independence, self-reliance, and confidence in one's means and skills. As an individualist it appealed to me at a profoundly affective level, just as it seduced the imagination of many others across the country ready to give up the rat race and go off-the-grid. But I knew that disconnection had its dangers and its price. Ezra—a Lasqueti Islander with deep awareness of the socio-environmental potential of the solar industry—had anticipated this a year before in few, but powerful, words. To live like Canadian off-gridders did was "a colossal luxury," he had stated dramatically. "What's wrong with that? We can't afford to have billions of people be that luxurious!" Ezra's words felt right. Would it make sense for every household in the world to be energy-self-sufficient? Wouldn't a world of off-gridders feel atomized, Balkanized? Wouldn't it be more efficient to cooperate and pool resources together?

We were on our way to find out. After a patient search I had gotten invitations to a couple of off-grid co-op farms. Steve, from the **Prairie Crocus Co-op Farm**,[iii] had said we could easily stay for a week or even longer if we wanted, in exchange for a little work. That was enough time, I hoped, to try and understand whether collaborative power constellations could function a bit less autonomously than single detached off-grid homes.

Growing, Storing, Cooking, Eating, Shitting Organic Food

Solar panels[iv] were chockablock on the expansive Prairie Crocus Co-op Farm grounds, powering common areas and individual dwellings. A single wind tower fed into a shared electricity generation system as well. Organic food was grown in individually owned lots. Right away Steve asked Jon and me to help with some carpentry work, since a new chicken coop needed to be built. Taking advantage of the cool morning temperatures we set to work while we talked and took turns at measuring pieces and hammering them together.

Besides chickens, the farm communally owned a small family of cows. In fact, a great variety of food was raised and grown: tomatoes, beets, parsnips, potatoes, carrots, leafy greens, zucchini, squash, peas, **beans**,[v] peppers, garlic, onions, cabbage, cucumber, herbs and just about any vegetable hardy enough to withstand the gelid prairie winters and dry summers. The Prairie Crocus Farm was not a profit-based enterprise. While some cash was generated selling specialized commodities—Steve, for example, sold the worms he

---

iii. http://lifeoffgrid.ca/wp-content/uploads/2013/11/Life-Off-Grid_Manitoba_02.jpg
iv. http://lifeoffgrid.ca/wp-content/uploads/2013/11/Life-Off-Grid_Manitoba_04.jpg
v. http://lifeoffgrid.ca/wp-content/uploads/2013/11/Life-Off-Grid_Manitoba_06.jpg

grew in his compost pile—food was harvested to be eaten by its individual owner or as part of common meals.

For nighttime Jon and I had found shelter at a cabin-style home at the southern edge of the farm. It was a small, rustic, wooden house situated amid tall grasses, poison ivy, and birch and poplar trees. It had tall windows facing southeast and an inviting fire pit right out front. Inside, two comfortable beds occupied the low-clearance loft, which sat atop the kitchen and living space down the steep staircase. Also downstairs was another bedroom, temporarily occupied by a WWoofer[1] by the name of Elizabeth. The absence of a fridge and an indoor bathroom, however, presented us with an interesting challenge in convenience, a challenge that was quite apropos, given our research interests.

Dictionaries tell us that convenience is the state of being able to proceed with ease or little effort. But in contemporary consumer culture convenience has taken on new meanings. Convenience is now synonymous with lack of complications and with a lifestyle rendered easy by countless consumer products and services.[2] A cursory analysis of the usage of the word in common parlance reveals that convenience is now essentially an assemblage of values and practices focused on *accessibility, availability, affordability, speed,* and *ease*.[3] A convenience store and its many convenience foods provide a good example. Within cities convenience stores seem to be ubiquitous and easily accessible. The products they sell are generally always available (often worldwide): 24/7 and year-round. Those products also tend to be inexpensive, and quick and easy to use.

In contrast, at first glance, off-grid food growth, storage, and consumption seemed so inconvenient to be downright intolerable: foods could only be available at specific times of the year, their growth would demand patience and involvement, and their storage and cooking would require creativity, forethought, and problem solving. Off-gridders' food-related practices challenged the dominant meanings of food production, distribution, consumption, and disposal in similar ways to individuals like modern homesteaders,[4] voluntary simplifiers,[5] back-to-the-landers[6], smallholders,[7] and followers of the slow food movement.[8] The meaning of off-grid convenience, in sum, seemed to denote something altogether different than it does in our 7-Eleven-habituated world.

The social, political, economic, and environmental consequences of the convenience of our food consumption are often hidden from view or poorly understood by most of us. Popular books and documentaries have started to change the way we think about food, but a great deal of awareness remains to be generated. Take the way foods are stored, for instance. The first self-serve grocery stores began to emerge in North America and Western Europe during the middle of the twentieth century, but larger self-serve supermarkets did not become popular until the late 1960s.[9] Supermarket frozen foods have since played a crucial role in the development of domestic food habits.

Before home refrigerators and freezers became popular, grocery shopping had to be done more frequently. The absence of prepared or semi-prepared frozen foods meant that cooking had to be carried out with basic ingredients and was therefore more time-consuming. And because commercial refrigeration has also been instrumental in preserving foods shipped across long distances, the typical dietary regimens of the pre-refrigeration and pre-freezing era hinged deeply on consumption of locally produced foods.

Recent statistics show that as many as 96% of people in the Western world own a freezer today, whereas only 3% owned one as little as 40 years ago.[10] During those four decades women's employment has increased dramatically, and in part women's growing "time squeeze"[11] may explain the rising popularity of these time-saving devices. But the normalization of cold storage technologies can also be explained as the outcome of urbanizing trends. In fact, at first marketers thought that the freezer would only be popular with farmers—people who faced the problem of conserving large quantities of harvested or butchered foods for long periods of time.[12] However, as freezers began to be manufactured as small compartments built into refrigerators, rather than as large stand-alone devices, their reduced price made them more appealing for the kitchens of urban consumers—who preferred to drive infrequently to stores to stock up on (and thus freeze) foods and take advantage of bulk-buying offers.

The gradual development of "fast-freezing" technologies that better conserved the taste of frozen foods also won many skeptical customers over, and soon frozen foods became the epitome of consumerist convenience. Yet, few people now seem to realize that a typical refrigerator/freezer combo constantly consumes 540 watts/hour and, therefore, accounts for about a quarter of the electricity used by all the domestic appliances found in a home.

* * *

While Jon finished his (and my) work on the chicken coop, Elizabeth and I raced with the growingly warmer sun to complete the time-consuming manual irrigation of Steve's garden. Steve preferred we dunk metallic watering cans into barrels full of water warmed up by sun exposure, rather that employ garden hoses. But soon enough the scorching sun became unbearable. The rest of the hot day, useless for work, was up for grabs. "Wanna drive to town for coffee?" Jon tempted me the moment I sat down, "that way we can stock up on ice for our cooler and get some snacks too."

Americanos for him and flavored lattes for me were turning out to be a serious fieldwork vice. It was something of which we were feeling particularly guilty in Manitoba because we were so invested in praising the virtues of local food consumption, but—in our defense—coffee house stops allowed us to take care of important email, telephone, and, . . . er, constitutional duties too. Yes, it may seem silly, but the outhouse behind our cabin intimidated me at first. Though the idea of an outhouse is unassailable—"why would you want to shit within the same walls where you eat?" we had been asked many times by off-gridders, "and why would you throw away all that good fertilizer?"—the habit of flushing ran deep within me.

The history of the bathroom reveals that such collective habit isn't an old one, though. The toilet bowl was patented in 1778 by Joseph Bramah. However, a toilet's functioning depends on plumbing, pressurized water, underground sewers, water mains, and municipal waste treatment facilities—an infrastructure that has only been common in the Western world as of recently. Therefore, latrines, chamber pots, or similar tools fulfilled the function of the toilet bowl until well into the twentieth century.[13] Prior to the advent of flushing, human waste had to be carried away manually or evacuated through gravity-based drainage into cesspits. Cesspits in turn fed into covered-over streams that paralleled streets, sometimes flowing directly into rivers or other bodies of water, and sometimes making their way to collection centers where waste would be collected and transported to the countryside to be used as fertilizer.

Off-grid homes across Canada were always disconnected from municipal mains and sewers and therefore had to take care of their own business. Many off-gridders solved this problem with a septic system: a simple and clean solution implemented in most rural homes of the on-grid variety as well. But septic systems are costly to install and need to be pumped out every three years. Outhouse-based systems, instead, were cheaper, easier to build, and more self-sustaining. Instead of shipping away years of intestinal output, fecal matter could be treated locally and eventually re-integrated into the food cycle— or at least fed to flowers, shrubs, or fruit trees—in the form of composted "**humanure**.[vi][14] Even more simply, urine could be easily directed at—or spilled on, if it was collected first in a bucket—vegetation, especially fruit trees.[15]

The word "outhouse" typically brings to mind gross memories of poorly maintained campground facilities, but most domestic outhouses are clean and function rather effectively. After depositing one's leavings and dropping nothing else but soiled toilet paper, the defecator simply needs to add a scoop of sawdust, peat moss, ashes, or similar material into the container and pull down a cover. Some outhouses have different chambers where poop decomposes slowly onsite, whereas others yield raw material needing the user's immediate involvement.

[vi.] http://lifeoffgrid.ca/wp-content/uploads/2013/11/Life-Off-Grid_Ontario_09.jpg

Our cabin's outhouse was of the latter type, hence my circumspection. There, a common five-gallon plastic bucket was placed under a toilet seat. After completing one's mission the job entailed sliding the bucket from under the toilet seat, delivering the goods to a fresh pile of composting material, and scooping a handful of dry leaves into the bucket, which was then put in its place again. The heap of dry leaves worked like a charm; preventing shit from sticking to the bucket and simultaneously covering the fresh load (thus covering the smell and protecting it from flies) when it was deposited into the compost pile.

Composting humanure was a meaningful practice too. Compost toilet usage allowed off-gridders to engage in alternate relations with place by conserving local water resources and by enabling them to re-frame urine and feces as "generative, life-giving matter."[16] Human waste is, of course, socially perceived to be disgusting, unhealthy, and polluting,[17] and therefore by their radical re-orientation toward it off-gridders managed to refute an assemblage that treated the municipal disposal of waste as a manifestation of an individual's right not to be inconvenienced with the consequences of one's consumption. This re-orientation marked the entire food cycle at the farm and in many other off-grid homes across the country.

De-Concession

With no bathrooms available, the communal pond and Steve's sauna served as our bodily cleansing sites. Perhaps prudishly—given the general tendency around the Prairie Crocus to freely disrobe—Jon and I kept our trunks on at both sites, but at no expense of intimacy with Steve and some of his fellow farmers. During a particularly insightful conversation Steve, kicking back by our **bonfire**[vii] after an intensely relaxing and somewhat mystical sauna, explained why he believed in the redeeming value of simplicity. Global capitalism, he found, promises comfort and convenience but it actually shortchanges us all. International trade, corporate greed, and consumerism are at the root of growing social inequality, war, and environmental degradation, he observed.

Locally grown food and locally harvested energy were partial solutions to much larger problems, he argued. This was one of the reasons why some three decades ago he and a few other people purchased the farmland and decided to invest in a future of food security, self-reliance, and sustainable living. Growing food locally was a simple and effective way of fighting against concentrated agricultural production, flavor standardization, crop hyper-specialization, and the carbon footprint generated by distant food

---

vii. http://lifeoffgrid.ca/wp-content/uploads/2013/11/Life-Off-Grid_Manitoba_02.jpg

distribution. Steve believed that small-scale, diversified, localized production was also a way of re-introducing a level of humanness into the cycle of food growth. This is why the Prairie Crocus farm was also organic and powered by renewables. The avoidance of pesticides and carbon emissions showed that growing and cooking food was something that could be done cheaply and simply.

Yet, not enough people do it. To be sure, alternative food networks are growing all over the globe,[18] and undoubtedly these movements have had a meaningful impact on the mainstream. But findings by researchers such as Silva[19]—who found that cooking ranges and ovens were rated the least useful domestic appliances by many London families—show that taking care of one's own food is an inconvenient activity for many people.

To not do something one is able to do is an interesting phenomenon, equivalent to a *concession*. After all, when we let others do something we can do, we *concede* to them. To concede means to give way; to yield to others; to grant them a right, duty, or privilege to do something for us, in lieu of us. At times concession is the result of defeat (as when territories are given away to foreign political and economic powers), and at other times it is the result of free bargaining (as in the case of concession stands operating under lease-like contracts), but regardless of circumstances, to concede is to surrender.

Concessions can be practically useful but they can also have unpredictable consequences. Some people may find it convenient to let others cook a quick meal for them, but fast-foods—an example of that concession—have contributed to a preoccupying growth in obesity, diabetes, and osteopenia.[20] And convenience foods, which now occupy more space in supermarkets than fresh produce,[21] have destabilized traditional diets as well as entire economies worldwide.[22] Conceding the task of cooking to the distant supply chains that make meals-on-the-go "creates a tragic disconnection between the general public and the social and environmental consequences of the food being grown and eaten."[23] As food chains continue to grow in more complex ways, production and consumption are split farther apart, causing loss of biodiversity, degradation of water and soil, weakening of community ties, concentration of capital, reduction in agricultural resilience, erasure of local identity-based and place-based foodways, and ultimately food insecurity.[24] These concessions contribute to "thinning the lifeworld"[25] by fracturing food practices, skills, knowledge, and values previously tied to sense of place, locality, and community.

The main reason why so many people make concessions to fast-food restaurants, ready-made food producers, and supermarkets is practical convenience. In fact, marketers effectively advertise fast-foods[26] and convenience foods[27] by extolling their time-saving virtues. In addition to speed, consumers find accessibility, affordability, and availability to be appealing qualities of fast-foods and convenience foods.[28] Many shoppers also view these elements of convenience as essential in their decision on where and when to shop[29] and are therefore prone to patronize large, easily accessible, one-stop supermarket chains over alternative distributors. Convenience also explains the popularity of cooking with "on demand" kitchen technologies like toasters and microwave ovens[30] over alternatives like more frequent shopping for fresh products, cooking from scratch, and consuming shared meals. Convenience, in a nutshell, seems to broadly justify concession.

Current dominant discourses on convenience "speak to the problem of living in a social world where people act in response to the feeling that they have insufficient time."[31] In this context, alternative time-consuming choices like growing one's own food, cooking from basic ingredients, buying at organic farmers' markets, and seeking out local and fair-trade products may be valued in their own ways[32] but can hardly be perceived as convenient. The persistent reputation of alternative foods such as organic and fair-trade products is in fact that of being more expensive, not always available, harder to find, and more time-consuming overall; a reputation that has gained them a degree of distinction among conspicuous seekers of taste,[33] but relatively limited market penetration. Now, this is not to say that critiques are non-existent or that counterhegemonic choices are unavailable, but more simply it is to suggest that fast-foods, convenience foods, and supermarket chain products have come to embody and even redefine the dominant meaning of convenience.[34]

As the bonfire flames continued to protect us from the mosquitos, Jon and I opened a second beer. Steve did not. There was a good deal of hedonism going on elsewhere on farm grounds, but in contrast Steve seemed more parsimonious, heedful, and solitary. Living like this can be hard work, he said. But it allowed for a genuine existence. It could be backbreaking to try to be self-sufficient, but it was a lifestyle that put him in touch with nature and the "creator."

"You know, I have a theory," he opined when I asked him how he dealt with the inconvenience of living without some of the creature comforts common to most contemporary homes. "I call it the ratchet effect."

I smiled, "You've got a pretty good academic-sounding name for it, watch out I might steal it!"

He laughed. "Well, tell me what you think. My theory is that our society relates to convenience the same way a ratchet works. We ratchet up the ladder of convenience by becoming used to . . . I mean, by taking for granted things that we could only dream of in the recent past. But then we become unable to go back. Just like the way a ratchet works; we can only go one way. We get used to eating bananas from Central America, kiwis from New Zealand, grapes from Chile or this or that place, every single day of the year and soon enough we become unable to live without those things."

He was right: that is why I felt so guilty about my favorite Arabica beans shipped from Costa Rica. And I wish I could have patented Steve's theory, but when I looked into it, it had already been claimed. Sociologists of consumption have articulated the ratchet-like escalating process whereby cumulating comfort and convenience become increasingly difficult to scale back from.[35] But over the last decade more than a handful of de-escalations—at least within the context of food—have actually gained favor with people. Alternative agro-food networks, community food security programs, democratic agriculture initiatives, post-productivist trends, shortened food chains, epicurean fashions, organic and fair trade markets, the slow food movement, and other similar plans have aimed to re-instill a sense of place in the gastronomic landscape.[36]

Such *de-concessions* from the world of distant production and drive-through convenience have resulted in partially re-localizing and re-possessing systems of food production and consumption, have raised awareness about food insecurity, and have enacted a strong resistance to concentrated agricultural corporatism. In small ways these are also the de-concessions practiced by off-grid smallholders like Steve. To *de-concede* is to redeem the right, duty, privilege, and even pleasure of doing something for oneself. A de-concession is a recapture, a re-possession, a reclamation of what used to be one's own. De-concessions re-spatialize and re-configure assemblages of materials, institutions, practices, representations, and experiences.

Off-grid de-concessions go two steps further than all the other counter-hegemonic attempts to re-configure food assemblages. The first step pertains to food preparation. Re-localized food programs, plans, schemes, and movements of all kinds make no mention of how sustainable food cooking should be. A potato may very well be locally grown, organic, and fair trade but once it's baked in an electric oven powered by a grid fueled by coal, the environmental score is far from settled. The second step concerns the meaning of convenience. To truly recapture a sense of food security and sovereignty we must believe that our meals are not only better for us and the planet, but also more convenient. This is hardly the case when organic foods continue to be more expensive and harder to find than their counterparts. By cooking local food with local energy resources and by re-framing that practice as truly convenient, Steve and the Prairie Crocus Co-op Farm were making important de-concessions.

Sun-Dried Everything

Convenience reigns supreme in the modern kitchen. Electric ovens and ranges, freezers, refrigerators, microwaves, toasters, blenders, rice-cookers, bread-makers, juicers, hot plates, grills, and a whole circus of other pluggable "labor-saving devices" do their gig quickly and with limited user involvement. But electric appliances devour a lot of power. When your generating capacity is limited, the quest for convenience has to operate by different rules.

Take food conservation, for example. Power-hungry refrigerators and freezers can easily be replaced by old practices like canning, brewing, pickling, salting, and dehydrating—all practices that our grandparents were probably very familiar with, but that most of us have never learned or have forgotten. Or consider the usefulness of root cellars as an electricity-free alternative to refrigeration and freezing. A root cellar is a structure the size of a small garage that is built underground or directly underneath a natural or human-made mound of dirt, wood, and rocks. Using no energy at all, root cellars work like natural refrigerators, preventing food from freezing during winter and from spoiling due to excessive heat during summer. In off-grid homes where refrigeration and freezing were nearly impossible due to the low power-generation of the systems in place, these old technologies allowed for food to last well into the next season.

* * *

The biting sun was about to bore a hole into my skull when Elizabeth asked me if I wanted to help with dinner preparation.

"Will you need to fire up a woodstove?" I asked hesitantly.

"No."

"Let's go then."

Elizabeth and Sarah had gathered the ingredients for a summer vegetarian meal: beet (yes with a *t*, not an *f*) burgers and tortilla wraps filled with fresh greens and homemade hummus. We began our work by peeling the beets. Then we grated them and added finely diced onions, garlic, eggs, and seasonings. In the meantime we prepared the hummus: mashing chickpeas and mincing more garlic, adding lemon juice, olive oil, and tahini. Everything was done by hand—even cleaning and washing with hand-carried jugs and buckets of water—and then carefully setting kitchen waste aside for the compost pile.

While many ingredients came from the farm, not all did. Tahini, chickpeas, olive oil, and wraps were nearly impossible to produce on site, so they were all acquired from the grocery store. Sarah and Elizabeth were pragmatic about it; while it's important to eat what you grow, the climate and soil only allowed what they could. Time and effort were critical factors too. While localization and sustainability were essential, so was enjoying life's simple pleasures. Militant industriousness and hardline environmental ideology can get in the way of carefree downtime.

Generally, off-gridders across Canada would cook with propane stoves, woodstoves, or both. Propane could be easily bottled and transported, with no need for pipelines for domestic distribution (as opposed to natural gas). However, propane is a non-renewable fuel and its burning causes a modest but detectable carbon emission, so not all off-gridders—especially the more environmentally minded ones—liked to use it. Woodstoves, in contrast, used a locally grown renewable resource and emitted only as much carbon as wood yields naturally by way of gradual decomposition,[37] so they were an environmentally preferable alternative (if used on a small scale). But wood burning for the sake of cooking had its downsides as well, like unwanted heat. Woodstove operation was also more time-consuming and complex than cooking with electric or gas-fueled ranges and ovens.

With no electric tools available, and in order to avoid both the use of propane and firewood, Sarah and I lined the beet patties on two large baking sheets and brought them outside to bake in one of the **solar ovens**.[viii] I slid the baking sheets inside and immediately the skin of my hands sensed the penetrating warmth of the sun trapped by the oven's glass cover. The temperature was certainly lower than a typical oven—it generally took twice as long to cook food in a solar oven of that size—but undoubtedly serviceable. These ovens were indeed much bigger than we had seen in Dave's backyard on Lasqueti, reaching up to eight feet in height and about six in width. Even more remarkable than their size was their makeup: all their components had been carefully rescued and recovered. The glass and plywood came from industrial construction sites, for example, and the metal sheets from an old printing press.

While the sun went to work on our burgers, **Gijs**[ix] offered to give us an extended tour. Duly shirtless, but covered in layers of charisma, Gijs spoke softly, with a faint Dutch accent. He was born in 1947 in Groningen, Holland, and had moved to Canada three decades ago. What appealed most to him about the Prairie Crocus culture was the "incredible potential for creative expression. . . . It's amazing what you can do," he said, "when there is nobody around telling you that you can't do this and you can't do that." He wasn't bombastic—Gijs was one of the most inventive and resourceful off-gridders we'd ever met.

A peek into his summer kitchen alone would have convinced anyone of that. The summer kitchen was a small building separate from his house: an airy, wooden shed set amidst tall shade trees. "Check out my answer to refrigeration," he said as he invited us in. With the flick of a button a low whirring noise sprung from the floor. Lacking the sufficient power for a refrigerator—his four solar panels only gave him 300 watts/hour on a sunny day—Gijs stored perishables in the natural coolness of the earth six feet

[viii] http://lifeoffgrid.ca/wp-content/uploads/2013/11/Life-Off-Grid_Manitoba_07.jpg

underground, beneath his summer kitchen floor. The whirring sound came from a home-built pulley that hoisted a wooden tray and rolled it all the way up to the floor level. As the tray reached our feet a small bulb lit up. "Cheese, anyone?" Gijs smiled.

The low-wattage food elevator wasn't Gijs's only invention. Using a fan from a discarded computer he had devised a gadget that blew air into a compartment of his summer kitchen's cooking woodstove. This caused a faster fire, which enabled him to make coffee more quickly, to burn less wood, and to create less unwanted heat in the kitchen. The bonanza of unpatented inventions was far from over.

Inside his house, a thermometer had been rigged to a door opener. When the temperature reached the desired level, the door opener clicked into action by shutting, or opening if needed, windows and doors—sort of an automatic, "natural" air-conditioning system. All of this was, of course, on 12-volt electricity, which he had learned to use from a 30-year-old typewritten manual picked up at Radio Shack. "When you have little money you allow for the release of creativity," he remarked. "You can't be afraid, you just have to try and do it," he said, "when you've got money to buy already-made stuff you learn nothing."

The piercing ding of an insistent bell suddenly interrupted our chat. Dinner was ready. Before we could sink our teeth in, the nine of us joined hands in the broad dining hall and sang our thanks. Equally unaccustomed to pre-dinner grace rituals or to celebrations of communal lovey feelings, Jon and I were relieved the fanfare was over quickly enough. The beet burger was charred to perfection and the hummus as tangy as it should have been, but their taste's true distinction was our sheer involvement in it. I knew from my home garden as well that food tasted different when you cared for its soil, grew it, and cooked it yourself. In the delightful words of another Manitoba off-gridder: "It's like living in a house you built."

* * *

As our experiences at the farm and elsewhere in Canada had shown us, off-grid food production and consumption were about re-inventing convenience and re-discovering the value of sustainably cooked local flavors. This was off-gridders' disposition to food, but such orientation to convenience pervaded every corner of their homes and every aspect of their lifestyle. But we need to be careful not to lionize off-gridders. As romantic as it may sound to try to live simply, more self-sufficiently, sustainably, and in a resilient and ingenious way, we must understand that off-grid living required many compromises. Similarly, we can't sing the praises of "the local" too

---

ix. http://lifeoffgrid.ca/wp-content/uploads/2013/11/Life-Off-Grid_Manitoba_08.jpg

much. Sociological and geographic research on "localism" has exposed the dangers inherent in a "romantic essentialism of place"[38] and criticized the parochialism, provincialism, reactionary conservatism, and isolationism that un-reflexive localism may possibly slide into.[39]

With this said, we'd also make a mistake by not learning from the important lessons that off-grid food production and consumption can offer to the rest of us. The key teachings can be found in the implications of the de-concessions made through off-grid food production and consumption. Off-grid food production and consumption—and off-grid living more broadly—reclaimed a sense of place by re-inventing convenience as *suitability, simplicity, unhurriedness, harmoniousness,* and *proximity.* Through this re-assemblage, convenience was de-conceded from distant corporate powers and their concentrated food supply chains. This de-concession prompted new socio-natural connections, new flavors, and new positive practices counterbalancing the "thinning out of the lifeworld."[40] Such de-concession constituted a reflexive but "militant particularism" that "seize[d] upon the qualities of place, reanimate[d] the bond between the environmental and the social, and [sought] to bend the social processes by constructing space-time to a radically different purpose."[41]

Off-grid food production and consumption aimed to be *suitable* by trying to fit with the characteristics of a place. Something that is suitable is convenient because it is appropriate, reasonable, befitting, and expedient. Mass-scale producers of convenience foods want their products to be the same everywhere, regardless of local conditions. Instead, off-grid food production and consumption were intertwined in profound ways with local knowledge, geography, and sense of place. Through its sensual qualities—smells, textures, taste, etc.—place-suitable food helped build emotional and affective ties between people and place.[42]

By producing and consuming foods that were suitable to their places, off-gridders worked within a "food-shed"[43] that realigned human activity with the natural and social elements of the environment, including weather patterns, water availability, soil and slope conditions, and local market demand and traditions. "Foodsheds embed the system in a moral economy attached to a particular community and place, just as watersheds reattach water systems to a natural ecology,"[44] so growing and eating food originating within one's foodshed—and fertilizing such food with humanure—was convenient because it was suitable with the social nature of a specific place.

Off-grid food production and consumption were *simple* in the sense that they were genuine, basic, rustic, and down to earth. Simplicity is a direct synonym of convenience, but whereas the uncomplicatedness of mass-marketed convenience foods resides in their ease of preparation, the simplicity of off-grid foods lay in their plain, genuine flavor. All the off-grid meals we had across the country—from Yukon potatoes and Saskatoon berries to Arctic char and Atlantic lobster—had a distinct *goût de terroir*, as the French commonly say: a taste of the earth where they came from. Traditionally, French cuisine has entailed either sophisticated, complex, and cosmopolitan flavors, or a kind of simpler domestic quality embedded in local ingredients, artisanal products, and farming traditions. The latter is a type of plain cuisine infused with *terroir*: with "the earth considered from the point of view of agriculture"[45] and with the flavor of specific locales. Thus the kind of simplicity inherent in a beet burger or a home-raised, free-range chicken cooked in a solar oven—as Steve prepared for us one night—allowed us to taste not only food but also soil, climate, and the fruit of hard work. It was a simple convenience that did not exempt you from involvement in growth and preparation, but rather asked you and rewarded you for your meaningful engagement with whatever you ate.

Off-grid food production and consumption were also *unhurried*. Commodified, quick-mart, and supermarket foods promise convenience because they are quick to buy and fast to prepare. All of these products appeal to us only insofar as we are in a hurry. Off-gridders instead got at the root of the problem by directly attacking the condition of hurriedness.[46] Growing, cooking, and eating food slowly made perfect sense within a slower lifestyle in general, and not as expedients to save time in order to get busy with something else.

Like the slow food movement, off-grid food production and consumption aimed to protect the values of mundane pleasures, to respect natural rhythms, to re-discover heritage, and to re-instill into everyday life the habits and rituals of a less frantic way of living. And like the slow food movement in general, off-grid food production and consumption re-imagined a kind of convenience that resided in a placid discontinuation of the current dominant work-spend-work-spend mode of living and in enjoyment of relaxed conviviality. Convenience, therefore, lay not in a quick pace but in calm and tranquility.

As well, off-grid food production and consumption unfolded in relative *harmony* with the elements of a place.[47] Harmoniousness is a less known, but historically well-established, meaning of the word *convenience*. The word derives from the Latin *com-* ("with," "together") and *venire* ("to come"). Something that is convenient is something that comes together in agreement and harmony with other things. There were two kinds of harmony at play in off-grid food production and consumption. The first was a kind of harmony with the resources available in a particular place, which ranged from indigenous vegetation to the refrigeration and cooking possibilities allowed by weather and climate.

The second kind of harmony was a social one. Like other local food systems, the Prairie Crocus resurrected the traditional idea of place-based communities as "basic building blocks and foundations of our society, making critical contributions to the quality of families, interpersonal relationships, education, health, environment, food systems, economy, and overall well-being."[48] Cooking in common kitchens, sharing food, pooling money to purchase staples, making collective decisions, and harvesting common resources like water, the sun, wood, and soil were ways in which the off-gridders we visited came together as a community to tackle food security.

Finally, off-grid food production and consumption re-invented the notion of convenience as something that is close-at-hand. The kind of *proximity* practiced by off-grid food producers and consumers was different from the accessibility typical of supermarkets, fast-food restaurants, and convenience stores. Whereas the latter promise convenience through ample parking lots, drive-throughs, and ubiquity, off-grid foods came from places even closer to the kitchen table—they were grown or raised in the backyard and stored and cooked with resources available within one's land. Proximity, as opposed to accessibility, shortened the relations between food production and consumption, re-configured the very idea of food distribution, and re-embedded food growth within the domestic space.

Off-grid food systems challenged large supply chains and managed to reduce food miles.[49] Proximity therefore also informed trust, environmental stewardship, and familiarity. Localized food growth was an important de-concession from the industrialized food systems that have breached consumer trust, exerted animal cruelty, introduced "Frankenstein foods," and homogenized flavor.[50] Proximity short-circuited the lengthy food chains of agro-capitalism, lifting the veil on the provenance of local food while casting shadows on the anonymity of the producers of mass-market products.[51]

* * *

It was certainly difficult to disagree in principle with all these values. It was easier, however, to differ in practice. Not all of us have the space to grow our own food or store it in root cellars, or cook with woodstoves and solar ovens. Not many people can compost food scraps in their city apartments, let alone their bodily waste. There simply isn't enough time in the day to do everything we should, or so it seems, and there are strong geographical and logistical limits to how much food production we can localize.

We had left Ontario earlier in the spring with serious questions about the feasibility and consequences of off-grid living on a large scale, and now more interrogatives were piling up. To de-concede, even a little, was better than to surrender and do nothing—that much was clear. Understanding and practicing convenience differently and more reflexively, as off-gridders in Manitoba and elsewhere did, was undoubtedly important. But was it enough to make a difference? Did it entail too much sacrifice—so much that it was nearly impossible for most of us to ratchet back to? Off-grid living also demanded a lot of work, and could everyone afford to invest that much time and bodily energy in their domestic life?

To boot, sharing resources for power generation seemed to work quite well for the two co-op farms we had visited, but the unique lifestyles and profound collaboration those arrangements required were obviously not going to appeal to many people in an individualistic culture like ours. Even I, with all my best intentions, had felt—in as little as a few days—that it was challenging to get along with every neighbor. In short, co-op grids offered no more superior solutions than detached off-grid dwellings.

Though we had now made it halfway across the country, it was obvious that we were nowhere near finding the answer to whether off-grid living could be a better way of life for all of us. Or perhaps this was just a wrong question to ask. It was certain that by virtue of their involvement with nature, technology, their homes, their beloved land, and their sources of energy, off-gridders were able to deeply affect the quality of their day-to-day lives, enjoying domestic comforts and conveniences as much as the rest of us, but in a radically different manner because of their lifestyle orientation, or better yet, the way in which they inhabited place. But was this for everyone? Could anyone do it?

Notes

1. WWOOF stands for World-Wide Opportunities on Organic Farms. WWoofers are those who take advantage of such opportunities, donating their agricultural labor in exchange for room and board.
2. Jackson et al., 2006; Khamis, 2006; Shove, 2003; Warde, 1999.
3. Crowley, 2001; Khamis, 2006; Rybczynski, 1987.
4. Kneale-Gould, 2005.
5. Chhetri, Khan et al. 2009; Chhetri, Stimson et al. 2009.
6. Halfacree, 2006.
7. Holloway, 2000.
8. Parkins and Craig, 2006.
9. Shove and Southerton, 2000.
10. Shove and Southerton, 2000.
11. Hochschild, 1989.
12. Shove and Southerton, 2000.

13. Rybczynski, 1987.
14. A minimum of six months is generally required for human solid waste to be chemically ready to be used as a fertilizer. More information available at: http://humanurehandbook.com/
15. Human urine is high in nitrogen, from which trees, benefit more than smaller plants. Even trees can suffer from too much nitrogen and therefore, pee is best spread around (see Pickering, 2010).
16. Pickering, 2010:34.
17. Jewitt, 2011.
18. Kneafsey et al., 2008; Parkins and Craig, 2006.
19. Silva, 2010.
20. Lydon et al., 2011.
21. Gleick, 1999.
22. Feagan, 2007.
23. Kimbrell, 2002:1.
24. Feagan, 2007.
25. Casey, 2001.
26. Brewis and Jack, 2005.
27. Khamis, 2006; Turner, 2006.
28. Khamis, 2006; Turner, 2006.
29. Jackson et al., 2006.
30. Shove, 2003; Shove and Southerton, 2000.
31. Warde, 1999:521.
32. Murcott, 1982.
33. Guthman, 2003.
34. Shove, 2003; Warde, 1999.
35. MacCracken, 1988; Shove, 2003.
36. Kneafsey et al., 2008.
37. Of course, wood burning is faster than natural decomposition, and therefore in order to be carbon neutral more trees have to be planted than otherwise would grow on their own.
38. Massey, 2004:11.
39. DuPuis and Goodman, 2005; Hinrichs, 2003.
40. Casey, 2001.
41. Harvey, 1996:306.
42. Longhurst et al., 2009.
43. Kloppenburg et al., 1996.
44. Starr et al., 2003:303.
45. Trubek, 2008:xv.
46. Also see Parkins and Craig, 2006.
47. Halfacree, 2006; Holloway, 2000.
48. Lacy, 2000:3.
49. Renting et al., 2003.
50. DuPuis and Goodman, 2005.
51. Compare with Renting et al., 2003.

Hélène and Construction.[i]

8
HOUSE-BUILDING, DIW-STYLE

"Well, Phillip, homes are an extension of who we are, you know."

"So, what in the world does living in an **ark**[ii] say about you!?" I inquired, feeling baffled. Mike paused to think. Like biblical Noah's Hail-Mary pass at end-of-the-world carpentry, Mike and Monique's 5,000-square-foot, 120-foot-long ark-like home in the Gatineau Hills stood as an impossibly creative display of resolve, vision, and whimsical problem solving.

"Well, I am the only one who knows how this house works because I built it myself," he answered firmly, "and I built it to suit *me*. If Monique and I ever broke up I'd have to take the house because she couldn't live here by herself! No one could!" he laughed loudly.

"Come this way, I wanna show you my second generator," Mike said, as he started walking toward the ground floor workroom. The second generator was a custom-built, small-block, four-cylinder Merck engine that he and a buddy rescued from a boat and converted to propane. The engine was equipped with a 200-amp 12-volt alternator that he had recovered from a military Humvee. Mike and his friend had rigged the generator to harvest the heat from the exhaust through an AVS pipe. The exhaust was then sent through a heat exchanger and efficiently delivered upstairs to warm up the living room and kitchen. As for the leftover fumes, a trip to the outside confirmed my hunch: an exhaust pipe sticking out of the side of his house sat ready to puff out the discarded noxious gas. "There is only one of those in the world!" Mike cracked while I scratched my head at the contraption.

[ii] http://lifeoffgrid.ca/wp-content/uploads/2013/11/Life-Off-Grid_Quebec_09.jpg

"I have two inverters for my solar panels," Mike explained, moving on with the tour, "this house is full of redundancies." His first inverter was a normal one, but his second one had been recovered from an ambulance. "Three kilowatts! This thing is just pure power, it's a workhorse!" he boasted as he switched it on to let a robotic, buzzing hum echo his argument. The device, which he concocted once again following the suggestion of the same "crazy-mad scientist" friend, allowed his electrical system to handle the "hammer" of power demand brought on by the starting-up of a power tool.

Mike was not only an electrical wizard, but also an ingenious carpenter. His house used to be a saw mill that—due to no more plausible a reason than the fact that the guy who initially built it was "crazy"—was curiously shaped like an ark. When Mike and Monique bought it in 2003, the mill amounted to just three walls and a roof. Raw logs used to be driven indoors, where the front entrance of their house now stood, and all the millwork would go on downstairs. Upstairs, some rooms had been roughed in for future office space, but the place had fallen into complete decay so it and the adjacent 164-acre property sold for a bargain $99,000. Undaunted by the massive renovation task, Mike did beam-and-post work, insulated the structure, added drywall, finished the rooms, and took care of the plumbing, painting, and flooring. Going off-grid was a simple necessity to avoid paying an exorbitant Hydro Quebec connection bill.

"How did you figure out how to do all these home improvement projects?" I wondered. It wasn't a token question; Mike had a MBA and a consulting business in corporate leadership and team building. He also ran a campground and organized youth outdoor education programs, snowshoe races, and weddings on his property. There was no architectural or construction training at all in his Jack-of-All-Trades background.

"That's what's so great about the internet!"

"You mean, you . . ."

"Yeah, I Googled plumbing and all that stuff."

We all roared in laughter. "It's common sense," he continued. "You don't need to know everything. I don't even know the terminology. What's the difference between a rafter and a joist?"

"I wouldn't know . . ."

"It's just common sense. With plumbing, water runs downhill, that's all you need to know. Electricity? Electricity is even easier. With kids sometimes I hear the word 'can't.' 'Can't?!?' That word doesn't exist."

We had been in Quebec for a week by then, and though it wasn't unusual for off-gridders to build their own homes, *la belle province* seemed packed with DIY builders like Mike: crafty individuals who—despite not being architects or professional contractors—managed to find ways to assemble their own houses. Like Mike, the average consumer interested in doing it oneself these days has the ability to source knowledge from a bottomless pile of DIY books for dummies, reference manuals, websites, YouTube videos, and ezines readily prepared to break down steps, exemplify, and demonstrate procedures.

Social historian Steven Gelber[1] has observed that the moniker "do-it-yourself" (or "DIY" for short) dates back to 1912, when an article in the popular magazine *Suburban Life* first used that expression to encourage homeowners to take on minor renovation projects on their own rather than hire professional contractors. DIY was set for an impressive uptake in popular interest. With the subsequent historical rise in suburban and exurban home ownership,[2] the articulation of ordinary maintenance and renovation with evolving ideologies of both masculinity and femininity,[3] the progressive commercialization of home-improvement tools and supplies,[4] and the explosion of lifestyle media promoting home- and garden-based hobbies and identity-based domestic consumption,[5] DIY has become part and parcel of contemporary consumer culture. Part self-expressive hobby, part ostentatious consumption and ego-boosting skill display, and part convenient utilization of handy money-saving skills,[6] DIY building and home-improvement symbolize and exercise practical knowledge capital, lifestyle choices, and autonomous control over possessions.[7]

Do-it-yourselfers are a diverse group of people. While the majority are men, women's participation has been growing steadily, outpacing the growth in men's rates.[8] Members of many different socioeconomic groups engage in DIY often for different reasons, such as to save money, or to spend disposable income in self-affirming hobbies or social status-enhancing projects.[9] DIY, however, is not exactly for everybody. Many everyday obligations compete with DIY projects for people's attention, including leisure options, family responsibilities, and paid work.[10] Heightened social and geographical mobility also end up reducing the transfer of skills across generations, friends, and neighbors, rendering it difficult for aspiring DIY practitioners to learn how to tackle projects through personal networks.[11] Formal building codes also make it impossible for unlicensed individuals to tackle certain projects, especially electricity-related ones. Ingenious DIYers who build their own homes with creative designs, innovative techniques, and alternative resources and materials, therefore, easily stand out among a mass of weekend handymen and handywomen carrying out smaller projects.

For the better part of the last three decades, the DIY ethos has been routinely lionized as the epitome of resistance across the cultural sciences.[12] As a result it would be tempting to suggest that DIY home builders are countercultural heroes fighting against the erosion of the private sphere, the compression of everyday time, the hyper-specialization of skill, the loss of orally transmitted lay knowledge, the massification of residential architecture, the homogenization of domestic design, and the commercialization of building trades. Such characterization would be an overstatement, however.

As it turns out, the off-gridders we met in Quebec and elsewhere revealed something altogether different about the nature of home building and DIY. Our encounters showed us that it always took a village to raise a barn, so to speak. Mike's example was a great one; despite his ingenuity, creativity, and resolve Mike could only build his house with the help of other people, such as friends willing to invest time and skills, professionals able to provide occasional advice, and internet-mediated experts waiting to be downloaded at a moment's notice.

The expression "do-it-yourself" connotes an individualistic, self-oriented, self-sufficient impetus that does not match actual practice.[13] It is therefore no accident that doing-it-oneself has taken on the aura of a lone, last-man-standing, heroic, resistant response to a stable structure of domination.[14] A corrective to this romantic bias is to view individuals such as off-grid home builders as people who did not break away from, or openly contest, greater social forces, but rather as people who articulated their practices with such forces through different associative relations, or different "entanglements."[15]

These different entanglements manifested themselves in ways such as the employment of sustainable design, the recovery of vernacular architectural traditions, and the quest for a different way of inhabiting place. Together these entanglements of people, materials, and places demonstrated how the building of an off-grid home was not a resistant or defiant DIY act, but rather a practical application of skill. This was a skillset residing in a self-consciously practical and pragmatic orientation to building as a way of establishing connections[16] rather than severing or resisting ties. It was a set of *regenerative life skills* through which off-gridders exercised modest but meaningful degrees of control over their life circumstances and through which they brought practical know-how, dedication, resolve, judgment, creativity, passion, and their lifestyle values to bear on their day-to-day existence.

Building with Dirt and Garbage

Jon and I had sketched a very reasonable itinerary this time. Second only to the territory of Nunavut, Quebec was simply too large to cover with any pretentions of wholeness. Language was an issue too, so we had figured our chances of meeting bilingual off-gridders would be greater by situating ourselves between Montreal and Laval to the east and Gatineau to the west. It was a prudent strategy. Besides, the Outaouais, Laurentides, and Lanaudière regions were spectacular, so much so that even off-grid tourism was booming there. Case in point, the upscale Fairmont hotel chain offered off-grid cabin accommodations in equally upscale Montebello. Since we could benefit from shoulder season rates, I phoned to book a few nights.

"Are you sure?" said the voice on the other end of the line in a heavily French-inflected English. "We are not the typical Fairmont, you know? To reach that cabin you'd have to drive for an hour on an unpaved road, and once at the cabins there is no . . ."

"I'm sure. We're in the business of writing about peace and quiet," I re-assured the lady.

"Well, then you're getting a bargain. There are hardly any other guests at this time. You'll have 65,000 acres of protected wilderness for yourselves."

"Did she just say 65,000 acres?" I thought.

She wasn't being grandiose. One of the largest game and fishing reserves on the continent, the land had been given away by the King of France in 1674. Countless moose, wild turtles, and 70 lakes—several of them stocked with trout—were shared by 20 cabins, most of which depended on the usual combo of solar, propane, and wood. With our relatively modest nightly rate we were also given access to two kayaks, a canoe, a barbeque, and our own undisturbed **private lake**.[iii] My sour mood and fatigue instantly evaporated with the first autumn morning mist. As for Jon, I would have asked him how he felt, but he was out fishing.

Tearing ourselves away from our luxurious base camp for the day, we reached Hélène and Alain's **earthship-like home**[iv] outside Laval after a singularly tortuous drive along dreamingly picturesque exurban hillside towns. Hélène and I had emailed in French and as we shook hands, nervous at having to beg for her indulgence in chatting in English, my red face was as bright as the early afternoon sun. Her accommodating disposition felt like a relief. Alain, however, was less comfortable with our language and since he had errands to run he excused himself.

"Just make sure you don't steal my favorite joke," he teased Hélène on his way out.

"What's the joke?" I inquired.

"Ask her what kind of tires we used," Alain smiled.

The couple had lived at their off-grid earthship for seven years. Once the cameras were rolling, I began with the usual question, holding off on seeking the joke's punch line for the time being.

[iii.] http://lifeoffgrid.ca/wp-content/uploads/2013/11/Life-Off-Grid_Quebec_08.jpg
[iv.] http://lifeoffgrid.ca/wp-content/uploads/2013/11/Life-Off-Grid_Quebec_06.jpg

"I like to be able to do everything, repair everything, make everything myself," **Hélène**[v] began.

"Is that why you're off-grid?"

"I've always felt that I'm never better served than by myself," she replied convincingly. Her short hair, her practical attire, and her skin naturally tanned from working under the sun confirmed she was not afraid of toil.

"Life is full of challenges," she continued. "I prefer the ones that I know where they're coming from. If you build your own house and there's a leak in the roof then you know why and how to fix it . . . that's why in this house there is no essential element that needs electricity to function, we're not dependent on anything in particular." Everything vital could always be done some other way, she explained, by applying a practical ethos of re-purposing, re-combining, and **re-using**.[vi]

Hélène and Alain's earthship-like home was built by ramming dirt and sand into discarded motor **vehicle tires**.[vii] The tires were packed and stacked on top of one another to form walls and then plastered over. Tires were easy to build with and provided remarkable thermal mass—slowly absorbing and releasing warmth when packed with earth. Earthships were invented and trademarked by maverick US architect Michael Reynolds, who has famously touted their passive solar advantage, cost-effectiveness, potential for energy autonomy, and reliance on abundantly available **resources**.[viii] The tires the Quebec couple used, as Alain's famous joke went, were the all-season type.

The wisecrack was well rehearsed—Hélène and Alain's earthship-like home had been in the limelight of the sustainable design world for some time. Mainstream and alternative media had brought much attention to this otherwise quiet and recluse 15-acre hillside property. That day it was a group of apprentices from French-speaking Africa who were there to learn new skills and pay back in volunteer work on the house and garden. Hélène and Alain's house was in fact both a home and a classroom. Like the learning process, Hélène liked to point out, a house was "always going on," never finished. The current 800 square feet would double sideways, eventually.

"You learn by doing," observed Hélène. But despite her practical and **generalist**[ix] leanings, she knew that "doing" was never a solitary undertaking. Filling tires—collected and delivered for free by Recyc Quebec—was nothing but a group effort, with friends and volunteers coming and going as their availability permitted. Dirt and sand had to be trucked in from a nearby pit

[v] http://lifeoffgrid.ca/wp-content/uploads/2013/11/Life-Off-Grid_Quebec_05.jpg

[vi] http://soundcloud.com/innovativeethnographies/helene-re-use

[vii] http://lifeoffgrid.ca/wp-content/uploads/2013/11/Life-Off-Grid_Quebec_03.jpg

[viii] http://earthship.com/

[ix] http://soundcloud.com/innovativeethnographies/helene-being-a-generalist

at the cost of about $100 per load. Even the choice of the site where the house would eventually be built was not a solo effort, as a dowser had been hired to locate the most ideal water source. Logic, intuition, and common sense, Hélène explained, were the key building blocks. And of course experience too: "everything you learn is things that you do, so if you're interested in building you're going to help somebody build their house, and then help someone else, and then eventually you'll build your own and ask people to come and help you."

Solar panels provided 300 watts of electricity for their modest domestic needs. Gravity provided water pressure. Composting replaced sewage lines. Propane fueled their hot-water heater. Re-purposed junk served as insulation. Wood harvested from their property worked as building material and fed their efficient and beautiful rocket stove. Their home backed deep into the hill at such an angle that almost their entire bedroom lay cocooned under warm dirt. It was so **warm indoors**[x] that they were able to grow fig, lime, banana, mandarin, and lemon trees. And a cellular signal—the city that occasionally dragged them away for work was indeed not too far—provided them with internet access. "If it wasn't for the internet I wouldn't have figured out that earthships existed in the first place," Hélène quipped.

Like Mike, Hélène and Alain had built their own house with the help of others. Making, for them too, was a way of "connecting."[17] "Acts of creativity usually involve, at some point, a social dimension and connect us with other people," media theorist David Gauntlett has observed.[18] DIY off-grid building was therefore more a kind of doing it *with others*. But Do-It-With, or DIW, was not just about interpersonal connections. DIW building was also about "connect[ing] *things* together (material, ideas, or both) to make something new."[19] In the case of Hélène and Alain these things included tires, dirt, sand, wood, and many more other materials. These were the objects they and their helpers had "woven"[20] together to shape their home—they could not have not done it without these things.

Arguing that the expression *DIY* is partial because it overly focuses on the solo human builder at the expense of material things is not a fastidious semantic quibble. Non-human agents matter greatly, as volumes of material culture studies attest. Human and non-human agents in fact generate new forms of life by becoming entangled together. According to Ingold[21] entanglements are processes through which humans and non-humans become intertwined and interdependent. We can think of an entanglement as a type of relational binding that erases all boundaries between the elements that comprise it. Take Hélène and Alain's home, for example.

---

[x] http://lifeoffgrid.ca/wp-content/uploads/2013/11/Life-Off-Grid_Quebec_07.jpg

Hélène and Alain's dwelling did not sit atop a piece of land, but was rather ensconced into it. In other words they did not build *on* a hill, but *with* a hill. Standing on the grassy roof with Hélène, admiring the landscape from the hillside, I could barely detect there was a house underneath my feet. They wanted to be inside the hill, she explained, to feel one with it, to feel its warmth and protection. By doing so, their home was not *outside* the ground in any clear way. The plants potted right into the floor and growing so lushly indoors seemed but to reconfirm this pervasive feeling of entanglement. There was no obvious division between the inside of the home and its outside—a blurring of boundaries also reinforced by how the southern sun penetrated the large windows to warm up the interior, as well as how water flowed from the hilltop into their faucets by sheer gravity. The entanglement of home, water, sun, and dirt annihilated the boundaries among them, thus "the land itself no longer appear[ed] as an interface" between the inside and outside of their home, "but as a vaguely defined zone of admixture and intermingling."[22]

Re-using discarded material like tires was another way of entangling things together to generate new forms of life. Within contemporary Western culture, garbage is generally perceived to be a source of unease, disease, and contamination.[23] Within our homes we routinely separate new material, which we store inside, from discarded stuff, which we relegate outside in the name of disposability and cleanliness. By re-using, however, we actualize the potential of discarded material to generate new relations.[24] So by using discarded tires, Hélène and Alain "restore[d] these things to life,"[25] returning them to a space where their material qualities could still be functional and productive.

It is by a logic of inversion, Ingold[26] has argued, that most of us have become accustomed to living life as if it was "reduced to an internal property of things that *occupy* the world but do not properly *inhabit* it." It is by this logic that most of us occupy homes already built for us. A home that is built for us and merely occupied by us is a home "furnished with already existing things[27]" that power it and fuel it. In contrast, a home of the kind woven by Hélène and Alain was bound together—knotted into place from the strands of the continual coming into being of the living materials entangled into it. It was a place of habitation, not mere occupation. It was a constantly regenerative building, as Hélène herself pointed out: a build*ing* (as the gerund denotes) always open to becoming entangled in new ways, with new materials, in novel formations. Buildings like these were "living things"[28] continuously generating new forms of life, contributing through their evolving weaves to forging new relations, new connections, and new growth.[29]

Regenerative Life Skills

Autumn had made a gentle and slow return in 2012. Daily temperatures in the Outaouais were well into the high teens[30] and the maples had only lazily begun to turn a leaf. Reds were not quite yet ruby, yellows still shied from amber, and greens only hinted at burnt umber. While it wasn't the main arboreal event we'd hoped to attend, the deciduous spectacle was still beguiling enough for our evergreen-accustomed eyes.

Michèle and Gilles had given us plenty of early warnings about reaching their home. It was a very steep and unpaved hill, they cautioned us, cragged enough that only a 4 × 4 could conquer it. Even though I was behind the wheel of a gritty Jeep, I felt on the edge. While Jon navigated the GPS with our withering cellular signal, I strove to shift the automatic stick into lower gear. And then, the asperous monster appeared in front of us.

While by then we'd seen our fair share of remote properties way back in the bush, we hadn't yet seen anything like this, er, "**driveway**."[xi] I floored the gas pedal. A few meters later suddenly the road disappeared. All we could see was the crown of the trees around us and the late September sky. The climb felt like a jumbo jet's take off. Somehow, we landed unscathed. The road was so precipitous, Michèle and Gilles later recounted, that when they had to deliver long pieces of construction lumber they had to back up all the way, or otherwise the gravity would pull them down from the beds of pick-up trucks. Altering the landscape to form hairpin turns would have clashed with their values.

Atop, the site was idyllic. Water was free and plentiful around their property, locally harvested timber kept their woodstove lit, and a photovoltaic system provided them with the electricity they needed. "I'm not a fan of big company control on grids," Gilles remarked. "You're vulnerable to them, they control what you're going to pay, and the system is always on the edge if you get bad weather." There was a feeling of "self-empowerment" that came from being independent from Hydro Quebec, one of the most powerful utilities on the continent.

Besides independence, Gilles and Michèle were drawn to the mountain by a deep connection with the place.

"Up here you can breathe," said Michèle.

"She wanted the view and the feeling of being on top of a mountain," Gilles interjected.

"Down below it feels suffocating, overwhelming."

[xi.] http://lifeoffgrid.ca/wp-content/uploads/2013/11/Life-Off-Grid_Quebec_02.jpg

How they found this place was a story in itself. Property-hunting during a Sunday drive they saw a hawk flying low above a rural road. They felt compelled to follow it. It was as if the hawk was leading the way, revealed Michèle—who had aboriginal blood and was keenly sensitive to this symbolism. The hawk finally stopped, of all places, right by a "For Sale" sign. They immediately bought the 25 acres, made space for their home on top of the plateau, and eventually started building. They had been at it for three years and aimed to be finished—if a house can ever be finished—in two years' time.

Michèle, a natural health practitioner, designed the house.

"How did you . . . I mean, natural health practitioners don't get training in architectural design, do they?"

"I do what I do," she laughed.

By taking an interest in the subject and by using a blend of logic and intuition they found a way to get started. They learned the rest along the way, discussing things together. Not everything was the fruit of their own labor. They hired a friend to help with electrical components and a small crew to help Gilles with framing, though "they put the rafters on backwards and Gilles and I had to turn them all around," Michèle grinned.

Self-reliance—however relative—felt liberating. The sense of accomplishment and responsibility they drew from taking care of their own needs put them in touch with the place they called home.

"You need to understand your needs and wants," and what "the available sources of satisfaction are," they observed. "When you understand all that, then you need to realize how much work it takes to gratify them, and whether you should, and whether you are able to, or not." All this wisdom came from careful **toil and exploration**,[xii] and from working *with* the land, they pointed out.

"I know every corner of this place," Gilles observed as we lazily followed a meandering path under a thick canopy of maples and young birches.

"And because it's yours I imagine you want to preserve it, right?" I prompted him.

"We don't say it's ours," Michèle gently corrected me. "We don't think that way. We're simply the caretakers of it, for a very short period of time."

Off-grid home builders like Michèle and Gilles were neither DIYers, nor professional architects, nor carpenters. Rather, as Michèle beautifully put it, they were simply people keen on learning how to build and live *with* a place, that is, with the potential for life that a place made available. This principle, fundamental to the idea of dwelling, building, and habitation,[31] is central to the architectural tradition of *regenerative design*.

Regenerative design is a type of environmental architectural design founded around the principle of ongoing renewal and rebirth.[32] Late Canadian architect John Lyle[33] famously explained that regenerative design "provides for continuous replacement" of energy resources, fuels, construction material, and organic life "through its own functional processes of the energy and materials used in its operation." Regenerative design hinges on cyclical flows that "maintain themselves by renewal," in the words of John Dewey[34]—one of the philosophical sources of inspiration behind this tradition. Regenerative design systems integrate natural and social processes by making minimum use of non-renewable resources and by maximizing the use of renewable fuels, energy, and building materials and by striving to facilitate the re-assimilation of waste into the environment via re-use, recycling, and reduction.[35] Advocates of this design view ecology as a process: a "dynamic living assemblage"[36] whose structural, functional, and spatial ordering, disordering, and reordering patterns generate renewal via mechanisms of conversion, distribution, filtration, assimilation, and storage.

Like other off-gridders, Michèle and Gilles understood these ideas heuristically and practiced them carefully. Building their home had been an open-ended exercise in exploring and getting to know the land they had chosen, learning about its potential for enabling the way of life they wanted to practice, and respecting the local eco-system. Gathering knowledge on the local microclimate, for instance, allowed them to understand the ideal building site, the necessary details of their passive solar design, and how their life needs could be met by locally available resources. This was a process of logic and intuition as well as trial and error: a "gradual filling up of capacities and shutting down of possibilities."[37] Home building for them was therefore a regenerative path toward creating and re-creating conditions to keep life ongoing, toward "finding a way through the myriad of things that form, persist and break up in its currents."[38]

To build a home like they did required skill—this much was obvious. But, surprisingly, off-gridders never seemed to acquire their skills from technical institutes where knowledge was conventionally distributed. Their skills, instead, arose from observation and from learning as they went. This was typical of their regenerative design, which began from practicing utmost respect toward life's inherent potential to renew itself. It was also something typical of the idea of habitation—according to which life-generating and regenerating skills consist of "growing" into the lifeworld, rather than transforming it, or of simply playing a part in the "world's transformation of itself"[39] and establishing the conditions for "ongoing growth and

---

xii. Listen at: http://soundcloud.com/innovativeethnographies/gilles-and-michelle-toil-and

development."[40] How to build and inhabit a home, and especially an off-grid home, in the end might have been truly a simple thing. It might have simply been a case of "letting nature do the work."[41]

Regenerative design and principles of habitation are the antinomy of DIY. Rather than conceiving building as the expression of a self-contained, independent mind that imposes a pre-conceived manual-like or blueprint-like design on a pliable world, these philosophies embrace the view that building and habitation are a way of working *with* the land. Off-grid building and habitation skills, therefore, seemed less an expression of prior knowledge than capacities generated and regenerated in the course of interacting with a continuously unfolding eco-system. Skills of this kind were thus *regenerative life skills* "arising as emergent properties of the fields of relationship set up through [builders'] presence and activity within a particular environment."[42] These skills—rather than generalized know-how, prescriptive techniques, or deductions—were *embodied, sentient capabilities to engage with, and relate to, an environment and the inanimate materials, animate beings, and becomings inhabiting it.*

Vernacular Architecture

"So, how exactly do we get back down now?" I asked Gilles when our visit ended.

"Going down is the easy part. Gravity will take care of you."

Encouraging. Luckily we didn't have to tumble too far. Their neighbor, **John**,[xiii] also lived off-grid and he was our next stop.

John, a tall and lean bilingual in his late fifties, was working on his house when we stopped our fall and spilled out of the car.

"Phillip? Jon? You made it. Would you guys like a coffee?"

A few minutes later we were sipping a delicious stovetop brew, comfortably chatting away on John's deck as a jet flew far overhead to Montreal's Trudeau Airport—a reminder that there indeed was a world beyond the hills and the lakes of this quiet land.

John had lived in that distant world for most of his life. In 2003, fed up with the anonymity and the frenzy of the city, he and his wife Guylaine decided to purchase this property and build their dream home here, 3 kilometers away from the nearest utility pole. "That's when Hydro Quebec gave me an estimate of $300,000 to connect to the grid," he chronicled with an aggravated smirk. With a background in law practice and a successful career in urban administration, John had no serious backwoods living experience or construction knowledge. But that didn't intimidate him. It's about "not sweating the details . . . it's about the beauty of the process," he reflected.

[xiii.] http://lifeoffgrid.ca/wp-content/uploads/2013/11/Life-Off-Grid_Quebec_01.jpg

First, John and Guylaine had to solve an exhausting legal boundary dispute with a corporate neighbor. Then, they had to bushwhack their way to the site. During winter the only option was to ski in. When spring arrived and the snow finally melted they had to carry building material in a trailer dragged by an off-road Jeep—getting stuck in the mud at nearly every turn. And until they managed to build a second[43] bridge over a nearby creek—with the help of family, friends, and neighbors—they had to carry construction material on their backs while they waded waist-deep through the cold waters. For the last two years now they had finally been able to sleep inside the home. It still wasn't quite finished but at least it was warm enough. Before the insulation was completed, the temperatures inside would hover between 2°C and 10°C (36°F and 50°F) on a good winter day. "It was so cold," John confided, "I had to have the cat sleep on top of me to warm me up."

The outside was something to behold. The gray, rough, rock façade looked as if it had been plucked away from the Scottish Highlands and transplanted here. It turns out it was. This particular area was settled by Scots, so John wanted to build a house that looked like it "belonged here," as if it had "**grown**"[xiv] in this place. But there was also another, more practical, reason for using rock as building material. The rock, coming from a nearby quarry, was remarkably easy to work with. Initially bent on building with cordwood, he thought he'd experiment first with that technique by building his workshop. It didn't work well. Significant gaps formed between the wood and the mortar due to the wood's shrinking. While a vapor barrier could have solved the insulation problem, he eventually selected rock because of its vernacular value and superior workability over other options, such as timber framing. "It was a style for a house that I could build myself," he explained. "I didn't have the time and the skill to build a full timber frame myself. I had built furniture before but my joinery is not so fancy. So I built post and beam by substituting rock for cordwood between the posts."

"And how exactly does one go from building furniture to building a house?"

John laughed. "I enjoy it. You have to enjoy it to learn. I started by making furniture when I was in university. Oh, and I built a spice rack in shop class in school too! It starts with little things," he continued, by "putting something together physically." Learning gradually more complex lessons creates the confidence necessary to tackle bigger projects. "You read tons of books too, but it's about growing experience."

Building was a form of growth. He simply "improvised" along the way, beginning from a loose sketch. Later on Guylaine convinced him to hire a professional to draw a building plan so that construction could go on even in his

---

[xiv] Listen at: http://soundcloud.com/innovativeethnographies/john-style

occasional absence (some contractors were hired to help out with stonemasonry, installation of the solar system, and to put shingles on the sharply pitched roof). After all, "there are some things you can't do by yourself," he acknowledged, but a little bit of passion and resourcefulness can build skills fast.

DIW builders like John acquired their skills in a number of different ways. Most often they learned as they went, through exploration or "wayfinding."[44] Wayfinding took form as a stop-and-go process of practical and open-ended problem solving, similar to the process of ordinary repair and troubleshooting.[45] Family and friends with relevant knowledge were also common sources for skill acquisition.[46] A loose body of historical tradition transmitted through collective memory also often played an important role, as was obviously the case with John's home. Vernacular architecture—the tradition of building with place-specific resources, style, and knowledge[47]— was not only a mechanism for the acquisition of useful skills, but also another important way through which builders "did it" with others. Far from mere DIY, learning from others and from the places and unique eco-systems where homes were built was a significant way in which off-grid builders regenerated—or gave birth againto—traditional styles and techniques.

DIW builders' dedication and passion also revealed how the acquisition of regenerative skills is something that can be relished. "You have to enjoy" building to do it well, in John's words. Craft—the making or fashioning of material through the exercise of skill, knowledge, and judgment—is in fact an important vehicle for self-expression, passion, creativity, mastery, and the will to accomplish.[48] Learning to enjoy craft is not easy within a hyper-specialized consumer society in which armies of professionals are available at our fingertips to make our lives easier and our learning of new skills unnecessary. However, the practical skills acquired, refined, and applied in the process of off-grid home building were at the basis of what many scholars would view as essential to the shaping of a creative cultural economy.[49] These skills also had "much in common with sustainability and environmentalism"[50] and, like these broader ways of envisioning the world, they had a definite orientation toward regenerating people's relationships with place.

Regenerative life skills had several properties.[51] They were intentional and functional since they were immanent in the nature of practices themselves. They were personal and temporal rather than abstract and universal, as they demanded the engagement of care, judgment, passion, and resolve as well as the application of vernacular lessons. They were practical and emergent, because they arose from the process of hands-on learning, troubleshooting, problem solving, and wayfinding. They were non-representational in the sense that they did not take place by a mechanical unfolding of a preformed vision but rather took form as they grew following the generative potential of the relations they were enmeshed within. Furthermore, regenerative life skills were relational since they depended on establishing relationships among people, places, times, and materials.

Skills were also creative—not in the sense that they constituted highly original contributions to the history of a civilization and the received artistic tradition—but in the sense that they resided in the capacity to tackle novel challenges in response to life's contingencies.[52] Buildings affect those who live, play, and work within them.[53] When builders and dwellers are the same person, a builder-inhabitant has the creative opportunity to infuse a dwelling with a very personally meaningful affective resonance. John's intentionality in giving form to a building that "fit" the local environment revealed a remarkable vernacular creativity[54] influenced by his particular vision of being and living. This vision of being and living—for John as well as other off-gridders—connoted a profound closeness with place. His was a form of creativity that did not impose a vision on an abstract space, in other words, but rather a form of vernacular creativity that regenerated the natural potential of place.

Regenerative skills demanded the application of improvisation and intuition, because building must be continuously attuned to place-specific conditions, the performance of others involved, and the response of materials employed. Like other off-grid builders, John used intuition to apprehend the consequences of a vision unspecified by a clear blueprint or architectural design. He also used improvisation to address the "conditions of a world in formation."[55] Through their creativity, intuition, and improvisation off-grid home builders did not manifest any kind of extraordinary genius. Rather, they simply exercised their capacity to keep life going by knitting together the common entanglements that everyday living demanded, making and re-making their homes and their places while at the same time making and re-making themselves.[56]

* * *

We spent the night at John and Guylaine's and departed on a sunny morning. After a few hours we reached the city of Gatineau. It was lunchtime so we crossed the bridge into downtown Ottawa in search of an English pub. After spending nearly a week off-the-grid, our subdued nation's capital assaulted our senses like a runaway train. Culture-shocked and rattled, we sped back to the bush and paddled the rest of the way on a placid lake separating our newest off-grid cabin from the madness of urban noise, traffic, lights, and speed. We opened a beer and spent the rest of the day working on our notes, recordings, and reflections and relishing the last shimmers of sunshine before autumn's overdue arrival. Next morning, we'd reach our last interviewee and then fly home before the rains began to pour.

The regenerative life skills developed by off-gridders had taught us a few important lessons. These lessons included using information and place-specific knowledge instead of interventionist, place-altering power; benefiting from what nature freely provided and letting nature do the work; matching technology and building design to actual need; searching for multiple pathways to a building problem; prioritizing sustainability; drawing from lessons from the past; adjusting the form of one's home to the existing characteristics of place and the flows occurring within it; and aggregating rather than isolating.[57] Building a home was not an exercise in imposing one's solitary vision and will on an object, but rather was an ensemble of sensitive practices resulting in numerous open-ended entanglements.

Quebec had dramatically changed, if not the direction of our research, then our attitude toward off-grid living in general. Ever since the first trips across the water on the West Coast we knew that off-gridders sought to live a better life, and that they regularly succeeded in doing so. The doubts sparked throughout our journeys in Ontario and Manitoba—our misgivings about the potential of off-grid living to make a global difference beyond the separate little safe havens of peace and quiet in which it took place— were beginning to dissipate. Sure not everyone could muster the necessary physical capacities and easily acquire the skills to build their own house, but re-inventing comfort and convenience and re-imagining our rapport with place was something in which we could all take heed.

According to Ingold,[58] life is a "creative unfolding of an entire field of relations within which beings emerge and take the particular forms they do, each in relation to the others." Life, in other words, contains the potential for its own regeneration. Our capacity to give continuous re-birth to ourselves and to the forms of our activity must therefore consist in harnessing those unfolding processes and carrying them forward. Regenerative life skills— which off-gridders across the country were teaching us—were thus first and foremost about the "education of attention"[59] toward meanings immanent in the lifeworld. "Only if we are capable of dwelling," as Martin Heidegger might put it, "only then we can build."[60]

Notes

1. Gelber, 1997.
2. Gelber, 1997; Powell, 2009; Tomlinson, 1990.
3. Edwards, 2006; Gelber, 1997; Hackney, 2006.
4. Atkinson, 2006; Roush, 1999.
5. Lewis, 2008.
6. Atkinson, 2006; Powell, 2009.
7. Powell, 2009; Shove et al., 2008; Williams, 2004.
8. Williams, 2004.
9. Shove et al., 2008; Williams, 2004.
10. Powell, 2009.

11. Powell, 2009.
12. See for example, Beaver, 2012; Culton and Holtzman, 2010; Duncombe, 1997; Dunn and Farnsworth, 2012; Levine, 2008; Portwood-Stacer, 2012; Schilt and Zobl, 2008.
13. Beaver, 2012; Gauntlett, 2011.
14. Crane, 2012; Luvaas, 2012.
15. Ingold, 2011.
16. Gauntlett, 2011.
17. Gauntlett, 2011.
18. Gauntlett, 2011:2.
19. Gauntlett, 2011: 2, emphasis added.
20. Ingold, 2000.
21. Ingold, 2008, 2011.
22. Ingold, 2008:1803.
23. Hawkins, 2006.
24. Crane, 2012; Soderman and Carter, 2008; Vaughan et al., 2007.
25. Ingold 2008:1797.
26. Ingold, 2008:1797, original emphasis.
27. Ingold, 2008:1797.
28. Strebel, 2011.
29. Ingold, 2008:1803.
30. Low 60's F.
31. Ingold 2000, 2008, 2011, 2013.
32. Lyle, 1994; McDonough and Braungart, 2001.
33. Lyle, 1994:10.
34. Dewey, 1919:1.
35. Lyle, 1994:11.
36. Lyle, 1994:25–27.
37. Ingold, 2011:3.
38. Ingold, 2011:4.
39. Ingold, 2011.
40. Ingold, 2011:8.
41. Lyle, 1994:38.
42. Ingold, 2000:4.
43. The first one washed away.
44. Ingold, 2011, 2013; Mall, 2007; Nakamura, 2007.
45. Dant, 2009; Graham and Thrift, 2007.
46. Harper, 1987.
47. Glassie, 2000; Vellinga, Oliver, and Bridge, 2007.
48. Campbell, 2005; Gauntlett, 2011; Shove et al., 2008.
49. Edensor et al., 2010.
50. Gauntlett, 2011:57.
51. Following Ingold, 2000:291.
52. Bruner, 1993.
53. Kraftl and Adey, 2008.
54. Edensor et al., 2010.
55. Ingold and Hallam, 2007:3.
56. See Ingold, 2011; Ingold and Hallam, 2007.
57. See Lyle, 1994:3845.
58. Ingold, 2000:19.
59. Ingold, 2000:22.
60. Heidegger, 1971:148.

Debbie.[i]

9

SLOWER HOMES

Rhythm: Patterned Movement Re-Occurring at Regular or Irregular Intervals.

The Atlantic had ebbed, just as the tables foretold, and temporarily undressed the tall shore from its mantle of water and silt. Now free to be seen, massive slabs of rock strangely clothed in layers of tangerine earth and shrouded by a flimsy coat of snowy powder leapt perpendicularly out of the pebbly beach. Near their apexes an unkempt plumage of evergreens hung askew, clinging to migrant topsoil wondrously blown over with westerly winds. Closer to the coarse and dark sand at the bottom, the motley-shaped pillars revealed painfully rough striations, as if receding cold waters had left hurtful algae and other nameless creatures to wound and tear away at their uneasy foundations. Standing at the cliff's edge, Jon and I were the only audience to the semi-diurnal ritual that the low tide performed that morning at Alma. On a summer day, the Bay of Fundy would have drawn thousands of spectators peering at the lunar-driven aqueous fluctuations from behind their digital viewfinders, but on that gray December day the blowing snow had kept even the park warden close to his warm hearth.

Bay of Fundy tides consist of 100 billion tonnes of seawater flooding and ebbing, rising up to 50 feet in height, then falling, twice daily. They are the mightiest in the world. Despite all their natural strength, their potential for energy generation remains largely untapped. Cupping my hands and blowing warm breath on them, I recalled a few off-gridders who would have gladly put them to work. But, alas, tides are entirely unexploited by Canadian off-gridders; too much infrastructure, too many regulations, too many headaches stand in the way. And yet, the regular rhythm that tides keep did strike a familiar chord with off-gridders and the two of us alike. Here one minute, gone the next. Back at it again, and away they went one more time.

Natural rhythms—of tides, clouds, sun, moon, atmospheric masses, or else—are no noteworthy events for most of us. Natural rhythms, especially of the seasonal and meteorological kind, however, affected Canadian off-grid homes very differently. Energy-independent households that relied on photovoltaic and wind power may not have been too badly affected by a couple of cloudy or windless days in a row, but whenever still and tenebrous systems of low pressure lingered, things got hairy. Off-grid homes used batteries to store electricity collected during propitious days, but batteries were no magic wand. Batteries were very expensive and fickle: they disliked being drained and could die early as a result. And though backup generators worked as somewhat of an insurance policy against bad weather, for the most part off-gridders tried relentlessly to minimize their use. A courageous few did not even own one at all. The day before, in fact, we had met such a Spartan couple.

Capable of generating a miniscule 300 watts on a bright sunny day, having no source of electricity other than twelve 50-watt **photovoltaic panels**,[ii] and relying on neither generator nor propane, **Debbie**[iii] and David could have easily qualified for the Olympics in the minimalist off-grid living event. We had arrived at their farm home on a cold but sunny Sunday afternoon. Lying near the top of a gently rising and mostly treeless hill, their south-facing home cast its gaze at one of Atlantic Canada's largest cities. You couldn't quite see it or hear it, even on a sunny day like this, but Fredericton was close and within commuting distance for Debbie, who owned an organic food store there. The couple had lived off-grid in their 1,200-square-foot home on a 125-acre organic farm for 20 years. Philosophies of local, slow, and healthy food, environmental sustainability, and renewable energy ran deep in their blood.

We sat down to talk at the living room table, nibbling on some munchies and bathing in the warm sun. Soft-spoken, even a touch timid, David and Debbie were well past their younger years but were unafraid of hard

---

[ii] http://lifeoffgrid.ca/wp-content/uploads/2013/11/Life-Off-Grid_Nova-Scotia-New-Brunswick_04.jpg
[iii] http://lifeoffgrid.ca/wp-content/uploads/2013/11/Life-Off-Grid_Nova-Scotia-New-Brunswick_07.jpg

physical work. "We cut most of our wood ourselves," David said, "so we don't need to join the gym." Passive solar design and two cords of locally collected wood per year were all they needed to reach thermal comfort. To put it in perspective, three cords of wood per year and 300 watts were about a tenth of what a typical home might consume in the area. "We just can't help marvelling at how inefficient people's homes can be," remarked Debbie.

Most of the firewood was burned in a masonry stove that served as the hearth of the house, connecting the kitchen, the living room, and the dining room area. Its heat naturally rose, and so the masonry stove warmed their upstairs bedroom as well. Masonry stoves were heavy, laborious to assemble, and expensive to buy but they made it all up in efficiency by emitting copious amounts of warmth and by serving as a cooker as well. In David and Debbie's home the masonry stove was in fact the sole cooking appliance—neither a propane-fueled range nor a microwave oven was available. Propane, after all, was a non-renewable gas, and microwaves—we were told—were not only gluttons for wattage, but also environmentally unsustainable because of the materials used to build them.

The unique setup, of course, created the conditions for some slow cooking in the kitchen. "It takes about 15 minutes to fire up the stove and get the water boiling for tea," Debbie explained. But when the stove was on, it could also double as a hair drier. Blow driers were a tremendous electricity draw, which their system could not handle. "In the summer the sun will do the job," long-haired Debbie had remarked with a peaceful smile.

Their pint-sized electricity system also meant they needed to be inventive when it came to refrigeration. Canadian off-gridders could generally get away from having to plug in a refrigerator by placing a thickly insulated ice box outdoors, or simply in an unheated room in the north side of the house, but Debbie and David had a more uncommon solution: a **California cooler**.[iv] The California cooler was invented and popularized in the Golden State in the early 1900s, before refrigerators became common household items. California coolers are essentially cabinets that bring in cool air from the outside through wall vents. The cabinet door is heavily insulated to keep the cold air in and to prevent the warm indoor air from leaking inside. Temperatures within their California cooler never reached freezing level, but this did not constitute a problem for the couple, who were both vegetarian and did not need to keep meat frozen.

[iv] http://lifeoffgrid.ca/wp-content/uploads/2013/11/Life-Off-Grid_Nova-Scotia-New-Brunswick_07.jpg

Debbie and David were busy, but they did not live hurried lives. Their everyday rhythms were simple: "We rise with the sun and go to bed early at night," David told us. "Summer days are longer and busier with farming," David found. "When you live off-grid you really change your routines with the movements of the sun; you can't be in a rush." While Debbie could work in town up to five days a week, their home was in a temporal space removed from the rhythms of the city. The limited electricity available meant there was no computer in the home, no internet, no satellite TV. "We have four channels and VHS," David showed us with a hint of pride in his voice.

Back at Alma, embattled by the wind, Jon and I gave up on the idea of waiting for the tide to rise again. We retreated to our car with our lunchtime parking lot special and revisited our fresh handwritten notes—the only trace remaining from David and Debbie's interview after our recording technology had spectacularly failed to work.

"Do you think you have just about everything now?" Jon asked me after remembering and dictating yet another quote almost verbatim from the day before.

"I think I do," I answered, still reeling from the discovery of the disastrous breakdown, a snafu that—as it turned out—had also affected three other previous interviews.

"What are we doing with these interviews in New Brunswick?"

"Time. Rhythm." I answered laconically. "There are several theorists that have lamented the consequences of the increased speed of modern lifestyles."

Most notably, geographer David Harvey[1] has outlined the existence of a "time-space compression" facilitated by technologies that make seemingly everything available almost anytime and anywhere. Similarly, Nigel Thrift[2] has argued that speed is imbricated in the same assemblages that have brought light and power to the modern world. Electricity grids, natural gas pipelines, communication networks, airways, railways, and motorways have left indelible marks on the timescapes of modernity and shaped the very nature of capitalism, democracy, and everyday life.[3]

"So, we're saying that off-grid living is a critical response to all that."

"Definitely," I replied, "one of many. Like slow tourism,[4] slow food,[5] and slow urban living."[6]

In fact, as others have observed, "hurry sickness, as a response to the acceleration of just about everything, has become a recognizable late modern malaise."[7] Slow food, slow urban dwelling, and slow tourism represent a multi-faceted set of responses to speed, involving the deliberate renegotiation of the different rhythms that make up our quotidian existence. "Slow living," as Wendy Parkins[8] has noted, derives from "a commitment to occupy time more attentively," investing time "with significance through attention and deliberation," and "engaging in 'mindful' rather than 'mindless' practices" in order to "differentiate [our]selves from the dominant culture of speed." The slowness of off-grid homes had clearly much in common with these trends.

The slowness of off-grid homes hinged on a unique factor, however: their relation to weather and seasonality. In the off-grid lifeworld, the sky's rhythms were a concrete and lived occurrence as well as a planned-for affective possibility: a space of anticipation.[9] In other words, if today the sky was overcast David and Debbie would act accordingly in order to draw less power and have some more left over for tomorrow. But the sky affected off-gridders' conduct even on a sunny or windy day. By anticipating the occurrence of gloomy weather and short winter days, off-gridders carefully conserved their stored power and "splurged" only when their batteries could no longer accommodate any further charge. Their anticipation took weather and seasonal rhythms into account as both continuous and repetitive events as well as indefinite and less foreseeable occurrences—rhythm after all is both repetition and difference.[10] As a result, natural rhythms were deeply woven into off-gridders' everyday consciousness and acted as a slowing-down factor on their way of life.

"I think we can see the strength of natural rhythms even more clearly in homes like David and Debbie's," observed Jon as he, habitually, wrapped and set away for later half of his uneaten sandwich.

"You mean because they have no backup generator?"

"And a small solar system too," he added, while he switched his attention to our itinerary on his iPhone.

Running out of stored power was practically improbable for most, if not all, off-gridders. But what truly affected their energy conservation was not the prospect of a blackout in and of itself, but its affective significance. To run out of power, even for an hour, would have been equivalent to getting caught unprepared, unskilled, and unable to practice self-sufficiency.

"You know what's interesting about people like David and Debbie?" I mumbled. "They're not *scared* into conserving energy because they fear running out of it. It's not fear that motivates them. It's their lifestyle, their beliefs. They think that there *is* enough renewable energy available to live a good life and so they feel they *should make do*. It's like an adaptive mechanism. Like trying to fit life to *what* nature provides and *when* it provides it, rather than the other way around, like most of us do."

"Yes. But speaking of rhythms, we should get going," Jon reminded me. "We have a long drive ahead of us."

It's Sunny. Tell the Kids They Can Come Inside and Play the Wii

Wendy was waiting for us at a busy gas station a few kilometers away from her home. "I won't bother you with impossibly complicated directions," she had wisely suggested. We followed her car home through slowly winding country lanes connected by wooden bridges. The snow had stopped falling, but it was a caliginous, foggy, damp day and the light and warmth begotten by the Franklin stove she immediately lit as we stepped in was dearly welcomed by the three of us. Like all off-gridders, Wendy was very mindful of the electricity draw of her appliances. She had efficiently placed the refrigerator away from the kitchen, far from the woodstove and other sources of heat, and her freezer out in the garage. She owned no TV set, no toaster, no microwave oven, no coffee machine, no bread maker. Her tidy kitchen counter was barer than an airstrip cleared for landing. She also tended to "live in the dark a lot," she admitted with a smile as we began to set up. "Actually," she wondered politely, "would it be ok if we switched off that light?" Because we were video recording we sheepishly begged for her indulgence.

Wendy had been living alone at her house since 2004, though she had been "camping" onsite for nine years prior to that. Moving in permanently felt like an escape. "I could hardly function anymore in the city," she disclosed. Unlike David and Debbie's, Wendy's 1.5-kW solar system was rather typical for an off-grid home. Modern life "is not sustainable," she answered when I asked her why she lived off-grid. "I just don't think it's necessarily good that you can turn on a switch and have everything at your fingers. And I like the quiet and peacefulness of it," she added. Her home was in fact a retreat from the busyness of her "crazy life." Wendy served as the executive director of a not-for-profit council and regularly logged 60- and 80-hour weeks, sometimes more. Yet, most of those hours were spent in the safe haven of her home, where she could simultaneously be attending a phone conference and pickling vegetables grown right here in her garden.

Despite the demands of her work and the fact that her internet-connected computer was plugged in virtually all the time, her life rhythms were undoubtedly measured. While it could be a challenge to accomplish everything she wished to, she still made time for gardening and for ritually strolling along the beautiful river that coasted her property. The sun imposed a definite sense of structure on her personal time too.

"Every day I get up and check what the weather is going to do, and decide what I am going to do accordingly, if it's possible."

"For example?" I asked, as I double-checked that all three of our recorders were working this time.

"Well, if it's a sunny day and my batteries are charged up then I'll do laundry. Otherwise all that power goes to waste, and I hate that. But I'd never do my laundry on a day like today." We had heard similar examples of efficiency before, elsewhere. Dark days were not the most propitious for washing machines, vacuum cleaners, power tools, or toasters. Some off-grid families were especially pugnacious about getting the most out of a bright day: after the point at which batteries could accommodate no further charge, excess power could even be dumped on frivolous things like video games.

For people like Wendy—motivated by environmental values, self-sufficiency, and the sense of challenge—back-up generators represented a last resort. Running a generator was a bit like getting a push on the steepest hill of a bicycle race: though the help was badly needed, it was something to be bashful about. Turning on the generator carelessly "would defeat the purpose," remarked Wendy. "I hate every time I turn it on because I know what it's really doing to the atmosphere." Making sunlight's power last, then, became a trial in curtailing personal needs and wants, and in mastering the "little things" that allowed for reductions in power consumption—starting by challenging dominant ideas of efficiency. "It's a fallacy that all these little pluggable gadgets can save time and energy," she observed. Saving time and energy was more about being organized, being skilled, and doing with less. "Simpler is more efficient."

In common talk *efficiency* is synonymous with ease and speed, but in the off-grid world *efficiency* denoted primarily something else: a more technical meaning relating the ratio of energy produced to the amount of energy invested. This is not to say that ease and speed were irrelevant to off-gridders, but rather that they were only desirable insofar as they cost no excessive expenditure of renewable energy. This meant that off-grid living was practiced at a distinct pace, a pace that was discernibly *slower* than grid-connected homes where connectivity, mobility, and availability of electricity were not dependent on sunlight, wind, or locally stored energy.

Consequently, different seasons tended to make different demands and opened distinct opportunities. "Winters are hard and you have to be really careful," Wendy found. "The days are so short and you have to be mindful of how you use your power." So, "If there are things that require light to be done then I'll do them in the daytime rather than at night when I would have to turn the lights on." Winter also brought on unique chores. Atlantic Canada regularly receives a lot of snow from November to April, and during those times snowfall accumulates on solar panels and solar hot water collectors, blocking ultraviolet rays. Removing the shadowing white stuff was as simple as brushing it off, but it required attention and physical presence.

Needless to say off-gridders generally found it difficult to leave their homes unattended for tropical winter getaways.

The "decompression" present in the atmospheres of off-grid homes was palpable, and off-gridders knew better than to take it for granted. As a matter of fact, they methodically took into reflexive account how quickly they could have accomplished things if they had been on the grid, and how different their lives could have been otherwise. Their relational position highlighted the conscious efforts they constantly made to slow down and to live in synchrony with the natural and technological patterns in which their lives were entangled. From the number of watts hour their batteries could last, to the number of daylight hours in a winter day, off-gridders were intimately aware of the temporal dynamics of their power constellations in a way most of us are not.

Off-gridders performed a deliberate deceleration in their everyday lives. The durations of their chores tended to be longer and their pace of life seemed to be less hurried than most. Theirs were discordant speeds, rhythms, and durations that posed "alternative modes of spending time, different pacings and pulses which critique[d] normative, disciplinary rhythms and offer[ed] unconventional, sometimes utopian visions of different temporalities."[11]

But let us slow down ourselves and practice a bit of reflexivity too. I live on the grid. Because I work from home my days are characteristically mellow. I write, I read, and whenever necessary I log on to the internet to connect with the rest of the world. I make time to cook, grow food, play, enjoy my island, and spend time with family and friends. And yet I am on the grid. Other people have a similar-paced lifestyle, on-grid. So, did off-grid homes truly live slower? And if so, slower than whom? And why? There is great deal of research to help us figure this out.

Broad social trends do point to the existence of a diffused time pressure, but these trends are neither clear nor univocal.[12] Feelings of stress, burnout, and time poverty are on everyone's mind these days, but people are not necessarily busier than they were years ago. They simply *feel* busier,[13] as evidenced by mundane chitchat and by the commercial success of books outlining these pressures, stresses, and their roots and consequences.[14] Being "busy" is nowadays a common excuse for everything. But why do we feel so busy all the time?

We like to think there are at least two reasons. First, increased media connectivity has come to mean heightened expectations to be always "on" and at the mercy of incoming digital information. These expectations have begun to seriously colonize private times such as evenings and nights.[15] "The drone is never-ending and ever-present,"[16] and this can cause fatigue, frustration, and anxiety. Second, the blurring of daily, weekly, and seasonal rhythms has manifested itself not only in private spaces but in public domains as well. Electrification and the diffusion of lighting technology have resulted in the progressive expansion of leisure, consumption, and surveillance regimes into the night,[17] almost obliterating darkness and the times and spaces when people can be "off." In this sense, the "unplugging" typical of off-grid places and lifestyles (and even some on-grid ones) could indeed be seen to be a discordant rhythm, and an alternate way of spending time and making place.

On the other hand we need to be careful. As said, a great deal of research shows that people are not necessarily busier than they used to be. Theoretical arguments that point to a uniform acceleration in the pace of everyday life simplify both the present and the past, unquestioningly assuming the existence of halcyon days of unhurried synchrony between natural and social rhythms and positing a clear shift to an industrial-style domesticity attuned to the new 24/7 consumer economy. These are facile polemics.

More critical and systematic research reveals instead that "natural and commercial rhythms have co-evolved and often complemented each other in the modern period,"[18] thus highlighting the coexistence of multiple and contradictory temporalities throughout history. "The great acceleration" was neither as comprehensive nor as disorienting as it is sometimes assumed.[19] Several historians have found that the diffusion of electricity, the acquisition and domestication of labor-saving appliances, and the consequent "industrialization of the home" were neither quick nor pervasive processes.[20] To say that social conditions have dramatically and uniformly changed with successive stages of the electrification and digitization of private and public spheres is nothing but a simplification of the case and an example of technological determinism.

A brief look at how labor-saving technologies intersect with the temporalities of different households confirms that domestic spaces are characterized by multiple and diverse rhythms, and that speed and slowness are no univocal phenomena. Even though appliances like microwave ovens, toasters, refrigerators, dishwashers, freezers, tumble driers, cooking ranges, and vacuum cleaners are customarily marketed for their potential to free homemakers from the busyness of domestic work, the reality is that their purchase, installation, operational demands, coordination, and the ways in which they raise expectations for convenience, cleanliness, and good housework tend to nullify whatever time-saving effect they may have[21]—just like Wendy opined. So, *not* having them—as was the case with off-gridders like her—was *not* the decisive factor in their slowing down. But if that was not the key difference, what was it then?

Synchronous Power and Unplugged Appliances

Sometimes ethnographic knowledge lies in the unsaid and the undone: in the happenings that could've taken place but didn't, in what could've been otherwise.

It was in the middle of a Saturday morning when we knocked on Marc's door. He welcomed us inside and offered us food. He had made brunch and he was delighted to share his breakfast burritos. Though grateful, we declined—the Holiday Inn Express had very recently treated us to stale cornflakes and rubbery pancakes. Marc's edge-of-the-city home was within easy reach of the airport hotel strip where we had spent the night. In fact, from his suburban home he commuted to his downtown business daily. But we've digressed; Marc had made himself breakfast—this is the point we could fail to notice.

As time feels more compressed, as dual-earning couples become busier at work, as appliances continue promising to make food faster, as people spend less time cooking and eating at home, Marc—a man, to boot—was preparing food from scratch. And not just for himself either. Within minutes of our ingress his wife Vera, showed up. Then there came Sumira, their older daughter, 15. Finally Jamuna, 12, their younger daughter walked downstairs too. Each added to Marc's meal and fixed up something to eat. Each nibbled on what everyone else had prepared. And each made the time to sit down to chat, not in their Acadian-inflected French—but in *our* preferred language with us: two strangers from the other end of the country whose research agenda should have ranked much lower in the weekend's order of priorities. It could all have gone very differently.

Marc told us they had been off-grid for two years, but the dream had inspired them for much longer. Vera grew up in Germany with the knowledge that solar energy does work. Marc himself was intrigued with the physics of electricity and enchanted by the power of the sun. A sculpture of the fiery star—made with recycled green wine bottles planted within the tan kitchen wall of their cob house—seemed to bask in the recognition of their trust and admiration. The sculpture lay where a TV screen or a microwave might otherwise have been, atop where a dishwasher might have stood. Again there was the telling absence of what could have been: the startling lack of a TV or other appliances.

And so inquired the wondering ethnographer: "How do you manage without a microwave?"

Quipped the witty younger daughter: "Microwaves are boring!"

There were more absences. There could have been a sedan and an SUV outside. Instead there was an equine friend neighing for our overdue attention, two compact cars, and an electric bike. "It's about making choices," explained Marc, "our money has gone toward the lifestyle we prefer. Sure it wasn't cheap to buy a four Kilowatt solar system, but it was the same money that many people prefer to spend on a pick-up truck." They could have bought the truck instead. They could have driven it to Starbucks to eat breakfast that morning. And they could have used the grid—which was just across the driveway—to power up a microwave, an electric toaster, and a couple of blow driers for all the long, blonde hair in the house. Instead, "we live in abundance," declared Marc as he finished off the last bite, "if you want to promote energy conservation you shouldn't scare people into having to make sacrifices. You want to show them that what is already available is more than enough to enjoy life."

Marc's powerful insight made a great deal of sense about energy, and it also resonated about another abundant resource: time. If you want to promote a deeper appreciation of time—Marc might as well have said— then you shouldn't feel you're missing out by not doing *everything*. Rather, you want to feel that the time that's already available to you is more than enough to enjoy life. Most of us don't feel that way, though. There's always another email to send off, another contract to take on, another holiday to book, another class to join, another party to attend. And yet there was an alternative, which off-gridders across the country passionately practiced: a radically different way of cultivating time and slowing down. "Less is more." "What we have is enough." "Take time to relish the little things"—herein lay the basic difference we had sought. Slower homes simply sought a different orientation to time and an alternative disposition to life itself.

Off-gridders were no meditative ascetics. They weren't monastic masochists either. They were simply opportunists. The most common definition of *slow* implies a chronometric shift: a reduction in speed. But the slower ways of life typical of off-gridders showed the importance of another dimension of slowness, one that was less based on *chronos* and more on *kairos*. Kairos is a rhythmical movement. Kairos refers to an *opportunistic* or a propitious time to do something.[22] Off-gridders were opportunists because they chose to become involved in certain activities at select moments in time in accordance with the rhythms of the sky (that is, with the patterns of weather, seasons, and availability of sunlight) and in strategic ways.

Interestingly, the word *opportunistic* derives from the original denotation of *opportunus:* a combination of *ob-* ("in the direction of") and *portus* ("harbor")—in essence the condition of enjoying a favorable wind for sailing into port. Opportunistic, therefore, has come to refer to a skilled, knowledgeable, and clever person who seizes the right moment to achieve one's goals. Off-gridders, then, were opportunistic in the sense of acting strategically while also being careful about sustaining themselves and their environment. Being opportunistic in their case meant being efficient too.

Grid-connected electricity was to off-grid power what fast food is to slow food. Whereas power is constantly, predictably, and uniformly available to grid-connected homes, off-grid power availability was more irregular, more intermittent, and more dependent on local conditions and resources. There are exceptions to this distinction, of course. Rotating blackouts, unexpected power outages due to inclement weather events, and other cuts in service prove that even grid-connected homes do not live in a vacuum from the outside world. But these are exceptions to the norm, and the norm is that to a great extent our on-grid power consumption occurs *asynchronously,* in a state of relative disassociation from weather-driven ephemeral mutations of our landscape. Off-grid homes on the other hand lived in a state of *power synchrony:* their energy generation and consumption unfolded in sync with the constantly changing availability of resources proximate to their surroundings. Power asynchrony and power synchrony meant radically different ways of practicing efficiency, as well as different rhythms, different speeds, different affects, different ways of assembling comfort and convenience.[23]

Some ephemeral qualities of place are short-lived and irregular, like the cloud formation obscuring the sky right here, right now. Others are seasonal, like the different climatic periodicities of light and darkness across the year at particular latitudes.[24] As the weather and the seasons change, so do light and darkness, and as light and darkness changed, so did the worlds of power-synchronous home dwellers. Hence the cyclical rhythms of weather and the rhythms of off-grid everyday life deeply intersected. Rhythms of darkness and light were "a rhythmpattern of timespace"[25] that meaningfully shaped electricity use and everyday rhythms. While these rhythmpatterns did not *determine* off-gridders' behaviors, changing amounts of ultraviolet rays interfered with off-gridders' domestic practices by increasing or failing to increase the amps they could deposit into their batteries. Light and darkness, therefore, variously constrained and enabled off-gridders, becoming embedded with their daily life over time, leading them "to follow particular courses of action, and produce an everyday practical orientation toward their taskscape."[26]

Thanks to batteries, power synchrony was only approximate. Synchrony and asynchrony were variations along wide continua, yet these variations were no less meaningful. While the oscillation of light due to the alternations of day and night, overcast and fair skies, and winter and summer does affect us all, off-grid homes were more immediately impacted than the rest of us. Darkness is easier to ignore when you can flick on a switch and turn on an appliance powered by distant resources. Weather and seasonality, in contrast, were key protagonists in off-gridders' lives. The rhythms of the sun rendered off-grid dwellings lively, in constant movement, in need of continuous synchronization with the outdoor world. Changing light patterns demanded that power-synchronous lives be "open to change through cae-suras operating between the existing ecology and external elements, both material and immaterial, human and non-human."[27]

Thanking Marc, Vera, and the girls for their hospitality and insights, we headed farther east. To make more efficient use of our time, and to pollute the sky a bit less, Jon and I had decided to cover neighboring New Brunswick and Nova Scotia in one single swoop from the West Coast. We had a looming kayaking date with Phil in Musquodoboit Harbour, near Halifax, Nova Scotia, but since the weather and tide were not ready for our crossing, we still had time for Jerry and Jo-Anne in New Brunswick.

New Age Homes for a New Millennium

After moving from pricey Alberta to affordable New Brunswick 19 years ago in order to get over a family financial crisis, Jerry and Jo-Anne at first had to resort to kerosene to light up their 14-year-old daughter's bedroom. They had now invested in a more powerful system. A four kW photovoltaic array powered all the electricity needs of their stylish, self-built, 2,600-square-foot multilevel home out in the country. Timber from their 20-acre property was used for space heating, cooking, and heating water.

"It's a new age home for a new millennium," Jo-Anne responded when I asked her about efficiency.

"What do you mean?"

"Put it this way. We don't need air conditioning because of the number of windows. We have very efficient pumps. Our refrigerator, our appliances, our stoves, and our cooking stove are very efficient. Our house is well insulated. Even our generator is very efficient."

"Can you show me your most efficient technology?"

Eagerly, they quickly rose from their indoor verandah and made a beeline for the kitchen, where their "**Cadillac stove**"[v] shone before our eyes. "There he is: Harley!" Jo-Anne beamed with satisfaction. The old-fashioned, country-style woodstove looked like it weighed a ton and was harder to operate than a 1931 Cadillac Series 355, but it was seductively beautiful in a way that only cars and stars from the celluloid era could be. It was also an ingenious, multi-purpose tool with a sharp character. Efficient meant resource frugal, and the woodstove epitomized that thriftiness.

Efficiency, in the off-grid lifeworld, was not about taking shortcuts to save time. It was not about speed and constant availability of everything. It was instead about investing time with care and exercising care over time. "This

---

[v] https://soundcloud.com/innovativeethnographies/jo-anne-on-harley-the-stove

is a far more labor-intensive life," declared Jo-Anne forcefully. The learning curve was steep; patience, attention, mindfulness, and knowledge were all crucial requirements. "This kind of home demands a lot more involvement," Jerry continued where she had left off, "you can't come home after work and turn the TV on and go to bed." The house demanded you. "There is no end in sight, there is always something to do," he went on, "but work is not a dirty word, work is something we do instead of watching TV, instead of going to the mall to chit-chat with friends, instead of going on a cruise."

It was resource-consciousness, involvement, and care that made this home efficient: a mix of old and new-age knowledge and values. Learning old skills, like growing food, canning vegetables, living in tune with whatever the seasons allowed, was a simple way of anticipating the challenges that the future holds for us. "Things have got to change," concluded Jerry. "I say this is a new-age home for a new a millennium," Jo-Anne clarified, "because we're not a throwback to the past. This is the way of the future."

Power-synchronous spaces often separate the domestic environment from the outside world. This detachment of the indoors from the outdoors supposedly makes us feel secure, sheltered, and comfortable.[28] Such separation of indoor and outdoor spaces is part and parcel of a general cultural orientation that routinely treats nature and society/culture as separate.[29] Power-synchronous homes did not treat the outside as an external background surface, but rather as an open space demanding direct involvement. In power-synchronous dwellings, the sky and the energy bestowed by sunlight were enmeshed in a "perpetual metabolism" that gave form to a hybrid and intimate *socio-nature*.[30] The sky and its light (or lack thereof) therefore became a place for everyday habitation, a going concern, a tool for everyday living. This opportunistic way of being-in-the-world was a mode of habitation that differed sharply from the mode of occupation typical of someone who may very well carry on ignoring the unfolding, dynamic, moody weather of the day and its ever-changing patterns. Power synchrony was a different orientation to time and place: a way of living life more "in the open," "within a weather-world in which every being is destined to combine wind, rain, sunshine, and earth in the continuation of its own existence."[31]

Power synchrony demanded care for what went on in the weather world. It required a sensibility toward changing levels, shapes, and shades of energy. It expected a continual "attunement" with its imperative demands.[32] It urged a capacity for immersion in the changing cycles of light and darkness, in the unfolding rhythms of the sky over the day, the week, and the seasons. It compelled a capacity for temporal reflection: a "critical capacity for reflexivity which is insisted upon as central to slowness."[33] The slower rhythms of power-synchronous homes, therefore, arose out of a realization that the inside and the outside were not separate, that the surfaces of a house—from its windows to its solar panels, and from the vents to the roof—were not boundaries but channels for the "comings and goings" of daily activities and of the formations, movements, and fluctuations of a temporally evolving landscape.[34] In this sense, living slower, in greater synchrony with sunlight and darkness, was a way of learning to be sensitive to the "vibrant matter" of the lifeworld and the vitality of the things inhabiting the interface between animate and inanimate life.[35]

Energy "is always on the move, always going somewhere, though where this will be is not entirely predictable."[36] Grids, however, limit that unpredictability and as a result most of us have settled for rather reliable power constellations that function in a seemingly independent way from diurnal, seasonal, and meteorological rhythms. Off-gridders, instead, chose to synchronize their lives with the "turbulent matter"[37] of these patterns to a greater degree. Their homes, therefore, were in many ways more deeply shaped by ephemeral qualities of place, more open to the continuous coming into being of light and darkness, less enclosed by surfaces aiming to separate them from the sky, and more "involved" and "engaged" with the "telluric, celestial, and organic" agitations of matter.[38] These were "new-age homes for a new millennium," if we are to believe Jo-Anne.

Jo-Anne is right if we believe that our future will demand more sensibility, more care, more involvement, and a greater attunement to the "vital connections between the *geo* (earth) and the *bio* (life)."[39] To become more attuned to the "livingness of the world," and to shift our attention from indifference to intimate involvement, requires a new orientation: a disposition that is sensitive to the ways in which our everyday lives are imbricated with lively matter and "co-fabricated" with the reverberations of the world.[40]

Perhaps these slower, supposedly more efficient, power-synchronous homes were utopian spaces. Maybe they were impractical experiments: microscopic lifestyle enclaves reserved for a few brave souls, or perhaps hopelessly romantic idealists. Or maybe they were the dawn of a new enlightenment: one not so keen on sacrificing natural rhythms at the behest of prepotent consumer desires. To be sure, we have no ultimate answer on this, but after nine provinces and our fair share of questions, discoveries, and doubts along the way, we knew that off-gridders—though they had no pretense of having found *the* sustainable solution—had at least assembled *one* path forward.

Off-gridders had reminded us that, like "the grid," the abstract clock time of the 24/7 economy is potent, but it is something we can choose to deselect. Most of us today "live with burgeoning temporal ecologies, which we often misread or just ignore completely."[41] If we wish to become more opportunistic, more efficient about energy production and consumption, then we can no longer afford to ignore cosmic and climatic rhythms. If the future will call upon our civilization to diversify our energy resources and to learn to rely more on renewables, then natural rhythms—from tides to the sky and everything in between—will open "a potential for change for everyday life to be interrupted and its organization to be changed."[42] A renewed attention toward the rhythms of the "patterned" entanglements of societies and natures[43] such as the rhythmpatterns of sunlight, wind, and power might then be one of the keys to regaining the sense of enchantment and wonder necessary for the sustainable regeneration of everyday life.

Notes

1. Harvey, 1991.
2. Thrift, 1996.
3. Nye, 1999.
4. Dickinson and Lumsdon, 2010.
5. Parkins and Craig, 2006.
6. Mayer and Know, 2006; Pink 2007.
7. Parkins and Craig, 2006:1.
8. Parkins, 2004:364.
9. Edensor, 2012; Thrift, 2004.
10. Lefebvre, 2004.
11. Edensor, 2010:16.
12. Shove , Trentmann, and Wilk, 2009a.
13. Shove , Trentmann, and Wilk, 2009b:1.
14. Schor 1993, 1999.
15. Nansen et al., 2009.
16. Nansen et al., 2009:188.
17. Gallan and Gibson, 2011; Melbin, 1987; Schivelbusch, 1995; Shaw, 2010; Thrift, 1996; Williams, 2008.
18. Shove, Trentmann, and Wilk, 2009:3.
19. May and Thrift, 2001.
20. Tobey, 1997; Parr, 1999; Schwartz-Cowan, 1983.
21. Hand and Shove, 2004; Lupton and Miller, 1992; Schwartz-Cowan, 1983.
22. Tam, 2008.
23. As in the slow food movement, the decelerations practiced in the course of day-to-day off-grid living were invested in diversifying and localizing resource generation and utilization. Implicit in this process was a "redemption of the quotidian:" (Felski, 2002:610) an affirmation of the value of everyday life as a productive, emergent, "hybrid timescape" (Simpson, 2008:824) in constant negotiation with "the little affected modifications that permeate [its] functional ecologies" (Simpson, 2008:824). Immanent in the experience of living in greater synchrony with the weather was thus an affirmation of mundane domestic spaces as place specific and place sensitive. In this sense, off-grid homes were deeply synchronized with the ephemeral qualities of place, qualities that "may change from minute to minute, or through the day, or over the seasons" (Brassley, 1998:119).
24. Palang et al., 2005.
25. Jones, 2011.
26. Edensor, 2006b:491.

27. Simpson, 2008:824.
28. Biehler and Simon, 2011; Hitchings and Lee, 2008; Kaika, 2005.
29. Kaika, 2005; Gunn and Owens, 2006; Swyngedouw, 1999.
30. Swyngedouw, 1999:447.
31. Ingold, 2007b:20.
32. Anderson and Wylie, 2009:326; Lingis, 1998.
33. Parkins, 2004:377.
34. Ingold, 1993, 2007b:28.
35. Bennett, 2010.
36. Bennett, 2010:28.
37. Anderson and Wylie, 2009:320.
38. Anderson and Wylie, 2009:325.
39. Whatmore, 2006:601.
40. Whatmore, 2006:601–602.
41. Jones, 2011:2287.
42. Simpson, 2012:448.
43. Harrison et al., 2004.

Phil.[i]

10
BREAKING WATERS

Morning comes
we're living inside a fridge
The radio batteries are frozen
and yesterday's coffee
a brown layer of stone
The orange saved for breakfast
does not bounce
The wood stove is still asleep
and windows are frosted
like a stained glass church
You tell me
underneath your army surplus
double down sleeping bag
the emperor has no clothes
and that it's my turn
to start the fire
Soon the tide will shift
the inlet ice
like continental drift
and we will be stranded
The floor makes exploding sounds
I hop in my cheap sleeping bag
rigid from the night's early sweat

and with my axe
try to break the water
in our kettle
It's the Canadian thing to do.

(Philip K. Thompson, "The Cabin in Winter")[1]

"Philip?"

"Phillip with two *l*'s?"

"Yes. Nice to meet you. And this is Jon."

"How's it going, Jon?"

"Really good. Thanks for bringing out the sun for us, Phil."

"Yeah, it's a gorgeous day. Looks like you guys didn't have to bring those life jackets after all, eh?"

"Oh well. They pack light."

"Cool. Well, if you guys are ready to go, I'll lead the way."

Philip,[ii] with one *l*, had been patiently waiting for us alongside the quiet road hugging **Petpeswick Inlet**.[iii] Armed with sturdy gumboots, unflinching enthusiasm, and a well-equipped arsenal of stories, he began blazing the jagged up-and-down terrain with ambitiously long strides. The precarious trail crossed a neighbor's property, curved around a small cape, and—after a few tricky steps—broke up at a tiny beach of pebbles and uneven rocks wetted on and off by breathless waves. There, Philip began untying three kayaks while Jon and I debated how to pool the camera gear.

"So you guys have ocean-paddled before, right?" Philip sought to reassure himself.

For leisure: yes. As far as work was concerned, this was a first. And it couldn't have waited much longer. Long days of driving through New Brunswick's foggy and snow-clogged backcountry roads, sojourns at unimaginative hotel chains, and scarring frustrations with recording technology had us clamoring for a relapse into raw adventure. There was no need to hurry—as our visit had been carefully planned around successive high tides—but it felt so good to be once again at eye level with the Great Outdoors that I felt an irresistible child-like urge to sprint to Phil's house with a few long strokes. In just moments, I left everyone in my wake. Being able to hear nothing but my panting breath

---

[ii] http://lifeoffgrid.ca/wp-content/uploads/2013/11/Life-Off-Grid_Nova-Scotia-New-Brunswick_11.jpg

[iii] http://lifeoffgrid.ca/wp-content/uploads/2013/11/Life-Off-Grid_Nova-Scotia-New-Brunswick_08.jpg

and the gurgling vibration of my paddle on the ocean surface energized me with serenity and clarity of mind. It was for moments like these that I cherished fieldwork.

Phil had been living on his small island since 1994. It was only a few acres, but it made up in bucolic beauty what it lacked in size. Tall coniferous trees, a gentle shoreline, pellucid waters, and soothing vistas over the sun-bathed inlet would have made this an ideal development site for insensitive tourist operators and commercial builders alike, had it not been for him. The property—in the family's hands since 1794—had been bequeathed to Phil by his grandfather who, on his deathbed, asked him to steward the place. Proud of his heritage and intimately close to his grandpa, Phil made a solemn promise to carry out the onus, and over the coming years he fiercely resisted insistent developers' pressures to sell out. Eventually, constantly rising property taxes made it obvious that if he wanted to afford keeping the place he had to make it his residence, and so he did. It took him and his three sons five and a half years and $50,000 to erect the walls of his two-story, 1,200-square-foot, elemental-structured, well-insulated home.

"It's a simple house anyone could build," Phil observed with obvious satisfaction in the efficiency and modesty of his abode. Modesty was underscored in everything he did and said. "I even had the chance of scoring a great deal on helicoptering building material to the island," he recounted, "but that would have been an ugly show off. I am not a rich man. So my sons and I just made trips back and forth on our little dinghy and carried lumber up the trails."

Unlike the helicopter deal, the connection to the local electricity grid would have been everything but a steal: $25,000 just for hooking up and on top of that a monthly power bill and a yearly lease to run a cable across the shore. His house instead now ran on a record-setting low 150-watt solar system and on locally collected wood for heating. The system used to be more powerful and reliant on wind energy too, but Hurricane Juan and Tropical Storm Noel had recently wreaked havoc and Phil and others in the area were still reeling from the devastating blows.

At the age of 62, Phil, who hardly looked a day older than 50, received a very small pension from his years of work in government energy conservation, which he supplemented with seasonal employment as a dockside fishery observer and year-round writing for the local newspaper. He published poetry books too, but—as poetry demands—chiefly as a labor of love. "I am comfortable here, I have all I need," Phil reflected at the dining table as he took a puff from his pipe. Other than telecommunications and taxes, he had no regular bills and, seemingly, even fewer worries.

I told Phil we were interested in ways of dealing with water during our Nova Scotia trip: how water was sourced, channeled, stored, used, and disposed of. I explained it was a very important issue for me, personally, as water conservation was one of the main reasons why I had become interested in off-grid living in the first place. Though it rains much on the West Coast during autumn and winter and my home's well is copiously replenished every year, long dry summers and heightened seasonal demand require extremely careful water consumption from all of us Gulf Islanders. So my well had taught me firsthand the practical and conceptual lessons of monitoring, care, and involvement at the service of conservation.

The water system was the "least convenient" feature of his home, he noted pensively. He used to have it "rigged up" with a pressurized system, automatic filtration, and a small marine pump, but over the course of the years mold had grown within the plastic pipes and he had to revert to a different solution. Rainwater was now harvested in 20-liter barrels placed on his deck under the roof's eaves. Potable water, instead, came from a friend's well on the mainland. It required a bit of planning and hauling but it was free, and it was something Phil could do when he went to town to take his clothes to the laundromat.

Due to the absence of a serviceable pump, the collected rainwater needed to be brought inside in buckets and warmed up—when needed—on his wood stove. The process got even more time-consuming in the winter when snow had to be first melted.

"All this bucket work reminds me of what my grandparents did," he smiled.

"It's a lot of work," I remarked.

"Yeah, but it's exercise too, and I enjoy it," Phil replied confidently. "I get more exercise in a day than most people do in a week."

Onerous Consumption

Phil had felt morally compelled to safeguard his island. His entire lifestyle had been born out of that profound personal connection with his family and his strong sense of responsibility for place stewardship. His day-to-day life and all the choices he made to consume resources in the modest way he did closely adhered to his ethics. Phil wasn't the only off-gridder to feel and act this way, of course. Across Canada we had met off-gridder after off-gridder who related to their home and their land not as real estate, but rather for their affective and moral significance.

"Ethical consumption"[2] has been the subject of much growing interest lately, especially in light of heightened public sensitivity to the moral, socio-political, and environmental consequences of fair and unfair trade and growing individual consumption.[3] Ethical consumption practices are "creative" and "reflexive" lifestyle positionings[4] and relationship-building consuming activities[5] that go beyond merely rational and economic deliberations of price and use-value.[6] As expressions of virtue, acts of ethical consumption allow individuals to establish meaningful relations with others and to fashion a sense of self that is grounded in heartfelt moral values.[7]

In the off-grid lifeworld, ethical consumption in the form of resource conservation and procurement stood in sharp contrast to a broader cultural paradigm that links the pleasures of the good life with consumerist ease, limited effort, and the widespread normalization of comfort and convenience.[8] In this sense, Phil's water pails and buckets were more than reminders of bygone generations. Not unlike solar panels, organic foods, or compact fluorescent light bulbs,[9] his water buckets made possible a unique way of life and equally unique practices of sustainability and place stewardship. The buckets that he and other off-gridders used functioned as "moralizing machines"[10] that "forge[d] specific socio-material relations"[11] and shaped an ethical commitment to place and to people,[12] ultimately translating into a parsimonious orientation toward resource usage and conservation.

Moral commitment and physical effort, however, did not preclude full enjoyment of life. Despite occasional minor hassles, the self-governance of consumption practiced by off-gridders allowed for the "making of one's own life as a project of self-cultivation."[13] Through their re-inventions of comfort and convenience, all off-gridders "exercise[d] freedom and responsibility" and realized a "private right of individual autonomy"—however partial.[14] Such combination of individual choice and moral responsibility to other people and the environment was a unique way of practicing hedonism.[15] So, as paradoxical as this may sound, buckets served as crucial tools for the ordinary gratifications of a modest but nonetheless fulfilling "hedonist imaginary."[16]

Off-gridders' everyday entanglements with water—that is, their direct, practical, embodied engagement with the resources needed to drink, wash dishes, do laundry, bathe, shower, and clean—constituted a type of onus: a burden. But the burden was an enjoyable one: a treasured outcome of their sense of responsibility and their relative enjoyment of self-sufficiency. Theirs was, then, a form of *onerous consumption:* a type of ethical consumption characterized by a willfully chosen burdensome involvement that—though it was a source of some degree of inconvenience, toil, and occasional technical problems—was uniformly appreciated as a fulfilling moral responsibility and even a treasured privilege.

Onerous consumption was a counter-hegemonic, self-reflective, and critical orientation that rejected the seductive appeal of an unrestrained consumerism promising a carefree, inconvenience-free, endless gratification of needs and desires. The burdens of onerous consumption were moral and practical obligations and orientations woven into ordinary routines and accepted and even embraced as inevitable necessities of one's existence. Onerous consumption affirmed the value of a good life that wasn't lived at the expense of social and environmental justice.

The word *onerous* denotes the condition of having an obligation or a responsibility and is typically synonymous with burdensome, heavy, and troublesome. Onerous consumption refers, therefore, to a type of consumption characterized by a problematizing stance toward the act of consuming: a moral stance that recognizes the broader socio-environmental consequences of consumption and that manifests itself through practices of alternative engagement with place, natural resources, technology, and the material world.

Off-grid onerous consumption depended on direct, embodied, and permanent involvement in the process of collecting, storing, channeling, and disposing of the subject matter of consumption. Onerous consumption was engaged, committed, and entangled. It unfolded through practical ways of incorporating an environment's features into everyday life. Such incorporation required "attentive engagement" and a revealing "exploratory quest for knowledge" through which off-gridders entered "actively into the constitution of their environments."[17]

Off-grid onerous consumption was marked by a deep involvement in the process of *procurement* of whatever was consumed. To *procure* is to exercise skill, attention, practical knowledge, sensitivity, and adaptability in the process of obtaining resources, materials, and goods.[18] To *procure* is "to bring about, to obtain by care or effort, to prevail upon, to induce."[19] When consumption entailed procurement, as it regularly did for off-gridders, the ordinary mode of everyday life became task-like. In this sense the objects of onerous consumption were anything but ready-made or taken for granted. Off-grid onerous consumption was rather a "taskscape" and "a project that had to be continually worked at."[20] The consumption typical of an onerous mode therefore entailed a generative capacity and a keen attunement to, and deep involvement in, a socio-natural environment.

Self-Sufficient Homes

Domestic consumption of water is constantly on the rise across the world, causing increasing environmental concern.[21] Countless policies, technological innovations, commercial strategies, and research studies are produced every year to deal with the problem of rapidly depleting fresh water supplies as a result of escalating standards of domestic comfort, convenience, and cleanliness.[22] Yet, for most of us, water remains taken for granted and of limited preoccupation—save for the rare times when scarcity surfaces as a result of droughts, power outages, or system malfunctions.[23] The sources of water, its distribution, and the infrastructures dedicated to its collection, treatment, and disposal remain largely separate from our ordinary mode of engagement with our homes. But what happens when water becomes the subject of ordinary consumption? What happens when the collection, storage, channeling, and usage of water shift from a distant assemblage operating in the background of our consciousness to a proximate and immediate set of concerns? What is everyday life like when people become entirely, or almost entirely, water self-sufficient?

We arrived at Andrea's house on a misty morning, quite late for our appointment. Betrayed by the dysfunctionality of the new digital maps created for the iPhone, Jon and I had obliviously driven 30 kilometers in the wrong direction. Fortunately, Andrea had been patient enough to re-direct us over the phone. Apologetic and embarrassed, we sat down at the kitchen table to drink a soothing cup of tea and fuel up on homemade cookies, as her 14-year-old son calmly got ready to go to school. Being able to spend quality time with him—she confided as he stepped out carrying his backpack—was one of the key reasons why she had chosen this lifestyle. "I practice homeopathy, I am a pet groomer, and I teach music," she said, but, "I carefully choose how much time I work and how I structure my days."

Anxious about unkind bylaw enforcement, Andrea preferred we use a fictitious name for her and that we maintain her area of residence entirely confidential. We stored our cameras away and gladly obliged. Her distrust of authority and large institutions was perfectly understandable, given what she had experienced. It had all started a few years ago back in Ontario, when she had received an erroneous $500 heating bill. Convinced of being right, she had fought it tooth and nail, but the struggle had proven futile. When utilities think they are right, right is what they are. Unwilling to surrender, Andrea was eventually disconnected. But it wasn't over. The utility pressed on and threatened legal action, so Andrea had to borrow money to pay off her bill. When she was finally reconnected, the company admitted fault and told her she had been right all along. Poetic justice had arrived too late, though. Andrea had been "turned off by corporate utilities forever" and had made a plan to move off-grid. Nova Scotia was home to some of the least expensive land in the country—and, incidentally, some of the most beautiful—and so here she was, seeking a taste of autonomy.

Invariably, off-grid homes were, however, far from being fully autonomous self-governing spaces. Due to lack of clarity in municipal regulations regarding whether she could build an off-grid residential dwelling on her property, Andrea and her son had initially called home an old school bus parked on their undeveloped lot just outside of town. A bus is, after all, a mobile structure and not quite a permanent dwelling. In the meantime she had been busy designing and building a barn and her current house: an ark-shaped "houseboat" floating on stilts above a swampy area, and seemingly floating above bylaws as well. "I love to work with wood," she told us. "I've designed and built my own houses before, it's really simple and fulfilling." The ark only cost $6,000 and she managed to do all the work by herself with the help of just two friends.

Like all "boats," Andrea's ark had a rudimentary plumbing system and used very little water. Water was mostly channeled through buckets. It was either first pumped from a 14-foot deep hand-dug well, or harvested in 10-gallon plastic wheelbarrows and then wheeled around. Drinking water, instead, came from the store. In town was also where Andrea did her laundry. As in Phil's case, a basic composting toilet eliminated the need for flushing. As for cleaning and washing, the kitchen sink drained outside into a holding tank, whereas a small 4-foot by 2-foot bathtub waited to be hooked up to plumbing.

"So, how do you bathe?" was my next, inopportune yet obligatory, question.

"We have sponge baths. Sometimes we bathe at friends' homes," her words quivered.

I sensed this was a difficult topic. Though Andrea was proud of her achievements, she was also profoundly aware of the constant challenges she had to tackle on her own.

"I used to bathe every night and had showers every morning before we moved here," she sighed, "long, luxurious, comforting baths. I miss that. I have a real shower once a month now."

"It's a compromise," she reflected as she tried to contain her emotions. "I see how much people consume in their homes, and how much they waste, and I know that if we can live with less, we can be more sustainable and independent."

"Can you ever be truly sustainable and independent?"

"Maybe I could, but I am aware of how much physical energy I have. I can't do everything on my own. What you see here is a compromise: a mix of self-sufficiency and a pragmatic attitude."

To be fair, self-sufficiency was nothing but a myth. Like Andrea, all off-gridders we met were well aware of the costs and challenges of practicing a completely self-sufficient lifestyle. Pragmatic compromises with their ideals were therefore always necessary.[24] Nevertheless, the ideal of self-sufficiency—even if it was "just" an ideal—strongly inspired and motivated off-gridders. Self-sufficiency promised them a sense of freedom and independence, and its daily practice yielded a re-affirming sense of self-reliance, self-confidence, and self-efficacy. Many off-gridders like Andrea, therefore, practiced as much self-sufficiency as they could, drawing a line whenever hardline idealist orthodoxy got in the way of life's enjoyment.

Lifestyles like Andrea's were always informed by a prideful sense of difference from the cultural norm, as well as by a self-affirming rejection of the wasteful ways of life practiced by so many others.[25] Frankly, they often had a point too; most typical modern homes are anything but self-sufficient. As urban studies scholar Maria Kaika has argued, in Western societies the private space of the contemporary home is typically alienated from nature. Homes are generally perceived as somehow independent and autonomous from natural elements like water; elements that are viewed as external, abstract, and "other."[26] There are exceptions to these trends, of course, but still way too many citizens rely on water that is mass-produced, standardized, and commodified by increasingly large corporate socio-technical networks.

For off-gridders, instead, water had to be routinely domesticated through painstaking efforts that "incorporated"[27] it in meaningful ways. So, whereas the sense of domestic comfort and convenience typical of on-grid homes arises from a partial separation from, and exclusion of, the rather unpredictable *nature* outside,[28] the sense of control typical of off-grid homes emerged from a partial disconnection from a wasteful, inefficient, and corrupt *society* seemingly incapable of establishing a more authentic rapport with the environment. It was from this orientation, and from off-gridders' disconnection from large infrastructures, that a coherent sense of off-grid self-sufficiency was born.

Self-sufficiency was obviously always partial. Andrea, for example, bought drinking water at the store and washed clothes at the laundromat. However, even a partial sense of separation from the ways of consumption of the "outside world," and even a limited self-exile from large infrastructures and utilities, were sufficiently powerful moves to justify a sense of autonomy and independence. This sense of partial self-sufficiency allowed off-gridders to feel that their use of resources occurred in greater synchrony with natural availability, in righteous contrast to a broader social mode marked by a care-less distancing[29] of consumption from production and procurement. As a result, complete self-sufficiency was not necessary to reap the self-affirming moral rewards of onerous consumption. What did matter for off-gridders was simply having undertaken the quest—the quest to internalize, rather than externalize as most consumers do[30]—the costs and externalities of domestic comfort, convenience, and cleanliness through personal responsi-bility and hard work.

I was wrong to think—as I had done for a moment back in Ontario—that off-gridders' quest for self-sufficiency was a form of selfish alienation. Rather, their partial self-sufficiency was a relational responsibility:[31] an onus to duly play one's part in socio-natural processes "wherein people and their environments are continually bringing each other into being."[32] As was typical of all forms of hedonism, concern with self-interest was evident among off-gridders, but their pursuit of the good life was always accompa-nied by a preoccupation with the greater environmental, social, and politico-economic externalities of individual action. In this way, off-grid hedonism always required involvement, ethical commitment, a sense of onus, and the carrying out of multiple tasks that demanded financial expenditures, continuous learning, and application of skill. So, rather than an ascetic bright-eyed idealism, it was a pragmatic hedonism that fueled the off-grid quest for self-sufficiency. But this was no hardened, irresponsible, decadent realism. Rather, it was an interesting form of hedonism that we might call "alternative."

Alternative Hedonism

Hedonists like to enjoy life. Alternative hedonists are equally keen on pur-suing pleasures but enjoy doing it in socially and environmentally conscious ways.[33] According to British social theorist Kate Soper,[34] alternative hedo-nism "is premised on the idea that even if consumerism were indefinitely sustainable it would not enhance human happiness and well-being." In fact, consumerism and the unrestrained hedonism it stands for are not only politically, economically, socially, environmentally, and culturally irrespon-sible, but also ultimately unsatisfying at a personal level. So we need an alternative, in Soper's view, an alternative that promises a positive vision of the good life as well as a sustainable future for all. That is the philosophy of alternative hedonism. This type of hedonism is an alternative to consumerism, but also to the ascetic sanctimoniousness and gloomy defeatism present in some currents of the environmental movement. Alternative hedonism "points to new forms of desire, rather than fears of ecological disaster, as the most likely motivating force in any shift towards a more sustainable economic order."[35]

As a form of alternative hedonism, onerous consumption was a quest for the good life, a quest that was both negative and affirmative. It negated the unchecked behavior typical of consumer culture and criticized the pursuit of an "unpleasurable and self-denying"[36] standard of living that forced a person to work more in order to spend more. At the same time, onerous consumption affirmed the values of comfort, cleanliness, and convenience and the gratification drawn from the basic pleasures of domestic life. Though it may seem incoherent to suggest that the cultivation of a burden was a hedonistic practice, off-gridders' experiences showed that the onuses inherent in relatively self-sufficient living were personally fulfilling. Involvement was onerous, yes, but not unpleasant because it generated a sense of self-reliance, self-efficacy, independence, and a feeling of pride in one's ethical commitments.

"It's all about consumption," Simon opined. "It's not hard to reduce what you consume, but there has to be a certain amount of self-control and self-discipline involved."

"You have to *want* this way of living, you have to *want* it enough because there is no 'push-button instant technology'," Simon's wife, Sue, added, "you have to work with nature."

We had heard these things, of course, but somehow they sounded different coming from Simon and Sue. Here and there throughout the country we had occasionally suspected that some off-gridders made virtue out of necessity—painting a somewhat rosier portrait of domestic life than the average middle-class citizen might have under the same circumstances—because of limited financial options or reduced opportunities. Not that making virtue out of necessity would have lessened the significance of their lifestyle, or the validity of our arguments, but there was sometimes a feeling that it would have been difficult to "sell" this way of life—outhouses, lack of plumbing, hand-operated blenders, and all—to a *lot* of people in our modern society. But in a way, it was houses like Simon and Sue's that strengthened the wider case for off-grid living as a hedonist and widely enviable lifestyle pursuit.

Not that there was anything decadent about their 840-watt photovoltaic and 1-kilowatt wind-powered, 1,500-square-foot, ocean-facing villa, but it was the type of home that could have easily graced the pages of a home-and-garden magazine. And yet, its operation was everything but hands-free.

"You have to think about what you do," Simon and Sue—two committed environmentalists with a long history in off-grid living across the globe—acknowledged.

Take their water usage, for example. Hidden under the kitchen rug, like a giant elephant in the room, there was a 12 × 8 × 4-foot polyurethane water cistern. Its name was Theodor, they joked, because when it arrived on the delivery truck it looked just like TV's Theodor the Tugboat. Theodor—we learned as we lifted the rug, unscrewed its top lid, and inspected its gaping mouth-like opening—stored up to 9,000 liters of the rainwater collected from the roof and channeled in through a pipe.

"It's deep," Sue described, "we take the stepladder and go down there when we have to clean it out."

"So it's not an out-of-sight, out-of-mind thing?" I asked.

"Not at all. We monitor how much water we have," Sue explained as she showed the "high-tech" gadget used to inspect storage: a wooden dipstick adorned by a variety of marks and reference points. The quarter-full mark was the cut-off point, she illustrated, because the last 10 inches of water sat below the reach of their 24-volt DC water pump.

To conserve water they used a humanure toilet beside their other conventional low-flush toilet, a low-flow shower, and a very efficient washing machine. As well, they recycled wastewater to the garden plants. And their tightly insulated passive solar house consumed no more than 3 cords of wood per year, thanks in part to a relatively unique way of using water. On the house roof there were two solar hot water collector systems that warmed up water and also heated up a glycol-water mix, then channeled it all underneath their main floor to radiate heat to the house. And because **it could take**[iv] a while for warm water to come out of the showerheads, they kept a bucket in the shower booth and collected 8 liters of cold water while they waited for the warm stuff to arrive.

"People want their housing to be easy," Sue remarked as she showed us the bathroom, "but the key is to be observant and mindful" if you want to conserve. To be mindful, observant, and involved sounds like a burden to most of us, as accustomed as we are to flicking on a switch and letting distant network infrastructures take care of us. But the "burden," to off-gridders like Simon and Sue, was a pleasant one: something they embraced and enjoyed as much as they endured as a basic necessity and responsibility of life.

---

iv. http://soundcloud.com/innovativeethnographies/simon-and-sue-excess-of-hot

In combination with large-scale socio-technical networks of water distribution, indoor plumbing has made it easier for constantly escalating standards of cleanliness, hygiene, convenience, and comfort to become normalized and taken for granted.[37] Consequently, the responsibility for managing water supplies and waste has been increasingly delegated to infrastructures and agencies—"Big Water/Big Shit systems"[38]—far removed from consumers' homes. The constantly growing consumption of water, combined with the existence of assemblages that allow individual consumers to feel separated at best and irresponsible at worst from the consequences of their everyday routines, does not bode well for the sustainability of our collective way of life.

In contrast, awareness of one's own consumption and of resources' inevitable scarcity is a crucial element of conservation practices.[39] As a result, many policies and programs aimed at developing environmentally sustainable practices emphasize the need for individuals to make their consumption habits visible and subject to personal scrutiny.[40] By becoming conscious of otherwise taken-for-granted practices and their consequences, consumers of energy, fuels, and water can experience "revelatory moment[s]" with the power of shedding light on, and hopefully altering, the wastefulness of their behaviors.[41]

In a way, off-grid living was precisely that: a protracted exercise in cultivating awareness of one's consumption and in constantly developing a deeper understanding of what it meant to utilize natural resources. In fact, off-gridders reversed the prototypical orientation toward a house as something separate from an untamed "nature" outside its walls by taking an active role in **collecting, storing**[v], utilizing, and disposing of natural resources and by becoming physically involved in how resources like water were channeled in and out of their homes. By doing so, off-gridders turned potentially unreflexive, habitual, and mindless routine activities into going concerns. Off-grid living, in short, consisted of making inconspicuous everyday domestic practices fully conspicuous and thus the starting point of self-affirming conservation.

* * *

A month before, back at home, I had insisted on searching for off-gridders on Nova Scotia's Cape Breton Island. For years I had fantasized Cape Breton as a windswept luxuriant land sheathed in gelid Atlantic currents

---

[v.] http://lifeoffgrid.ca/wp-content/uploads/2013/11/Life-Off-Grid_Nova-Scotia-New-Brunswick_09.jpg

and echoing melodies of time-forgotten Gaelic and Acadian traditions, and I felt a deep urge to go there. When Air Canada's small DeHavilland dropped us off in Sydney—Cape Breton's capital—I realized my romantic imagination hadn't been too naive. On the Cabot Trail abrupt cliffs and **dark woods**[vi] dove down the ice-grey waters underneath them. Dormant fishing villages punctuated the meandering road, resounding with signs of bygone folklore. Swiftly drifting billows chasing each other in the sky alternately obscured and then lit up snow-covered peaks and narrow valleys, intermittently hiding and highlighting the route ahead of us. Closer to Sydney, we then spotted a far less hallowed sight—and yet a profoundly reverent one to us—the road sign indicating the ferry route to the island, at last nearby, of Newfoundland. Few roadside treasures could have brought greater satisfaction to two weary travellers in search of their final destination.

It wasn't all bliss and rugged beauty, of course. Many barren homes and padlocked doors silently recounted stories of exile and heart-breaking out-migration—for after all there were as many Cape Bretoners to be seen on their haunting homeland streets as one could find any day or night melancholically shoveling tar out of Northern Alberta's unforgiving oily earth. And yet, other people were moving the opposite way: relocating to seductive Cape Breton from distant lands. Among them were Brian and Gina, who had moved from the US Midwest to Canada 12 years ago—Americans were by far Canadian off-gridders' largest ethnic minority group—to seek a simpler, better way of life. After they had completed building their straw bale home, both in their 30s, Brian had become a renewable energy specialist and Gina a potter.

Their abode, while humble in ambition, was a challenge to the descriptive word. Almost Steampunk-like in atmosphere and wildly creative in its most minute detail, its main feature was a massive jagged boulder that served as the home's astonishing hearth. The rest of the house, it felt, had seamlessly clung and grown around it.

"You want us to show you how we get water?" Gina asked, as our first mugs of hot coffee ran dry.

We began by walking outside to the water operations' headquarters: the tower and pump. Upstairs, the 20-foot tall, wooden water tower hosted a 250-gallon cistern that during the warm months collected rainwater harvested from the roof. Gravity fed water down from the second floor of the tower—where the cistern was placed—to a hose used to fill buckets. The buckets were then carried wherever needed: inside the house for washing

---

[vi.] http://lifeoffgrid.ca/wp-content/uploads/2013/11/Life-Off-Grid_Nova-Scotia-New-Brunswick_01.jpg

dishes, to the bathhouse for body washing, or to the garden for nourishing plants and animals. I walked the 15 steps up the steep ladder to take a quick glance from up high: an idyllic 23-acre property sitting near the top of a gently rising shore overlooking the mainland. "What you see out there is what some old islanders still insist on calling Nova Scotia," Brian commented with a smile. "You might want to make Cape Breton a separate chapter in your book."

Back downstairs, Gina proceeded to demonstrate how the pump worked by grabbing a "foot valve"—a 3-foot-long cylindrical metal container about 5 inches wide in diameter—and lowering it through a manual pulley. By handling the rope Gina dropped the foot valve into a narrow opening in the ground marked by a metal canister. Four seconds later the container hit the 15-foot waterline of their 204-foot-deep drilled well. A few bubbling sounds bounced against the metal and reverberated through the opening. It was a signal the bucket was full, so Gina hoisted it up and released the water into a pail.

Bucket in hand we walked a few feet to the bathhouse/sauna: a 15-by-15 foot wooden building heated by a small woodstove. On shower days Brian and Gina placed a bucket on top of the woodstove and warmed it up to the desired temperature. They then took the bucket and dumped the warm water into a portable, eBay-bought, US Army-issued, field shower bag. The 5-gallon bag was then hung high above their heads to trickle down water.

"We usually shower every other day," Gina said, anticipating my next nosey question, "and we make sure to use non-toxic soaps" so that the gray water, drained right outside, would not pollute the soil.

"It's our own waste," Brian said, "and I feel we have the responsibility to deal with our own waste."

"We don't use much water," Gina continued, "but it's not because we don't have enough. We just don't need much."

"And it takes work too," Brian added, "it takes some planning and a little bit of time, especially when we have to filter it to drink it."

In most of our homes water flows out of the tap almost magically, demanding little aside from a timely bill payment. But things were different in off-grid homes. Being independent from municipal water mains meant having the responsibility to harvest rainwater or extract groundwater, which required relying on muscle power or on electrical pumps and a plumbing system capable of meeting demand. And it also meant finding ways to dispose of gray water and human bodily waste. The majority of

---

vii. http://soundcloud.com/innovativeethnographies/brian-gina-outhouse

off-grid homes had plumbing, but even many of those relied on an out-house and other unconventional solutions that most people might find somewhat inconvenient. The onus was not a light one; Brian and Gina, and many other off-gridders, had to solve many demanding and potentially overbearing technical challenges. Yet, their responsibilities brought them not a sense of discomfort and inconvenience, but instead a deep apprecia-tion for the basic pleasures of their home life.

Our last stop on the tour of their "compound" was the outhouse. Approx-imately 8-by-8 feet in size, covered by a steeply pitched, low-hanging roof, the outhouse was suitably far from both their home and their well. The placement was ideal for hygiene but it was no less than a whole minute's walk from their front door. It required involvement but it was clean and worked simply—**Brian explained**[vii] as he pointed at the square wooden con-tainer mounted underneath the toilet seat.

I strove to imagine what that might be like during a blustery winter night: "Is it a hassle to come all the way here to do your business?"

"Nah! There are many worse things in the world," Gina replied.

"What's the problem, really? I pee anywhere. I walk outside and pee," Brian laughed, "humans have been peeing outside since . . . since the beginning!"

Bathrooms are the primary sites of domestic water consumption. A typi-cal power shower can utilize 20 to 50 liters of water per minute, whereas a common toilet can use up to 15 liters per flush. In Canadian homes, baths and showers account for 37%, and toilets for 30%, of water usage.[42] Though the tradition of the weekly bath is not so historically distant, showering is now perceived by most people as a normal daily routine.[43] Daily showering epitomizes the rapid escalation of contemporary standards of cleanliness.[44] As body washing has transitioned from a public activity to a private one, and later on from a hygiene-informed practice to one focused on the cultivation of well-being,[45] daily shower routines have come to symbolize the perva-siveness of socio-technical networks of water distribution and consumers' dependence on their reliable operation.

Like other household objects, water has a physical life: it is intro-duced into the home, used, and disposed of using specific conduits[46] over which most of us have little or no control.[47] But while it is true that divestment and disposal are not totally un-reflexive activities,[48] for most people the flushing of the toilet generally takes place with little regard to its consequences. In part this is because of the generalized attitude toward human waste as pollutant dirt transgressing the social order.[49] But in part this is also because flushing waste out to sewers pushes urine and feces away, beyond the boundaries of the home, toward an unknown elsewhere undeserving of concern.[50] The off-grid consumer of water couldn't afford to be so cavalier, as discarded matter always acted back in direct, visible ways.[51]

By becoming responsible for the "sinks"[52] where their gray-water and solid waste were disposed of, Brian and Gina did not so much "use" water, as "brought it into use" by incorporating it into a system of deeply inter-related activities.[53] As a result of their involvement in water procurement and disposal, off-gridders' domestic work truly became "integral"[54] to the whole process of consumption. Thus Brian and Gina reframed their rela-tion to local water resources and enacted counter-normative relations with place, resources, conduits, and their meanings.[55] By doing so, dirt became not something out of place, but rather matter *in* and *of* place[56] that was subject to the their direct "accountability."[57]

Onerous consumption hinged on a principle of sentient ecology—the idea that living beings gather reflexive knowledge about their environments through orientations and sensitivities continually honed in the practical experiences of living life.[58] As such, the concept of onerous consumption highlighted how the inconspicuous consumption of natural resources could be made conspicuous, meaningful, place-sensitive, and therefore immedi-ately consequential.[59]

The escalating global quest for domestic comfort, cleanliness, and conve-nience flies in the face of environmental conservation.[60] However, we real-ized as we left Nova Scotia, the pursuit of a good life does not have to result in environmental damage. As onerous consumers in the tenth province had showed us, and as Soper had opined: "We need a new political imaginary that dwells explicitly on the satisfactions to be had from consuming differ-ently. [. . .] We need visions of a future consumption built around environ-mentally less damaging methods of farming and commodity production, the use of renewable energy resources, the pleasures of unpolluted air and water, the recycling of all waste, the shortening of the working week, the decline of shopping."[61] A new possible imaginary to practicing conservation could entail not the sacrificing of good living but rather the sensitizing of our attention to what an environment makes available and the need to work with it—and not in spite of it. All this won't necessarily be easy, but whoever said living and housing are always meant to be?

Notes

1.   Thompson, 2013:48. The poem depicts an un-insulated cabin where Philip lived before he completed construction of his current, winter-ready home.
2.   See Clarke, 2008; Newholm and Shaw, 2007.
3.   See Glickman, 2009, for earlier manifestations.

4. Parkins and Craig, 2006:7.
5. Miller, 1998.
6. Barnett, Barnett, and Clarke, 2010.
7. Cherrier, Black, and Lee, 2011; Clarke, 2008; Newholm and Shaw, 2007.
8. Borgmann, 2000.
9. Hobson, 2006.
10. Jelsma, 2003.
11. Hobson, 2006:325.
12. Barnett et al., 2005.
13. Barnett et al., 2005:31.
14. Barnett et al., 2005:30.
15. Soper, 2007, 2008.
16. Soper, 2008:571.
17. Ingold, 2000:57.
18. Ingold, 2000:58–59.
19. Bird-David, 1992:40.
20. Ingold, 2000: 97.
21. Strang, 2004.
22. Shove, 2003; Strengers and Maller, 2012.
23. Kaika, 2004; Kaika and Swyngedouw, 2000.
24. Also see Connolly and Prothero, 2008.
25. See Cherrier, Black, and Lee, 2011; Soper, Ryle, and Thomas, 2009.
26. Kaika, 2004.
27. Ingold, 2011.
28. Kaika, 2004.
29. See Hawkins, 2006; Luna, 2008.
30. Luna, 2008.
31. They weren't even the only ethical consumers to act this way. Just like off-gridders did, homeowners keen on reducing domestic water usage (Allon and Sofoulis, 2006), or various groups involved in "co-provision" of resources (Van Vliet, Chappells, and Shove, 2005) have viewed their self-interest as involving more than the pursuit of material pleasures and the satisfaction of one's needs and consumer desires (Soper, 2008:579–580).
32. Ingold, 2000:87.
33. Soper, Ryle, and Thomas, 2009.
34. Soper, 2007, 2008, 2009.
35. Soper, 2009:3.
36. Soper, 2009:3.
37. Gandy, 2004; Hawkins, 2006.
38. Sofoulis, 2005.
39. Strengers and Maller, 2012.
40. Chappells, Medd, and Shove, 2011; Sofoulis, 2005.
41. Chappells, Medd, and Shove, 2011:703.
42. Babooram and Hurst, 2008.
43. Hand, Shove, and Southerton, 2004.
44. Shove, 2003.
45. Lupton and Miller, 1992; Quitzau and Ropke, 2009.
46. Gregson, Metcalfe, and Crewe, 2007.
47. Gandy, 2004.
48. Gregson, Metcalfe, and Crewe 2007.
49. Douglas, 1966.
50. Gandy, 2004.
51. Bulkeley and Gregson, 2008; Gabrys, 2009; Munro, 1997.

52. Gabrys, 2009.
53. Ingold, 2000:352.
54. Hetherington, 2004:158.
55. Gregson, Metcalfe, and Crewe, 2007; Pickering, 2010.
56. Pickering, 2010.
57. Hetherington, 2004:163.
58. Ingold, 2000, 2011.
59. Other than describing the practices of off-gridders, the concept of onerous consumption could also describe the active role taken by individuals invested in saving water through small-scale and improvised solutions (Head and Muir, 2007), and more broadly the activities of ethical consumers (Clarke, 2008) and alternatively hedonistic, sustainable consumers in general (Jackson, 2006).
60. Shove, 2003; Van Vliet, Chappells, and Shove, 2005.
61. Soper, 2007:222.

Timmun and Niviaqsi Lay the Net.[i]

[i.] For more photos, visit lifeoffgrid.ca.

11

CAMPING, OUT ON THE LAND

It never fails. You're out camping and right in the middle of the night you feel an irresistible urge to go pee. The outhouse is only a few steps away, but you dread losing sleep momentum by getting out of bed and scavenging for your shoes and lamp. You ignore it for a while. Yet, it keeps you awake. The pressure is too strong. It's nippy outside, and getting dressed is a hassle. You eventually surrender.

It's −30°C (−22°F) on the Arctic tundra. You have been cautioned to be on the lookout for polar bears, especially at night. So you try and speed up urination flow—however a futile physiological effort that may be. As you go on about your business, you anxiously scan the immense horizon glistening in the precocious pre-morning dawn.

And then it happens, just like you feared it would. The light cast by your headlamp hits two beady, fluorescent eyes gazing hungrily at you from some 50 meters away. Standing still, shaking, you stare. The beady eyes stare back, equally motionless. Your entire life flashes before your sleepy eyes. Then it jumps. Then you jump. Do you run now?

* * *

Iqalugaaqjuit[ii]—a "place of many little fish," in the Inuktitut language—is one of a handful of outpost camps scattered around the southern shore of Baffin Island, in Canada's Nunavut territory. Most of these camps were built

---

[ii.] http://lifeoffgrid.ca/wp-content/uploads/2013/11/Life-Off-Grid_Nunavut_09.jpg

in the mid-1980s, when the Canadian government thought it behooved them to encourage—after decades of systematic eradication of traditional nomadic lifestyles—hunting and fishing and the intergenerational transfer of language and skills that goes along with them.

Our *illugalaq* was a newer edifice. Built 17 years ago by Timmun and Kristiina, just like all the other neighboring cabins, it hosted its owners, family, friends, and occasional guests for short weekend or weeklong camping getaways. Escape, not subsistence, was the purpose of those getaways. "It's for our mental health," in Kristiina's words, "we come here to get away."

They weren't the only ones to go camping for that reason. Camps are unique spaces, and camping trips unique times. They are ephemeral pauses in the rhythms of everyday life. They are changes of pace and place, which allow us to experience time as duration and flow.[1] Yet, as fleeting as they are, camps endure year after year, becoming points of return, familiar escapes, comfortable safe havens, existing "between the temporary and the permanent."[2]

Camping is also the most common way in which at one point or another in their lives people experience a taste of off-grid living. We may have never thought of it that way, but camping—one of the most common forms of outdoor leisure in Canada and the US, and a "widely ramified institution linked to national character"[3] in our continent—gives us a small but often enjoyable sense of the real off-grid life. After all, when we camp we are generally disconnected from electricity and natural gas networks and we are responsible for making light and heat, generally accomplishing both through a simple, cozy campfire. Camping also entails collecting water by hand, cooking our food differently, and enjoying the comforts of sleeping away from the light of the urban night.

Camping may also mean having to walk a quarter of a mile to find an outhouse, showering with lukewarm water, fighting with ants and mosquitos, and constantly having to tinker with a campsite: chopping wood, fixing tarps, washing dishes by hand, and drying irreparably wet firewood. The pleasures of the camp life as well as its obvious discomforts and inconveniences are what make it such a good exercise in off-grid living.

Leisure camping comes in many shapes and forms. There is tent camping, of course, in both organized and wilderness campgrounds. But there are many other forms too: there are jamboree camps, peace camps, children's summer camps, field camps, base camps, festival camps, re-enactment camps, backyard camps, RV/caravan camps, and many more.[4] Then there are the more permanent camps where families may return year after year: the lakeside houses, the cabins in the woods, the upstate cottages, and all those countryside "campsteads"[5] that aren't quite a home, and yet more than just a tent. What we actually do at all these sites may differ from person to person, from place to place, from year to year, but a few important things do remain common.

We live in homes, towns, and cities over which most of us have limited or no control. Though our grandparents or great-grandparents may have been deeply involved in collecting water, tending to the hearth, growing food, or making do with what was at hand, nowadays our homes provide us with everything we want without much involvement on our part. We have limited control over the places and the resources that make our homes what they are. And camping unsettles that relation. By taking charge of a small site and reinventing how we bring comfort to our shelter, even if only for a few days, we play and experiment with a different sense of daily order, temporarily re-imagining our lives.

Camping is an event with a recurring structure: "we leave home, we arrive at a site, we clear [or clean] an area, we make and then finally break camp before departing."[6] Camping—no matter what precise form it takes—is then a dual process of deterritorialization and reterritorialization.[7] Deterritorialization is a process of taking control and order away from a place, from a territory. This is generally followed by reterritorialization: a process whereby weakened ties between people, culture, and place are re-organized, re-assembled, and subject once again to new forms of control and order.[8] Camping is therefore generative of space—camping indeed, like off-grid living, *makes* place.[9]

And like all good things camping must end. The essence of camping resides in its very temporary and transitory nature, "to put down any sort of camp in a place is to hammer out a truce between passage and permanence."[10] Camping is fun because it ends. Camping is meaningful because it eventually stops being meaningful. The reterritorialization it plays out simply must give way, once again, to powerful deterritorializing forces.

* * *

We left Cape Dorset right before lunchtime on a cold but sunny April day. For four hours we rode our **snowmobiles**[iii] over lakes, ponds, rivers, creeks, and the ocean. At times we steered away from frozen waters and conquered overland trails, often none the wiser of the topographical substitutions. We arrived at Iqalugaaqjuit in the late afternoon.

We had departed British Columbia with borrowed parkas and untested gloves two days before. Because of the unwise gear choice the first few minutes of Skidoo driving had turned out to be atrocious. My right hand had more or less frozen stuck on the accelerator handle, gripping it steady at such an angle that it worked like a human-mediated cruise control, set at precisely 21 mph. Thankfully, at the first cigarette break, local knowledge had saved me. A pair of spare beaver fur mitts had been kindly provided by Kristiina, who introduced me to their superiority over my cheap polyester

---

[iii.] http://lifeoffgrid.ca/wp-content/uploads/2013/11/Life-Off-Grid_Nunavut_05.jpg

gloves while Timmun un-dramatically switched on the heat on my snow-mobile handlebar—a mix of old and new world solutions.

Snowmobiling is an acquired taste, much like getting lashed in the but-tocks with a leather whip: once you see past the sore lower back and the bruises you actually realize that it's just another way of getting around and that in fact, for some people, it's the normal way of doing it. Given its wide-spread and enthusiastic uptake, it makes you wonder how rougher dogsled transport must have been, back in the day.

Other than a few stretches of pavement within the boundaries of tiny hamlets, there are no roads in Canada's Eastern Arctic. Snow and ice make snowmobile travel possible during the colder months: from November to May. Boats are used to navigate the ocean separating Nunavut's communi-ties from one another and from outpost camps during July, August, and September. During the shoulder seasons, when ice is breaking or freezing up, only airplanes dares to go out on the land.

"Going out on the land," the locals' favorite expression to indicate going camping, is a bit of a misnomer. The "land" is actually snow. Some of it is frozen solid, some fluffier but dry, some slushy, some icy and translucent, some resplendently turquoise even under the most timid of suns. The actual "land" is a different entity altogether, and an evanescent one for most of the year. I imagined it—for that was all I could do—as myriad soggy colorful meadows and shallow mosquito-stocked lakes, but I only actually witnessed it as lifeless and **cold granite dots**[iv] littering the unimaginatively bitonous—tritonous at best on a sunny day—icescape.

On land—or water, who knows?—our speedometer snuck past the 30 mph tack once or twice, but it was a short-lived thrill. Though wintery Arctic ice-scapes are generally easily amenable to speeding, tidal forces dancing underneath the ocean constantly pushed and pulled trails up and down, creating ridges and walls requiring twists and turns not unlike Formula 1 chicanes. Among them, most spectacular though immensely vexing, were 2-ton popsicles known as pres-sure ice. Near shores—where these small communities of Lilliputian locked-in icebergs appeared, grew, shrunk, and then almost vanished twice daily with the ebbing and flowing of tides—snowmobile travel was rendered labyrinthine, requiring low speed, patience, and a peripheral attention to distances that was parallel in nature to the task of merging onto a gridlocked parkway.

All of this slipping and sliding around was a fun adventure, and it had a point too. Jon and I had been pursuing the opportunity to go camping in the Arctic since we had discovered its popularity on our earlier trip to the Mackenzie Delta, in the Northwest Territories. For the thermally unadven-turous, Arctic camping seems like an unconscionable thing to do, but for

---

iv. http://lifeoffgrid.ca/wp-content/uploads/2013/11/Life-Off-Grid_Nunavut_10.jpg

residents of Northern Canada it was the typically preferred way to escape the hustle and bustle of increasingly busy and conspicuously loud communities (snowmobile engines aren't as quiet as you might think).

Camping in the Arctic was a bit different in context, but not terribly dissimilar in actual practice, from "regular" camping down south. And interestingly enough, even up here it was a way of escaping the rat race. Take Iqaluit, for example, the territory's capital city. Pizza Hut, KFC, and not one but three coffee-and-donut shops of the quintessentially Canadian Tim Horton's franchise chain competed for attention with *shawarma* eateries, hotels, government offices, schools, health centers, restaurants, flower shops, and crowded four-way intersections begging for the arrival of the Eastern Arctic's first stop light. No wonder then that local women and men—like our friend Niviaqsi put it—really "needed a break" from all this every now and then.

Camping up here had a deep historical significance too. Throughout most of the twentieth century the Canadian government gradually took control of the land away from Inuit people, destabilizing their traditional semi-nomadic ways of life, and forcing upon them a sedentary existence dependent on government assistance.[11] Going out on the land was a way of regaining that control, a way of reterritorializing traditional culture by practicing once again old skills and re-building ties with place. Like all forms of camping, going out on the land worked "between mobility and fixity, locality and foreignness, temporality and permanence."[12]

Frozen Fishing

After unloading the two enormous trailer-sheds of all the camping gear— no station wagon or SUV trunk can really compete with the cargo space of a *qamutiik*—we hurried to the lake to lay down our **fishing net**[v] before nightfall. Though Timmun is said to have pulled it off by himself in his younger years, ice fishing with a net was no one-*inuk* job.

You start by excavating a hole, approximately 2 meters wide, in the snow. With as many as 2 or 3 feet of snow cleared off the icy lake surface, you begin drilling two holes immediately next to one another. You then merge the two together with a 6-foot ice chisel. Next, you shove an ice crawler into the hole and send it floating under the ice. This is the tricky part; you must listen for the crawler's metal hook rubbing against the ice from underneath and determine, from the snow-muffled sound transmitted above, where it lies. That is the precise spot where you want to dig and drill two more holes through the ice. If you guessed right the crawler should be there, so you fish it out and grab on to the rope that it carried from the first hole. That is the

v. http://lifeoffgrid.ca/wp-content/uploads/2013/11/Life-Off-Grid_Nunavut_01.jpg

rope to which the fishing net will be tied, after being **stretched**[vi] from the first to the second hole and secured in both places with a simple knot around a shovel or an ice chisel. That's it. Overnight the char will magically fill the net to reward you for your good effort.

Kristiina and Timmun's **cabin**[vii] was unpretentious and small—at 16 × 12 feet it was just big enough to accommodate cooking space, a bunk bed, and a foldout couch tucked behind the dining table. Heat was provided by a combination of a propane-fueled camping stove and an electric space heater powered by a generator. The temperature inside could get as high as 21°C (70°F). The contrast with the outside required ventilation by way of two air exchangers: simple plastic-covered openings through the wall that almost managed to stop the unrelenting condensation. All of this made for a visually arresting explosion of steam every time the door was opened, so that stepping outside not only felt, but also spectacularly looked, just as if you walked into a meat locker.

Kristiina was a gold mine of information. Listening to her camping stories made every evening fly fast, and games of Scrabble helped when the stories ran out. Camping out on the land seemed like a mix of relaxation and busyness, but even the busyness—directed at securing basic comforts and sheer survival—was playful enough to be a diversion from the daily rituals of life in town.

When you camp in a remote place you carry on as if you were playing house. Playing is marked by few rules. You must imagine the camp to be the human race's last self-reliant outpost; and you must endeavor to make your temporary dwelling as comfortable as a permanent one, but different enough from a normal home to be challenging and exciting. Good campers play the game ostentatiously, as if their reterritorialzing skill display was subject to the scrutiny of scrupulous judges. Those new to camping, or those like Jon and me who had played the game on far away territory, mostly just listen, learn, and try not to get in the way.

Uninterruptedly Timmun and Niviaqsi, like two grown children seemingly incapable of sitting down, would spin their wheels outside the cabin as if keen on corroborating our game metaphor. The small cabin's atmosphere made this possible. Cabins are hardly ever built for comfort; they are "built to motivate people to get out of doors."[13] And so our cabin did, every time bursting out in frozen vapors to dramatically underline every ingress and exit.

The first clear night gave way to a scrimmage of early morning clouds, which then quickly dissipated as the winds rose. Temperatures hovered in the -20s with the wind chill. After a hearty breakfast of bannock and raspberry jam, it was time to check the net. It was a simple enough job that even

---

[vi.] http://lifeoffgrid.ca/wp-content/uploads/2013/11/Life-Off-Grid_Nunavut_02.jpg
[vii.] http://lifeoffgrid.ca/wp-content/uploads/2013/11/Life-Off-Grid_Nunavut_04.jpg

two clumsy southerners like us were allowed to help. It was fun too. After ensuring that the first hole was free of any cutting edge we pulled the net out of the ice in its entirety while Timmun, in dramatic suspense, recorded the outcome with his iPad for later posting onto Facebook.

The fish were still alive but visibly fatigued from a long night of wrangling with the nylon net, then shocked by the sudden exposure to the cold air. Quickly, un violently, **they passed**.[viii] We untangled 16 the first morning, **and then more**[ix] at sundown and in the following days, until we reached the contented conclusion that five dozen took enough space on our *qamutiik*.

Arctic char tasted like a genial pastiche of Pacific salmon's delicately sweet flesh and lake trout's juicy and tender meat. It was at its best eaten raw, chunked into steaks cut sideways or into long fillets cut lengthwise and salted overnight. Kristiina taught us to make the rubbery skin optional, carve each bite sashimi-style, and then dip the pieces into lemon pepper or soy sauce. At the **messy table**[x] we all agreed that one of the best things about camping was eating good food.

Though no more than 200 meters away there was a small cluster of cabins, six in total, no *illugalaq* other than ours received visitors during the time we were there. Alleviated of the responsibility to exchange a salvo of small talk with neighbors, hunt for a wireless signal, or catch the six o'clock news, Iqalugaaqjuit felt—and the more so as time went on—like a lunar substation where life could stand still and silent. And perhaps such was one of the greatest appeals of camping: the incontrovertible sensation that you were *here, and nowhere else*. The mobility and vagrancy enabled by growingly omnipresent media of communication ends abruptly at camp. It's temporary, to be sure, but the unplugging of that TV, computer, and mobile phone root us deeply—even if only for a short span of time—in a distinct place. The reterritorialization of camping locates us, gives us a place to call our own, and gives a sense of the here and the now.

And here you could unmistakably perceive that the Arctic tundra had a strange way of acting. Its few visible traces—the odd raven, bear, wolf, **white Ptarmigan**,[xi] or fox—would go about the land reservedly, looking disconcertedly surprised every time you spotted them. But the Arctic tundra was not as inhospitable as it's reputed to be. Far from being a bleak, desolate, or barren wasteland, it was more like a very large pond in which it was remarkably easy to be a big fish. It was as if the tundra wished to cast a spotlight on every little animal, plant, and human life that managed to find its way there. As if it wanted to say, "here you are the main feature, this is your chance to be a star."

[viii] http://lifeoffgrid.ca/wp-content/uploads/2013/11/Life-Off-Grid_Nunavut_03.jpg
[ix] http://lifeoffgrid.ca/wp-content/uploads/2013/11/Life-Off-Grid_Nunavut_07.jpg
[x] http://lifeoffgrid.ca/wp-content/uploads/2013/11/Life-Off-Grid_Nunavut_08.jpg
[xi] http://lifeoffgrid.ca/wp-content/uploads/2013/11/Life-Off-Grid_Nunavut_11.jpg

One afternoon, as we shadowed Timmun's skidoo-powered zigzags in a fruitless search for caribou tracks, I came to the realization that I had been wrong all along about the "land." The granite rocks that I proclaimed guilty of rendering the icescape featureless with their redundant shapes and unimaginative traits turned out to be much richer upon close inspection. As Timmun exploited their patterns in the course of wayfinding through the island's interior, I began to appreciate the rocks' diverse characteristics: the charcoal ones, darkened by a fungus named tripe; the verdant ones, vegetated by a lichen capable of keeping caribou alive in the winter; and the reddish-beige ones, shrouded in a blood-like splattering of a microscopic plant whose identity I questioned ignorantly. And more than just eye candy for my color-starved sight, the rocks also held enough solar warmth to serve as temporary stools in an otherwise seat-deprived place. Once, upon sitting down, I nodded dreamingly to the rocks as if to apologize to them—they too played their part eloquently here. I too was beginning to find that our camp was more than a site. It was a place.

Though we caught no caribou we netted plenty of fish. Eight- and ten-pound char came to the surface not only by way of the holes dug for our nets but also via smaller bores pierced for the leisurely pursuit of jigging. "Some people can jig from morning to night when they go camping," Kristiina pointed out after I admitted defeat, puzzled at the whole bloody thing.

The fun, I was told, was in seeing the fish. To make eye contact with the scaly beasts you had to be comfortable enough with shoving your head down the ice hole in order to shield away the glare from the milky sky. Neither Jon nor I were able to lie down for too long on the snow, stomach first, and seduce the poor things with morsels of orange peel and then clobber them in the head. Overcome by claustrophobia and by empathy for the vitamin C-starved vertebrates, while the rest of the gang jigged away I spent my time wandering about the place, fascinated by the supine dedication of my fellow campers as much as by the arrival onstage of an unexpected star above: an overhead jet.

The Arctic is a busy place these days. Many of us have indeed travelled above it, at 36,000 feet of altitude, en route to Europe or North America. I spotted my first plane the second afternoon at the lake. "Taken aback" does a half-decent job at capturing my bewildered feeling. Curiously, as the plane zoomed by, I began wondering whether anyone from the cabin of the wide-bodied jet could see me. I knew they couldn't, but I badly wanted them to notice me, to wonder what I was doing, whether I was lost.

Then something eerie happened: I saw myself.

From down there I spotted myself on that very plane: pausing the movie playing on my personal monitor to lift the curtain to see where I was. And from up there I laid eyes on myself, staring back from all the way below.

"What are you doing?" I asked.

"Why did you step out of the plane, don't you know you're not supposed to?"

"Why are you there, instead of home with your family?"

"What are you trying to prove?"

"Are you trying to show off?"

In my defense I mumbled away a few accounts. I said I wasn't there to show off. I said I wasn't even there because I found this place particularly comforting, at least in comparison to my home. I explained that maybe I too just needed to be out in the open, on the land, off-the-grid, away from the tank farms, North Marts, and busy co-op stores of northern towns. And as I rambled on, I finally found my line.

"I'm just here for the quiet," I stated solemnly, and convinced myself of it.

It was loud in Cape Dorset, with its snowmobiles. It was loud in Iqaluit with all its airplanes. It was loud everywhere, with cars, ferry boats, people, dogs, and everything else clamoring for attention: "Me, me, me, watch out for me, here's my pic, here's my update, here's my tweet!"—everyone screamed, all the time, everywhere.

Instead, it was comfortingly quiet here: a sonic emptiness, an explosion of quiet deadened by snow, choked by ice, walled-in by cold rock, and wrapped in beaver fur.

As the jet quietly streaked away and the sky's depth eventually muted her engines, I was once again in possession of the exclusive power to control and order noise. I was the only sovereign territorial power over silence. The only one with the sonorous might to make snow crackle, to chisel ice, and to let out a loud and obnoxious sneeze. It was only me: the star of a stage whose ears were all mine, a big fish in the largest, but most unscripted pond on this planet. There and then, while camping out on the land, I had found respite from the electric buzz, the noise of words and thoughts, and the cacophony of our busy world. For in the end camping out on the land, not unlike off-grid living, was simply a pursuit of rejuvenating peace and quiet.

Oh, and . . . no need to jump and run. It was just a cute Arctic fox.

Notes

1. Hailey, 2008.
2. Hailey, 2009:4.
3. Brereton, 2010:12.
4. Hailey, 2009.
5. Brereton, 2010.
6. Hailey, 2008:2.
7. Hailey, 2008.
8. deLanda, 2006; Deleuze and Guattari, 1972.
9. Hailey, 2008:1.
10. Brereton, 2010:61.
11. See Damas, 2002.
12. Hailey, 2008:1.
13. Brereton, 2010:12.

Judy With Goats.[i]

[i.] For more photos, visit lifeoffgrid.ca.

12

The New Quietism

For our first interview on Prince Edward Island we switched our usual roles: we—not the other way around—took care of answering the questions. A CBC Radio host did all the asking. This wasn't the first time. Over two years of fieldwork, Jon and I met with scores of journalists across the country to reveal the most interesting stories and discuss the practical pros and cons of off-grid living. Though we were actively seeking out publicity for our public ethnography,[1] and though we fully understood the timeliness and newsworthiness of research on renewable energy, the sheer volume of media attention had surprised us from the very beginning. Time after time, our journeys across the provinces would yield anywhere from a half dozen to a dozen radio appearances, print media stories, and TV news reports.

We mainly attributed such intense media attention to the "human interest" element of our work: the "colorful characters" (as journalists would often put it) that we met, and the many off-of-the-beaten-path and unique places we travelled through. But, more broadly, it was obvious that off-grid living held a great deal of public appeal and that most people were curious about it, with more than a few even keen on eventually trying it out themselves. The popularity of the topic wasn't always good, however. As part of the process of dealing with news media from all walks of life, we had noticed that journalists liked to play in particular a pair of different but closely related "angles" to make their stories appealing to their readers. At first, this reporting bias annoyed us. Then, over time, we learned to exploit those presumptions to better portray on our own terms the ethnographic knowledge we wanted to share. In other words, we learned to hijack those angles.

The first of these two angles was the "hermit" myth. Journalists and much of the general public alike somehow assumed that off-gridders were recluse, antisocial, and isolated from the rest of the world. One of the most common questions that revealed this attitude was the recurring, "How do you even find these people if they're off the grid?" "Well," I would shock inquirers with a flippant reply, "I Google them and then I email them." Being off-grid did not preclude someone from being online or having a phone, radio, or television. Most off-gridders were not hermits at all, and by aggressively defeating that stereotype we would give journalists an easy—and, more importantly, insightful and truthful—headline to focus on.

Of all communication media, off-gridders in fact enjoyed the internet the most. We knew this well in advance of what happened one spring evening on Prince Edward Island, but the events of that day drove this point home well enough to outright ridicule any further hermit stereotypes.

While at our off-grid **cabin at Goose River**,[ii] on the eastern end of the island, every evening at **dusk**[iii] dozens, perhaps hundreds, of the loudest crickets would punctually break out in a discordant chorus, shrilling at a pitch so high that no jumbo jet could match. The noise was short-lived—perhaps half an hour at most—and therefore not annoying at all but rather quaint enough to be enchanting. Even more captivating was the fact that the little critters were utterly invisible, despite our best efforts to locate them in the **swampy area**[iv] near our cabin and photograph them as they presumably hopped from blade of grass to blade of grass.

One day, intrigued more than ever by the ruckus, Jon decided to record the crickets' cacophonous performance with his video camera. I happened to be Skypeing my family back home and having a difficult time communicating through the noise. Then, in a matter of minutes, Jon quickly edited a **short video**[v] and posted it on Facebook, just to be cute and funny. Within moments, an off-gridder whom we had met during our fieldwork in Ontario Facebooked Jon to correct him. It was not crickets we heard, she was adamant, but actually spring peepers: a species of small frogs. To double check, we Googled spring peepers—beasts unknown to our eyes and ears—and played a sound clip of their chirping. Or better yet, croaking. It was a perfect

[ii] http://lifeoffgrid.ca/wp-content/uploads/2013/11/Life-Off-Grid_Prince-Edward-Island_06.jpg

[iii] http://lifeoffgrid.ca/wp-content/uploads/2013/11/Life-Off-Grid_Prince-Edward-Island_05.jpg

[iv] http://lifeoffgrid.ca/wp-content/uploads/2013/11/Life-Off-Grid_Prince-Edward-Island_04.jpg

[v] https://vimeo.com/42330830

match. The mystery was solved. While the little critters were fascinating enough in and of themselves, the instantaneous act of communication between off-grid homes—situated in remote rural communities across the country to boot—felt simply mind-boggling. Off-grid homes were far from being recluse hideouts, and thanks to vivid stories like this one more than a few journalists managed to bust the hermit off-gridder stereotype.

Despite the baselessness of the myth, we knew very well that Canada had its fair share of off-grid homes where neither communication media nor electricity at all could be found. Until our arrival on Prince Edward Island, we had run across only two offline households, but unsurprisingly both had electricity. So, when a local gatekeeper told us about Walter and his internet-free, TV-free, and most notably electricity-free home, we did not wait a single minute to make the long drive across the island.

Non-Users

We arrived at Walter's house at 11 o'clock in the morning, accompanied by Rob, one of our local gatekeepers. Rob thought it would be a good idea to accompany us to Walter's, despite the fact that his house was extremely easy to find, even with the most basic directions. He preferred to introduce us personally, he stressed, and hang out with us at Walter's place for a few minutes. "I'll leave shortly after if everything is ok," he said, putting us somewhat on edge.

Rob's loud knocks on Walter's front door were met with silence. Nervous with anticipation, we held our ground a few steps back; the 10 seconds of un-answering quiet seemingly dragging on forever.

"His car is not here. He must be out," Ron guessed. "This is the time of the day when he occasionally drives to town to run errands."

"Ok. What should we do then?"

"Hang out for a while and come and get me again in an hour or so."

"Ok. Are you sure? I mean, we know where the house is now and . . ."

"No, I'll go with you," Rob insisted, adding fuel to our fire. Why was he so bent on coming along? Did he doubt us? Or Walter?

The next hour passed languidly, our intimidation growing with every minute. As the clock finally struck noon we repeated the process from the start. Again: no answer.

Moments later, Walter quietly surfaced from his workshop's door. "How's it going, Walter?" Rob inquired. "Are you busy right now? These are the folks from BC that I told you about." We ambled toward him, shook hands, and introduced ourselves. Copious sweat drowned my forehead. Walt mumbled "hello," with a confused look. Sensing surprise and perturbation, I explained very gingerly our reason for being there and launched into the informed consent ritual. We generally made introductory contact with interviewees and "read them their rights" well in advance of showing up at the doorstep, but in this case no such option had been available.

"Oh yes, I remember now. That's fine," he said. "Come on in, I have nothing to hide, I enjoy visiting with people." We walked up the creaking wooden stairs to his workshop as he held the door open. The large, rectangular-shaped, dimly lit building was filled with a **melee**[vi] of old machinery, discarded TV sets, gardening tools, junk-filled containers, and tables overcrowded with tools, parts, and flotsam and jetsam dating from each of the last five decades. Heaps of sawdust were scattered everywhere on the floor, and a faint smell of mildew and WD-40 infused the air. It was a photographer's paradise and Jon wasted no time in drawing out his piece and firing **shots**.[vii] As he did that, Rob began to chitchat with Walt, while I endeavored to orient myself and gather my thoughts.

Walt wore a blue and black flannel shirt and dark denims. He also had an indigo ball cap, eyeglasses, and a bushy gray beard, which together with his hunched posture made him difficult to scrutinize. I surmised he was in his late sixties. His benign manners had quickly dissipated our feelings of intimidation, though his old-time island accent and mordant one-line answers to our queries still had us feeling uneasy. If there is one thing that I hate more than asking an interviewee to repeat their words, it is long drawn-out moments of awkward silence, and alas both were aplenty. Together with Rob we managed to hurl a few rapid questions about what he was currently working on, just to keep the conversation going. It turned out he was fixing a broken-down weed-whacker. More meaningful inquiries ensued. Wisely, Jon, who had more experience with World Englishes than I, sheathed his camera away and took it upon himself to lead the dialogue. Rob, in the meantime, liked what he saw and excused himself.

Walter had no electricity and that had been the case for some time. A wind turbine he used to own had broken down, and though he planned on fixing it, he was still in the midst of saving the necessary funds. Unbothered by the absence of electricity, Walt used a kerosene lamp to make the light he needed in order to read at nighttime. The rest of the day was kept simple, "real simple." "That's the way it used to be," he observed, "it was fine back in the day when there was no choice, so why wouldn't it be fine now?" (Ironically, that's the very same reason I give to people for not owning a cell

---

vi. http://lifeoffgrid.ca/wp-content/uploads/2013/11/Life-Off-Grid_Prince-Edward-Island_08.jpg

vii. http://lifeoffgrid.ca/wp-content/uploads/2013/11/Life-Off-Grid_Prince-Edward-Island_09.jpg

phone). Things get more and more complicated, he went on, cost more and more money, and then break down. And what's the point? The voluntary simplicity principles underlying his argument revealed him to be reflexive and informed, far from the simpleton his unsophisticated cadence would have given him off to be.

Walter grew up on a farm with his family, less than 10 miles away from where he resided now. It was a mixed farm—they grew a little bit of everything, unlike the potato-obsessed crops of today's PEI. He moved to his current house 30 years ago. Back then you'd hardly see a car in these parts, he recounted. It got busier and busier with time, especially with the growth of tourism and the wind industry. The hum of the **large turbines**[viii] generating grid electricity near his house—PEI notably depends on wind energy for about one-fifth of its electricity needs—didn't bother him one bit and he thought highly of their effort to produce clean power. In fact, he said, it was much better to get power from the wind than to rely on oil. While he didn't think of himself as an environmentalist, he made it a point of not owning a gasoline generator and he planned on investing in a 1-kW off-grid system—part wind and part solar.

As for television, he was more interested in the challenge of fixing the innards of TV sets than in watching their content. "Too much grief," he said, dismissing news coverage wholesale in three words. "I don't need it." The internet did not hold much appeal either. "People don't mind their own business on that thing," he stated laconically—and if he referred to the Web 2.0 his critique was perfectly adequate too. "I listen to CBC Radio all the time, though, day and night."

Homes, like all kinds of places, are not necessarily tied to location. Communication, information, energy, water, and many other flows entangle domestic environments in far-reaching powerful webs. A house is not a container but a "membrane," "a filter of exteriorities continually entering it and traversing it." "Awash in transitivity the home is a node in an indefinitely extended field of immanence, to which the technologies of transmission give body."[2] To sever those flows as extensively as Walter had done was a way of engaging in a reactionary "politics of connectivity"[3] in an attempt to anchor his house in this location.

Going off-the-grid was then like moving away. If migrating is a way of "voting with one's feet," going off-the-grid as Walter had done was a way of voting with one's walls: locking one's domestic membrane away from the flows and inputs of the broader society, and sheltering it from the global exteriorities otherwise constantly traversing it.

[viii.] http://lifeoffgrid.ca/wp-content/uploads/2013/11/Life-Off-Grid_Prince-Edward-Island_07.jpg

The vocabulary of self-sufficiency held no appeal for Walter. He drank "just a little bit" of alcohol, and cooked himself store-bought "fish, meat, and potatoes." For that, he used a woodstove in the winter and a propane-based one in the summer. He had no refrigerator—an ice box did the job—so his food was always fresh from the nearby grocer's. During winter the ice box in which he kept perishables sat outside in the cold, whereas during summer and spring he shopped for ice twice a week. He didn't mind this system too much, but if he ever got around to installing solar panels or a new wind turbine—he said with a yearning smile—the first and only electrical treat he'd get would be . . . a refrigerator. We all had a hearty laugh at that.

"Would you get anything else?" I asked.

"No, that's all I need," he muttered.

Outside I had spotted really old-looking twin solar panels, unusually pointing straight east, right underneath a strangely shaped moss-covered satellite dish.

"I noticed that you have solar panels and a satellite dish. Did those things work at some point?"

"No, you didn't," he stumped me.

"I didn't?" I thought with a funny look on my face. Jon glanced at me funny from behind his viewfinder. Neither solar panels nor satellite dish worked. Had the solar array functioned it would have only generated about 200 watts or so. Currently also out of order was his plumbing, and as a result there was no running water in the house. The source of groundwater would otherwise have been a 60-foot-deep well. He had to get around to solving the problem, as normally the water he'd pump would be enough for his needs. The water would then be heated on his woodstove and that's how he'd wash himself, whereas the "laundryman" took care of washing his clothes. In the absence of running water, he borrowed water from a nearby provincial agency, where he would occasionally take a shower too. Walt seemed unperturbed about all this; he looked as if he had a million projects to complete in his garage, including restoring TVs, engines, and taking apart other pieces of machinery for scraps—like two 1950-era metal panels sitting obtrusively in his front yard. He received a pension, but he could always use some extra cash and maybe that was how he generated it. Or maybe he just did that out of vocation, we could not tell for sure.

Walter was quite different from all the off-gridders we had met. Neither particularly well educated nor driven by an articulately critical philosophy, he was difficult to frame into our existing lens on the off-grid lifeworld. Yet, the more I struggled to comprehend his speech, the more I realized that my inability to peg him into a pre-existing category was merely lexical. Walt may not have cited classics of voluntary simplicity or political autonomism, but his ideas jelled with those ideologies like lobster and butter. For those reasons he was a "non-user"[4]—in a spectacular sense of the term.

Non-users are non-adopters of a particular technology: people who choose not to own or utilize a consumer object or service. Non-users are a diverse group. For some the non-adoption of a particular technology is driven by lack of interest and perceived advantage.[5] For others non-adoption is the result of historical patterns of social and individual difference and exclusion.[6] For other people non-using is part of a motivated countercultural stance. Cyclists who refuse to own a car, for example, do so in order to reduce their carbon footprint and to protest against the dominance of the automobile and against environmental degradation.[7] Then there are non-users whose non-adoption of a particular technology originates in lack of skills or knowledge. Several individuals who have never been on the web, for example, perceive themselves to be insufficiently proficient with computers.[8]

Walt had both the skills and enough financial means to bring communication media into his house, but he chose not to. He owned a car, for example—a mid- to late- 2000 domestic model that he had recently bought. But he chose not to travel much. The last time he went off island was at least two years ago, when he journeyed to Halifax to visit family. "Too many strangers, too many dope peddlers, too many people you can't trust," he concluded in his unsympathetic review of the city. Much more trustworthy were his friends at the nearby provincial agency and one of his neighbors, who checked up on him regularly.

Without a phone to call for help he knew these friendships were crucial. Telephones can be useful but they are just too much trouble to own, he reflected. He used to have a telephone back in the day when there were still party lines. People would stick their noses into his business, and that bothered him to no end. "No privacy," he found. "You'd pick up the phone and you'd hear a click—someone else was getting on the line," for the sole purpose of eavesdropping. That turned him off the whole telecommunication business and he never felt the need to have that in his house again.

Off-gridders were non-users of centrally generated and distantly managed electricity and natural gas. That much we knew from the definition of the term. But throughout our travels we had learned that many of them also chose not to use, or at least to use very selectively, communication technologies as well. Though the internet was nearly always present in off-grid homes, television wasn't. Only about a quarter of 175 off-gridders had a cable or satellite TV subscription. Well more than half had a TV set, but they used it only for DVDs. In a society dominated by the logic of light, speed, power, instantaneous information, and the virtual mobility afforded by connectivity,[9] to be as "unplugged" as deeply as Walt was constituted a revolutionary move.

Fifty minutes into our visit with Walt I started to get the feeling that his vernacular one-liners were all the data we could get out of him. I decided to make a bold move and asked him, with a sense of trepidation, whether he could give us a tour of his house. His workshop, after all, only held so much interest to us.

"I wasn't expecting you this morning, so I haven't cleaned up," he answered embarrassedly.

"But that's ok," I replied, trying my luck with a joke, "it's more realistic that way, isn't it?"

His reply was inaudible, then silence followed. Jon turned around toward me—while Walt looked away focused on his weed-whacker—and shook his head quickly. I took my hints and decided it was time to thank him for his hospitality.

"Yes, t'was my pleasure, come again some other time. I'll have my wind turbine up by then."

Lifestyle Migrants

The next off-grid stereotype we wanted to debunk was the hippie myth. Not that there is anything wrong with being one, but most of the off-gridders we met would have denied being hippies. And yet, many members of the general public and several journalists alike were surprised to hear that today's off-gridders were no flower children. "There is a crucial difference between 1970s hippies or back-to-the-landers of that day and contemporary off-gridders," I explained every time.

The day after our meeting with Walt we had an equally unforgettable visit. Jim and Judy's **farm**,[ix] well hidden at the end of a 1-kilometer-long driveway, sat amidst a field of short grasses caressed by a cool ocean breeze. After ensuring their manically hyperactive dog was more interested in playing catch than in blood-drenched guarding, we slowly stepped outside our rental car and immediately spotted Jim on a small tractor, mowing grass in his gorgeous blonde horses' pen. Judy was inside waiting for us, he hollered over the tractor's loud engine, and he'd soon join us too.

There are two basic groups of people on PEI: locals and CFAs. You are a local if your family has lived here for five or six generations. And if not, you are a CFA: a "Come From Away." Jim and Judy were CFAs, we learned as we sat down at their living room table, with the warm early afternoon sun

ix. http://lifeoffgrid.ca/wp-content/uploads/2013/11/Life-Off-Grid_Prince-Edward-Island_14.jpg

shining through the large south-facing windows. They had migrated here
from Guelph, Ontario, to follow a dream. They had *escaped* here—more precisely—shortly after 9/11, fed-up with their "meaningless" lives filled with
Saturday afternoon car washes, military and corporate careers, and empty
preoccupations with "matching countertop colors and kitchen accessories."

"I found my lifestyle in the suburbs too . . ." Hong-Kong-born **Judy**[x]
pondered pensively in search of the right word, made to sound even more
impeccable by her polished British English accent, ". . .robotic; as if we were
part of a cult, without wanting to be part of it."

Jim quit his job on that fateful September day. His branch manager
refused to listen to his insistent request that employees be sent home to
be with their families while towers crumbled and planes fell out of the sky.
That display of corporate insensitivity was the last straw. While Jim took a
new temporary job as a groundskeeper, together he and Judy painstakingly
weighed their escape options. Then one night, while Judy was fast asleep,
Jim stumbled across a property for sale on the internet—the property was
on West PEI. A former non-commissioned military officer—Jim was a
man of few but deliberately chosen words and clear decisions—he briskly
woke Judy from the bed, consulted with her, and bid on the property on
a whim.

Jim and Judy were prime examples of what anthropologists, geographers,
and sociologists call amenity migrants or lifestyle migrants.[10] Lifestyle
migrants move not out of economic necessity but out of choice for a different way of life; they wish to begin anew, to start over, and to reinvent
themselves.[11] These often highly educated and financially stable individuals
are known to move to warmer and gentler places, often far and abroad, but
the promises of a lifestyle migration can often be found even within one's
own country.[12]

Just about all the Canadian off-gridders we met on our journeys were
invariably seeking the amenities that many other lifestyle migrants sought
elsewhere in the world, whether in Costa Rica or in Costa del Sol: a slower
pace of life in tune with natural rhythms, a more intimate communion with
place and the natural environment, the opportunity to be one's own boss or
to enjoy retirement or semi-retirement, a more basic or "simpler" form of
living, and the time to downshift and dedicate oneself to one's hobbies and
passions.[13]

If buying property half a continent away without as much as a quick visit
seemed absurd, seeing the newly purchased land for the first time struck
Jim and Judy as even more surreal. "There was absolutely nothing here, just

---

[x.] http://lifeoffgrid.ca/wp-content/uploads/2013/11/Life-Off-Grid_Prince-Edward-
Island_13.jpg

trees," Judy smiled. "My dad—who was here with me—felt like we were in the Burmese jungle." Judy's father, sitting at the table next to her, smiled as he heard Judy tell the story. Nevertheless, up for the challenge, they immediately cleared space for the driveway and a lot for the house. The internet taught them how to build their new home with the lumber from the trees they cut. A few conversations with local renewable energy suppliers gave them the additional knowledge needed to set up a small hybrid system—solar and wind—to power their domestic needs. Next thing you know their teenage daughter—literally pulled from a "normal" suburban life filled with swimming lessons and shopping mall outings—was furnished with homemade snowshoes to trek to the end of their snowy driveway and sent to school out in the country. "She wasn't impressed."

Though they articulated it in different tones, Walter and Jim and Judy shared a common aspiration for a better way of life. Walter's quest was for a simple way of living unencumbered by unnecessary technologies, uncomplicated by material possessions, and undisturbed by the "grief" carried by communication media and the rest of the world, dope-peddlers and all. Jim and Judy's pursuit was instead focused on a more sophisticated practice of healthy and sustainable living, mixed with a DIW ethic and a critical stance toward consumerism and corporate greed. But both households, in the end, sought nothing but quiet and peace of mind.

Just like them, so many other Canadians had moved off-the-grid to get away from a postmodern culture and neo-liberal society that constantly spreads its tentacles farther and farther into private homes and personal lives through its seductive images of "the good life." A good life that is, unfortunately, also superficial, commodified, and unsustainable. And what they found by moving away was often the same—an alternative, semi-autonomous, and protected zone: a "stilled" place feeling like a refuge from the dromophilia of the outer world,[14] an oasis, and a safe haven of personal authenticity. This stillness was a pause, a bracketing, a friction in the onflow of everyday life.[15] It was a "willful unmoving" that took "a stand" as a "counterpoint to the nomadic metaphysics of flow."[16]

Similar to the "hippie" generation that "dropped out" of mainstream society in the late 1960s and 1970s and sought a better life by getting back-to-the-land,[17] modern-day off-gridders chose to disconnect from "the grid" and all "it" stood for in a Quietist attempt to take control of their personal lives and take care of themselves and their families. "Quietism" is an old doctrine. Within both Christianity and Islam, Quietism refers to a retreatist withdrawal from political affairs motivated by disinterest and skepticism in one's ability to affect change. Instead of open rebellion toward heresy and sin, and instead of militantly pushing for collective amelioration, religious

Quietists generally sought personal serenity by way of contemplative still-ness and communion with God.

Quietism is a label that was also applied to the 1970s back-to-the-landers who abdicated their former activist commitments to social change and sought instead personal peace in rural refuges.[18] In their case, godly devotion was generally substituted with variably intense pantheist forms of mysticism and non-institutionalized spiritualism. Like their 1970s counterparts, Canadian off-gridders had obvious Quietist-like tenden-cies. Disenchanted with mainstream living, neo-liberalism, consumerism, large institutions, the power of the state to affect change, and many of the currently available political alternatives, off-gridders sought personal contentment by migrating to idyllic and peaceful surrounds away from grief and noise. In these spaces they took care of their own existence by cultivating peace and quiet, and by rarely engaging in direct, collective struggles.

In contrast to the Quietist godly devotion and mysticism of earlier back-to-the-landers, these "New Quietists" simply drew great sensual enjoyment from the secular pleasures of life and the comforts and conveniences of renewable energy and domestic technologies. And instead of the asceticism of earlier Quietists, as we have seen, New Quietists practiced an alternative hedonism that valued sources of pleasure that were as sustainable and as local as possible—sources of pleasure that had been carefully wrestled away from the production and distribution networks of global capitalism. So, in short, off-gridders were no hippies.

Then again, no off-gridders defined themselves as New Quietists, of course. New Quietism was not an existing movement, but rather an idea we made up: a creative name that encompassed very diverse lifestyles and many different quests for a better way of life. New Quietism therefore was not a structured ideology, but rather a series of practical "tactics"[19] through which off-gridders reshaped relations with distant exteriorities, chipping away at the dominant infrastructures of consumption without challenging them head-on. Through their artful ways of "making do,"[20] off-gridders across Canada merely created domestic spaces where they enjoyed a safe remove from "the law of a foreign power."[21] There, they took some degree of autonomy,[22] building contained alternative power constellations in which they sought and often found, if nothing else, per-sonal fulfillment.

Again these were modest, but meaningful and powerful, tactics. Generating clean electricity, creating heat through renewable resources, growing organic food, harvesting water, and minimizing waste were just some of the many ways in which New Quietists drew gratification from their lifestyle. And so, through their tactics and their enjoyment of all the amenities they managed to obtain responsibly and often renewably, New Quietist off-gridders indirectly offered the rest of us constructive answers to global problems generated by shortsighted consumerism. Their cultivation of peace, quiet, and stillness "as a capacity to do things" thus posed "a solution to the problems of consumption, movement, and activity . . . and a powerful trope for environmental, economic and ethical sustainability."[23]

In Search of Stillness

The coffee percolator had been gurgling on the two-burner propane stove for a while, but first there was a story to finish. Seated tensely on the edge of their kitchen table chairs, Jim and Judy spoke with heavy hearts and sharp words. They had a sobering perspective on off-grid living they wanted to tell the world about, they said. Driving to their place that morning I had a feeling this would be the case, as I knew their house was up for sale. Their lifestyle plan, as it turned out, had a serious kink and they were right in the midst of considering another lifestyle change, but this one deeply unwanted. It was the first time we had come in direct contact with the disillusions of off-grid living. I was well aware that no off-gridder found their life to be perfect, of course, and in the past I had even managed to find and interview a few individuals who had given up on off-grid living for health, work, or other practical reasons. But never before had Jon and I witnessed a dream imploding right before our eyes.

With a small military pension to serve as a steady cash flow, all that Jim and Judy initially had to worry about was generating a small but meaningful income from their off-grid eco-tourism business. A lovely wooden cabin had been built to accommodate visitors interested in a bucolic energy-independent getaway, and an educational and health program—inclusive of horse-assisted therapy and organic agricultural teachings—had been put in place. A well-designed website and a thorough marketing plan had been launched. But this was West PEI: not exactly the kind of place you stumble upon on your way to Disney World. The world from which they had run away had never bothered to show up at their doorstep, or at least not in sufficient numbers. The people who had come were touched and perhaps forever changed, especially the children, Judy explained, but it wasn't enough. Soon afterward both Jim and Judy had to take up full-time jobs in town to make up for the missing cash flow. And with that adjustment their off-grid lifestyle had forever changed.

As the oblivious rooster continued to chant blissfully outside, Judy excused herself to finally fill her cup of coffee. The small and laborious camp-style propane stove was just one of the many inconveniences they were no longer tolerant enough to endure. Coping with the many infant-like demands of an off-grid homestead was troublesome enough when they had time to spare, but it was simply unbearable after they had resorted to making time for paid employment too. With every day that Jim and Judy worked away from home, their everyday life became more and more exhausting, their domestic technologies more uncooperative, and their busy rhythms increasingly discordant with the natural cycles they had sought. Moreover, Judy's father had fallen ill and had moved in with them, he too needing their attention. All that just couldn't go on much longer.

It was almost time for lunch. We reassured our hosts that we were in no rush. They had a long story they wanted us to document. It was an aggravating narrative filled with upsetting turns of events. There were "$2,000 bills here, $2,000 upgrade estimates there," Jim recounted, "there is something about that number, everything seems to cost no less than $2,000." And with every expense came more disheartening realizations and broken promises. The plot was thick: a solar hot water collector that never worked, which caused Judy to take "bird baths" with stove-warmed water and Jim to shower at work; a tiny and inefficient woodstove, which would force them to wake up to an alarm call in the middle of the night to restock it; a greater reliance on purchasing propane and ready-cut firewood, which challenged their values of self-sufficiency; and a temperamental groundwater **well and plumbing system**,[xi] which required aggressive monitoring and harsh conservation practices. "It's just too much," Judy confided, sounding hurt and deflated. "We came here for a simpler life, and what's simpler about this? Absolutely nothing."

It was a tough pill to swallow for Jon and me too. Our encounters with off-gridders had been so uniformly upbeat and positive that at times it was hard to remember that centrally generated heat and electricity could be a good thing for anyone. Our fledgling impression of the lifestyle had been positive but balanced up to that point, but now more than ever it was evident that off-grid assemblages weren't going to work under every circumstance, and that the lifestyle they enabled was at times deeply limiting and constraining. Jim and Judy's reminder that it was very difficult for a busy dual-earning couple to find the time to take care of off-grid domestic duties had also challenged both of our personal dreams to get off-the-grid with

---

[xi.] http://lifeoffgrid.ca/wp-content/uploads/2013/11/Life-Off-Grid_Prince-Edward-Island_12.jpg

our respective families one day. I quietly ate the sandwiches that Judy had prepared, absorbed in reflective thought.

In large part, the cause of Jim and Judy's troubles could be attributed to the destination of their lifestyle migration. Despite its beauty, West PEI was not a prime tourist site. Because of its limited development for sizeable tourist flows, Jim and Judy could never sufficiently profit from the place where they sought escape. They had just gone too far. Without relocating very far at all, Walter might have gone too far too. His non-use of electricity and many communication media had obviously caused him some degree of inconvenience and created a somewhat uncomfortable level of isolation, which was particularly risky at his age in case of a health emergency.

You may try to seek them, but pure stillness and remove are impossible to achieve. The ideal—the very aspiration—of stillness and remove was irresistibly motivating, and that's why most off-gridders dreamed the world could be slowed down and maybe even stopped and forgotten in the right slice of paradise. But by moving farther and farther away from the rest of the society, in the end, it was easy to need it more. Stilling can never be an utter separation, a final severing, a complete disconnection. Stilling simply "institutes a connection,"[24] creating the conditions for newer, different relations. The New Quietist quest for stillness had its obvious shortcomings, disillusions, risks, and challenges. Stillness, like other forms of immobility[25] was always relative and inevitably characterized by multiple flows, contradictions, compromises, and tensions. Stillness could never quite be a full "gesture of refusal."[26]

Like Jim and Judy, off-gridders all over Canada had plenty of reasons to be enamored with their idyllic islands of peace and quiet. But by disconnecting from distant providers of power, heat, and water, off-grid households invariably took on a great deal of domestic work that on-grid households need not tackle. Work like collecting wood, growing food, maintaining fickle technologies in stable working conditions, tending to repairs and regular maintenance, monitoring water, and exercising patience when resources were not available, not working, or not affordable could take a serious toll on anyone. To boot, by moving far away from urban centers, off-gridders exposed themselves to the risk of isolation, which challenged them in case of emergencies and financial need. So, despite their skillful quest for a more self-sufficient and simpler way of living, it was common for off-gridders to experience a greater deal of mundane challenges than the rest of us. While these demands were generally met with unwavering resolve and often even embraced as a necessary part of life, off-grid living was more laborious and time-consuming than some people would like their domestic life to be.[27]

Off-grid lifestyle migrants were able to carve out stilled safe havens by strategically adopting New Quietist tactics and by assembling unique power constellations. By doing so they achieved various degrees of the peace, quiet, stillness, harmony with place, contentment, slowness, simplicity, and serenity they aspired to. But their homes were neither fully autonomous from the ills and the perils of the world they left behind nor immune to its forces. Off-gridders' quest for remove and stillness—just like many other lifestyle migrants' quest for a sea change—always came with a revealing lesson. No act of disconnection, no remove, no escape can ever be complete. No off-grid household could last long without understanding that, in the end, no home can be an island.

We slowly walked outside to throw the dog something to chase and to give the goats and the horses somebody to show off to. A tall, grey, metal smokestack stood upright on the dark chestnut-colored roof of the house, pointing straight to an azure sky. Next to it four blades belonging to a small wind turbine rested still, on standby for a moment's whiff. I strolled with Jim toward the fence and wordlessly we together shot an eager glance at the ocean, the aroma of low tide lingering in the air. We would soon be called upon to cross that body of water, Jim to find work and an uncertain future in Alberta's tar sands, and Jon and I to drift to Newfoundland for the last leg of a long journey that had finally yielded clarity for our quest.

"You know, Jim, you could always upgrade your system and bring it up to a couple of kilowatts and make things a bit easier on yourselves . . ."

He replied with a few moments of silence, and then reminded me about that magic 2,000 number. That's all the answer I could bear to hear.

* * *

Before this book went to press, I wrote an email to Jim and Judy. Jim was now working in Alberta hauling water for the oil rigs, occasionally returning home to PEI to be with Judy. Though the compromise with his values was a jarring one and the work unfulfilling, the relatively well-paid job was allowing them to save money for the upgrades their house needed. In the meantime, the farm was still for sale. Jim and Judy's dream for independence was on hold, but for the moment still alive.

"As far as our future, oh for a crystal ball," Judy wrote. "It has taken a year just for the fall out of my dad's death which happened this week last year, to feel as though there is any semblance of relief both emotionally and financially. My mum is still in a nursing home nearby and I am still dealing with an injured back and unable to return to work. We have to hire a handyman to do what Jim used to do for the horses and the outside work, as I am unable to do anything physical. I don't know what to tell you except I love the farm and the feeling I have here is very rooted to the earth. The nature surrounding me somehow feeds me, it is an organic feeling. But without adequate financial resources and factoring in injury, age, health and the necessity for Jim to work in the oil patch I am sure that if a young couple were to magically want to start their own dream of small scale farming off the grid I would be able to step aside and know that what we created would continue and this existence has been worthy."

Notes

1. Vannini, 2013; Taggart and Vannini, 2014.
2. Massumi, 2002:85.
3. Amin, 2004.
4. Kline, 2005; Wyatt, 2005.
5. Selwyn, Gorard, and Furlong, 2005; Tufekci, 2008; Wyatt, 2005.
6. Kline, 2005.
7. Aldred, 2010.
8. Chia, 2006.
9. Elliott and Urry, 2011; Thrift, 1996.
10. Benson, 2011; Moss, 2006; O'Reilly, 2000; O'Reilly and Benson, 2009; Osbaldiston, 2012.
11. Benson, 2010, 2011; Benson and O'Reilly, 2009; Hoey, 2005, 2006; Osbaldiston, 2012.
12. Hoey, 2005, 2006, 2010; Jobes, 2000; Loeffler and Steinicke, 2007.
13. Benson, 2010, 2011; Hoey, 2005, 2006, 2010; O'Reilly, 2000; Osbaldiston, 2012; Torkington, 2012.
14. Bissell and Fuller, 2010.
15. Bissell and Fuller, 2010.
16. Bissell and Fuller, 2010:2.
17. Young, 1973.
18. Young, 1973.
19. deCerteau, 1984.
20. deCerteau, 1984.
21. deCerteau, 1984:37.
22. Holloway, 2010.
23. Bissell and Fuller, 2010:6.
24. Bissell and Fuller, 2010:10.
25. Adey, 2006.
26. Bissell and Fuller, 2010:3.

27. Off-gridders were not the only lifestyle migrants to face these kinds of problems. Many people who have moved to places like Montana in search of the rural idyll of the American West, for example, have often found their new lifestyles to be more arduous than they had hoped (Jobes, 2000). Many of the problems these lifestyle migrants had to face also originated in economic difficulties (Jobes, 2000). British amenity migrants to Spain and France also had difficulties becoming integrated into local interpersonal networks, finding work, and achieving financial security. For some of them, connecting with and working for other British expats became the only available option (Benson, 2010, 2011; Benson and O'Reilly, 2009; O'Reilly, 2000).

Phillip Exhausted.[i]

_____

[i.] For more photos, visit lifeoffgrid.ca.

13
A Better Way of Life?

It was in the early morning of the 10th of June, 2013, that the last journey began. Desultory and sleepy-eyed, I dragged my frayed rucksack into the domestic departure hall of the Vancouver Airport, scouting for the fastest way past exuberant vacationers and equally erratic rolling suitcases tightly leashed to their button-down business owners. A glance at the bright and uninviting electronic glare of the self-check-in terminals reminded me that, thankfully, by now I had accumulated enough air miles to qualify for the privilege of human contact. I made a beeline for the deserted frequent-flier counter and the bored-looking agent behind it.

"Where are you flying to, sir?"

"Deer Lake."

"Deer Lake," she confirmed in a sullen tone. "It's a very popular destination today."

"I can only imagine," I smiled and heaved the several pounds of extra baggage—tent, inflatable mattresses, and the rest of the camping gear—on the scale.

"Have a good camping trip."

Camping, this time, wasn't part of the research agenda. With a few spare dollars in the budget it wasn't a fiscal restraint, either. It simply was, Jon and I agreed, a more fitting experience. Unable to find off-grid cabins for rent this time, we had surmised that camping in national and provincial parks would provide us with final, longer-lasting tastes of the off-grid life: a warm fire, a simple but efficient shelter, self-catered meals made from unpretentious ingredients, and a **clear sky**[ii] for evening entertainment. To boot, for some obscure reason incomprehensible to both our scientific minds, we found that a cold creek kept a bottle of beer infinitely cooler than a hotel's mini-fridge.

Many hours later we settled into a fir-shaded grassy site, as the early evening Newfoundland sun slid shyly behind the western mountains. Gros Morne National Park's Lomond campground was tucked alongside the fjord-like East Arm of the Gulf of St. Lawrence, meandering away into steep hiking trails and hidden kayaking routes. It was a pity to be on a schedule. While a tinfoil-wrapped dinner of fish and potatoes slowly roasted over the campfire, we idly compared notes about that afternoon's interview.

Karen and Mike had met in industrial southeastern Ontario 11 years before and tied the knot in 2005. Mike had grown up in Western Newfoundland and, like many other islanders, had migrated to seek work elsewhere in mainland Canada. Karen hadn't left her native Ontario but had been dreaming about a radically different life for most of her life. "Homesteading has been my dream ever since I was six years old," she confided. "I didn't know what off-grid meant but my original dream was to go into the woods, build a cabin by myself, and do it all by hand." Increasingly fed-up with noise, traffic, and the hustle and bustle of southeastern Ontario, Mike looked back wistfully to the pleasures of simpler times on the island, remembering with fondness the time he spent with his large family at his grandmother's rustic cabin.

After their wedding in 2005, they decided to honeymoon in Newfoundland, since Karen had always fantasized about visiting the Atlantic rock that her husband used to call home. "We got here by ferry," Mike told the story, "and half an hour into the drive from Port-Aux-Basques she slapped me into my right arm and said, 'How could you possibly leave all this?'" The year after, they deserted Ontario. By the time of our visit they had lived at their solar-powered 600-square-foot cabin—set within a forested 1-acre property—for three blissful years. They had never felt so relaxed, so much at peace before. "It's the simplicity of the lifestyle," Karen explained. "I'd rather spend as little time at work as possible and spend my time here doing my gardening, my reading, my learning, and the things I enjoy. . . . I could even live more primitively than this," she confessed, "spending less money on propane on more on books." Despite the vicinity of the nearest electricity pole, going on-grid was never even a consideration; the prospect of going off-the-grid was as unintimidating as they had dreamed. "It was natural for us," Karen explained. "We knew we'd be comfortable with oil lamps and a woodstove. It was just very natural."

Call it "simple," "basic," "primitive," or whatever you wish, but it was obvious that there was a feeling and an atmosphere of "romance" about both camping and off-grid living that had a uniquely powerful appeal. Not the

---

[ii] http://lifeoffgrid.ca/wp-content/uploads/2013/11/Life-Off-Grid_Newfoundland_01.jpg

sappy romantic draw of a Tinseltown first-date flick, of course, but a more transcendentally romantic love of place that had pulled hundreds of off-gridders into the lifestyle and that constantly seduced many on-gridders to daydream about it. It was evident not only in our latest encounters, but in many of the conversations we had with people across Canada. It was a frontier spirit, a rugged sense of self-reliance and adventure that had also profoundly inspired Henry David Thoreau, who in *Walden* famously explained:

> I went to the woods because I wished to live deliberately, to front only the essential facts of life, and see if I could not learn what it had to teach, and not, when I came to die, discover that I had not lived. I did not wish to live what was not life, living is so dear; nor did I wish to practice resignation, unless it was quite necessary. I wanted to live deep and suck out all the marrow of life, to live so sturdily and Spartan-like as to put to rout all that was not life, to cut a broad swath and shave close, to drive life into a corner, and reduce it to its lowest terms.[1]

I suppose this romance consisted of a feeling of communion, of belonging, of **oneness with time**,[iii] place, and nature. It was the antinomy of the romance and adventure one could find under the tarry roofs of exotic resort chains, gated McMansions, or rows of houses shadowing one another in the anonymity of peripheries worldwide. It was the promise of life lived in the open, nothing more and nothing less.

Karen and Mike thought everyone could manage to live off-the-grid. "It just takes the right attitude," they believed. Others were similarly optimistic. It doesn't take much more than common sense. Skills can be acquired. Help is always available if there is something you can't do on your own. It just takes willpower and motivation. Such were the key ingredients these optimists felt were necessary. And of course, you might argue, why couldn't everyone do it? After all, our species has survived off-the-grid since the beginning.

Kathy and Fred, whom we had met the day before, belonged to a less optimistic group. "It takes an especially stubborn person to live off-the-grid," Fred thought, "someone who doesn't give up easily." Someone who is not easily intimidated. Someone with a great deal of self-efficacy and confidence. And someone "with a strong interest in the lifestyle," they believed, "and with many skills too: you have to be handy, you have to be someone who grew up around family and friends who taught you how to fend for yourself."

As someone who grew up without those skills and confidence in my domestic self-reliance, I began the fieldwork in 2011 in full agreement with

---

[iii.] http://lifeoffgrid.ca/wp-content/uploads/2013/11/Life-Off-Grid_Newfoundland_02.jpg

Kathy and Fred's argument. But it wasn't just about my own skills. As a level-headed social scientist, I was also well aware that certain personal and social barriers would prevent more than just the unskilled, the easily-defeated, and the self-doubting to live off-grid. People with severe physical challenges, for example, would find it impossible to live such a self-reliant and demanding lifestyle. Families and individuals dealing with demanding and inflexible work schedules would equally be hard-pressed to move into TLC-needing off-grid homes. But as time went on, and as I encountered more and more off-gridders like me without a particularly qualifying background or a definable talent for self-sufficiency, I began to feel that with the right disposition learning to live off-grid wouldn't be prohibitively difficult. Not easy, of course, but far from impossible. Living off-the-grid was something you learned along the way because you needed to, just like you learn everything else in your life.

Amidst (Fallen) Trees

Morning came. Air hissed out of our thin mattresses and metal tent pegs squeezed out of the earth. Lock, stock, and barrel we made for town, retracing our footsteps on the muddy banks of the river. We crossed the village boundaries with the mid-afternoon sun's sharp blades knifing through our parched skin, and set out to look for a man who would be willing to drive us across the island. We knew it wouldn't be an easy proposition. At this time of the year, the few hirable drivers willing to brave the fiery heat and the constant threats of separatist hijackings along the route were few and far between the scores of senseless adventurers trying to reach St. John's busy port. We eventually settled with Bruce, a cantankerous old man whose local tongue escaped our most basic comprehension and prevented all attempts at dialogue along the way, negotiating penny by penny and ultimately agreeing on a fare that seemed to anger us all immeasurably.

The next 36 hours of *travail* lingered in a toxic blur of dust and blistering sun, which we relished from the half-squatted comfort of a wooden plank bolted across the bed of Bruce's 1980 Toyota truck. The *piste* we followed through the mind-numbingly vast landscape—with occasional detours through desolate outposts to scavenge odd pieces of chicken wire or motley rusting parts to repair Bruce's irascible Toyota—turned out to be safe but far from sound. Crater after crater, the shock-less Toyota exerted a bumpy revenge on our hard bargaining, delivering us at the edge of town in the middle of the dark night bruised, rattled, and more disoriented than a moose on a parkway.

No, actually, it didn't go like that at all. Rather, our Air Canada flight—which we had booked weeks earlier on the net—departed and landed on time at YYT, where our reserved rental SUV equipped with AC, GPS, and XM radio awaited us. I wrote the passage above while bored on the plane, wondering what it might have been like to do fieldwork in a distant continent where off-grid was the norm and friction-less mobility the exception. But in spite of the reduced potential for relaying an adventurous narrative, I concluded, I liked our field site just fine. Surely it made for a less than glorious arrival into **our final destination,**[iv] but our feelings of elation and accomplishment were no less intense for it. Soberly, we delayed all calls for rest and celebration to first make time for a few interviews with local media outlets.

We began the last interview by reflecting on what had surprised us most over the two years of fieldwork. Jon and I agreed that it was off-gridders' inventiveness and resourcefulness. It had been remarkable to step into home after home and observe how comfortable and convenient an existence off-the-grid could be. The most beautiful province we had visited, we both confessed, was the Yukon—without counting our own British Columbia, of course. As for regrets, I wished we had managed to be hosted by an off-grid Mennonite or Hutterite family, but both religious groups constantly get more than their fair share of attention from prying researchers of one ilk or another. Then the questions became more poignant.

"No, I don't think *everyone* can do it," I opined about the feasibility of off-grid living on a mass scale, playing out the script I had loosely rehearsed in my mind during the last year. "It's easier than it may seem, but it would still be very difficult for many people to abandon, or at least redefine, the sources and meanings of comfort and convenience that our consumer culture has allowed us to get used to." I explained that our expectations for an easy life have escalated a great deal, and even though the required attitude change is something we can all pull off, for some people it would be extremely difficult.

"So, what's the point then?" I was quizzed unsympathetically by the skeptical man. "If not everyone can do it, how is off-grid living the solution to our energy-scarce future?"

"It's not *the* solution," I responded, defending myself and off-grid living alike, suddenly feeling like an unofficially appointed spokesperson. "There is no single magic pill solution to problems of energy scarcity. There is no single alternative future. Environmental scientists would be the first ones to argue that any solution to both present and future energy scarcity problems will require a richness of different approaches and a multiplicity of diverse energy sources and lifestyles."

"Then you're not saying that we should all live off-the-grid?"

"No, I would never suggest that." I sounded a tad grumpy but hopefully convincing. I generally hated this devil's advocate style of journalistic questioning, but by now I didn't mind being challenged. Given that the fieldwork was almost over, I actually appreciated taking stock of the last two years of

---

iv. http://lifeoffgrid.ca/wp-content/uploads/2013/11/Life-Off-Grid_Newfoundland_09.jpg

research and the chance to wrap things up. I went on: "Off-grid living is a lifestyle. Just like I believe in cultivating a variety of energy sources, I believe in the value of a society made more vibrant and stronger by a large variety of lifestyles. Just like it would make no sense to suggest we should all work at the same job, pray to the same gods, wear the same clothes, or live in the same kinds of places, I don't believe that we should all live the same way."

"Do you think that in the future we will all be living off-the-grid?"

"No. Given the kind of society we live in today it would make no sense for each and every one of us to live independently from one another. By pooling together our energy resources most people, especially those who live in densely-populated areas, can potentially live more efficiently. . . . In the future though," I uncharacteristically hazarded to predict, "we will need to learn to rely more on renewable sources of energy and conserve more. We will need to be more mindful and respectful of the limited resources our planet can offer."

I gathered my thoughts for a moment as his shorthand writing caught up. "We will need to be more sensitive, flexible, adaptable, and quite frankly less spoiled," I preached. "People who live off-grid can teach the rest of us a lot about our collective future. They can teach us many serviceable skills and useful attitudes. Their homes are less some kind of subcultural or utopian space than they are as a learning lab where a more sustainable tomorrow is being experimented on, today. And we can all learn from that." On that last point we shook hands and parted ways, setting out on the road for our final house call.

* * *

Flash forward to the next day now, to words lifted from Jon's field journal:

From my cot late in the morning I lift the corner of a makeshift curtain and see the source of the racket that woke me up: Tenzing feeding branches into a gas-powered wood-chipper before disappearing along a wooded trail on an ATV, soon to return with another wagonload of deadfall. **Hurricane Leslie**[v] brought surprising devastation to the shores of Newfoundland, we learned from Ian and Meranda last night. The two are in the finishing phases of building cabins and assembling other technologies—including the generation of methane gas through biomass naturally decaying and rotting into fuel—for the yoga, artist, and spiritual community they host on their five-acre site. Along with Tenzing, a long-time friend visiting from Tibet, they have spent the last little while clearing wind-blown trees from future building sites and milling logs into lumber suitable for construction.

Besides functioning as an alarm call the curtain also serves as a baffle against draughts in the unfinished main building we've been sleeping in, but the chilly

---

[v] http://lifeoffgrid.ca/wp-content/uploads/2013/11/Life-Off-Grid_Newfoundland_05.jpg

coastal air pushing its way through an invisible gap in the envelope is quickly defeating my reluctance to get out of bed to help with the yard work. Overhead, the soaring ceiling of this architectural marvel—hand-hewn beams joined without any metal fastenings—reminds me of the day's agenda: I had promised Ian I would lend a hand with the milling of logs on his **18" bandsaw mill**.[vi] Eager to learn more about this process and its implications for sustainable building, I tumble out of bed and towards the coffee promised by the plume of smoke rising from the chimney of Ian and Meranda's cabin across the compound.

Phillip is already up and is doing his own milling around the log-sorting site while Ian prepares logs to be cut into slabs by the motorized saw. Milling lumber is not a skill Phillip or I possess, but as I ready the camera on the lightweight tripod that doubles as a steadicam I can see that he has learned a great deal already: I zoom in and follow the whirling dust of the saw as it slides the length of the log, and, pulling back, record as Phillip hammers a wooden wedge into the space left behind to ensure the weight of the offcut doesn't pinch the blade.

Milling lumber was not something Ian had been formally trained for, either. With a PhD in biology and a career spanning two decades in federal environmental conservation, Ian—donning a blue rain jacket, sturdy leather gloves, and a trucker hat—"wasn't making enough change," he calmly reflected as he paused from unwinding his red Hud-Son Oscar back into the milling position. "After a while," he continued, "you come to understand that all this process that we have in our society that's supposed to make this a better place, a better environment, is not really working." Disillusioned, he realized that "the only thing you can really change is how you can bring yourself out in the world."

And precisely through his land is how he brought himself out in 2005. Three years before, he had met Meranda, who had recently returned to Newfoundland from a 17-year-long stint in India practicing yoga and meditation. Meranda and Ian looked to this parcel of land on the Avalon Peninsula as the ideal place to cultivate spirituality and environmental sustainability: a harmoniously symbolic and material cut from the outside world, "a place where people can come to experience an alternative way to be" either for a short retreat or a longer period of time. "People who live in the cities," Meranda had explained the day before at mealtime, "don't have a place to go to take a break, so when they hear about the **Tree of Life**[vii] and what we're doing out here, their eyes pop out of their head, like 'wow, this is exactly what I want.' They can come out here and rest in nature," away from the overwhelming busyness of their day-to-day lives, in search of a sense of community with one another and with place.

[vi] http://lifeoffgrid.ca/wp-content/uploads/2013/11/Life-Off-Grid_Newfoundland_07.jpg
[vii] http://www.thelotuscentre.ca/tree-of-life.html

Interrupted by nothing but the usual suspects—unevenly available resources, a few technical setbacks, uncooperative elements, and an unwillingness to rush things through—the process of building both living space and intentional community was unfolding slowly, without the pressures of mortgages, contractors, profit, or an uncompromising sense of deadlines. Like a tree, it was simply growing organically, at its own pace. And, as a matter of fact, by lending a hand with the milling we had become part of that growth too.

We had been milling for over two hours and it was time for a break. Tenzing was eager to show us his favorite hideout in the forest—a picture-perfect **waterfall**[viii] whose gushing had formed a natural swimming hole amidst moss-covered rocks and verdant shrubs—so **I followed him**[ix] and Ian along for the short jaunt, Jon trailing behind us hoping to record the last bytes of digital footage. Our interview and visit were just about over, and so were months in the field.

It isn't part of this ethnographer's job description to state conclusively whether this was definitely a better way of life across the board—a task better left to existential philosophers and best-selling off-grid manual authors. But it was clearly a better way of life for Tenzing, Meranda, Ian, and several dozen off-gridders we had met throughout Canada. A better way of life that was, depending on whom you'd ask, relished in the heightened sustainability, the self-reliance, the involvement, the sense of responsibility, the remove, the skillful confidence, the comfort, the convenience, the sense of place, and the small pleasures of a newly found "freedom:" the simple "freedom," in Ian's words, "that you're waking up in the morning and that you don't need to be anywhere else," the genuine freedom to choose how to occupy yourself, how to invest your time and utilize your energy, your own energy.

So, maybe off-grid living wasn't for all of us, and maybe it wasn't always as sustainable as it could have been, but it was certainly a better way of life for those who had managed to make their wish come true; a wish "to live deliberately, to front only the essential facts of life . . . to live deep and suck out all the marrow of life, to live so sturdily and Spartan-like as to put to rout all that was not life."[2]

The Way Back

"If you don't like the weather, just wait fifteen minutes," was the locals' favorite expression everywhere we went. Newfoundlanders liked to say it too, more rightly so than anyone else. And actually they could have made the same point about their landscape: "If you don't like the landscape, just drive

---

[viii.] http://lifeoffgrid.ca/wp-content/uploads/2013/11/Life-Off-Grid_Newfoundland_04.jpg
[ix.] http://lifeoffgrid.ca/wp-content/uploads/2013/11/Life-Off-Grid_Newfoundland_03.jpg

for fifteen minutes." Keen on seeing more of the island that had preoccupied our minds for the previous two years, we left Ian and Meranda's place en route to a long loop back to St. John's, winding south around the **Avalon Peninsula**[x] and then up the coast through Chance Cove and Witless Bay. Despite the fatigue, the small but measurable loss in attention, the home-sickness, and a shared eagerness to move on with the next creative phases of the ethnography—the writing, the editing, and the distribution—the slow drive back gave us a chance to cling on to the now rapidly dissipating jour-ney. Ethnographers like to wander as much as they like to wonder, after all. So as misty barren highlands sequined by stray rock gave way to rainy timberlands, and then as muffled pebbly shores of time-forgotten fishing outports gave way to dizzyingly windy cliffs seemingly plucked away from the green meadows of Ireland, Newfoundland and its skies and seas surged and transformed before us one last time.

Mid-coast, at Ferryland, we pulled over for a quick hike around the narrow cape and historic lighthouse. As our fieldwork was finally behind us, we set the tripod against a sharp-pitched matted bluff and recorded a final on-camera self-interview, describing "the making of" the film in methodological detail. Like a constantly evolving landscape, ethnography jolts you at every turn. It's easy to draw an itinerary, to sketch in advance a clear sense of direction as well as a starting and an ending point, but like the undertaking of every journey, the doing of ethnography never unfolds too linearly, too predictably. Sure there are lines you can draw across the map of a field, but through the actual process of wondering and wandering you always take those lines for a walk.[3] Or better yet, the lines take *you* for a walk, changing you as much as you change them.

Someone once said that the mark of a good journey is not whether it yields answers to the questions you had in the beginning, but instead whether it gen-erates questions you never thought of asking in the first place. And so this journey did. The disenchantment and disillusion with shortsighted global eco-nomic and political leadership and with the stunted evolution of international environmental policies to meet a growing demand on the planet's resources had me wondering at the outset whether off-grid living was an answer—a better way of life than the defeatism and dependency so many of us have suc-cumbed to. Now I knew it was at least one very small answer, a difficult but prodigious personal way forward on the path to a more responsible future. But before this journey started I never thought of asking how it might feel to detour from our broad collective path and go back, how it might feel to question the inevitability of the future and oppose, through a positive alternative, the blind march onward we collectively seem to have surrendered to join.

---

[x] http://lifeoffgrid.ca/wp-content/uploads/2013/11/Life-Off-Grid_Newfoundland_08.jpg

As more forests are slashed and burned, as new pipelines, dams, and mines are being planned and developed around the world every day to feed a growing appetite for worldwide consumption, we are reminded by cool-headed politicians that we can't stop progress and development. But can't we, really? Wouldn't we want to stop and turn around if we finally realized we are nearing the edge of a cliff? Wouldn't we want to go back and re-learn basic regenerative life skills made oblivious at the hands of careless concession? Wouldn't we want to re-discover the alternative hedonism of a modest and onerous consumption? Wouldn't we want to re-learn to appreciate a life lived in deep involvement with the resources made available by the places we inhabit, rather than in spite of them? And above all, wouldn't we *embrace and enjoy*—rather than *endure*—such regression? For the next 12 months, back at our respective homes, we worked on the implications of these questions— I mainly with the memories and words and Jon with the sounds and images we had painstakingly collected through our travels.

I typed the last pages of the first draft of this book during a long, foggy autumn from the comfort of my island home. On one November day the grid that fed electricity to my laptop and heat to my living room went down. It was a planned daylong outage required by BC Hydro to upgrade tension lines crossing the water and connecting us to our nearest substation. Our island's elementary school closed and many of my fellow islanders caught the morning ferries and went to town for the day. I stayed home. No emails, no phone calls, no TV, no buzz, no noise. I read a book slowly, reviewed my handwritten notes, played a board game with my daughter, and when it got a bit chilly in the house we both went out for a long, heartwarming hike in the forest.

When dusk arrived we lit candles and huddled by our propane-fueled hearth. The grid sprang back to life in the evening, but neither of us cared much. I recalled Daniel's words, spoken on Lasqueti Island two and a half years before: "If you want to understand if you can pull it off, you should try and go for a week or two without electricity of any kind. If you enjoy it, then you can be off-the-grid." It had only been one day, and I felt I would have welcomed thirteen more.

Notes

1. Thoreau, 2008:66.
2. Thoreau, ibid.
3. See Ingolda, 2007.

REFERENCES

Adey, P. 2006. If mobility is everything then it is nothing: towards a relational politics of (im) mobilities. *Mobilities*, 1: 75–94.

Aldred, R. 2010. "On the outside": constructing cycling citizenship. *Social and Cultural Geography*, 11: 35–52.

Allon, F. and Z. Sofoulis. 2006. Everyday water: cultures in transition. *Australian Geographer*, 37: 45–55.

Amin, A. 2004. Regions unbound: toward a new politics of place. *Geografisker Annaler*, 86: 32–44.

Anderson, B. 2006. Becoming and being hopeful. *Environment & Planning D*, 24: 733–752.

Anderson, B. and P. Harrison. 2006. Questioning affect and emotion. *Area*, 38: 333–335.

Anderson, B. and J. Wylie. 2009. On geography and materiality. *Environment & Planning A*, 41: 318–335.

Atkinson, P. 2006. Do-it-yourself: democracy and design. *Journal of Design History*, 19: 1–10.

Babooram, A. and M. Hurst. 2008. Uptake of water- and energy-conservation devices in the home. *Canadian Social Trends*, 11: 12–19.

Barnett, C., P. Cloke, N. Clarke, and A. Malpass. 2005. Consuming ethics: articulating the ethics and spaces of ethical consumption. *Antipode*, 37: 23–45.

Barnett, V., C. Barnett, and N. Clarke. 2010. *Globalizing Responsibility: The Political Rationalities of Ethical Consumption*. Hoboken, NJ: Wiley-Blackwell.

Beaver, T. 2012. "By the skaters, for the skaters:" The DIY ethos of the roller derby revival. *Journal of Sport and Social Issues*, 36: 25–49.

Bell, D. 2006. Variations on the rural idyll. Pp. 149–159 in P. Cloke, T. Marsden, P. Mooney (eds.), *The Handbook of Rural Studies*. London: SAGE.

Bell, D. and G. Valentine. 1995. Queer country: rural lesbian and gay lives. *Journal of Rural Studies*, 11: 113–122.

Bennett, J. 2005. The agency of assemblages and the American blackout. *Public Culture*, 17: 445–465.

Bennett, J. 2010. *Vibrant Matter: A Political Ecology of Things*. Durham: Duke University Press.

Benson, M. 2010. The context and trajectory of lifestyle migration: the case of the British residents of Southwest France. *European Societies*, 12: 45–64.

Benson, M. 2011. The movement beyond (lifestyle) migration: mobile practices and the constitution of a better way of life. *Mobilities*, 6: 221–235.

Benson, M. and K. O'Reilly (eds.). 2009. *Lifestyle Migration: Exploration, Aspirations Experiences*. Farnham: Ashgate.

Biehler, D. and G. Simon. 2011. The great indoors: research frontiers on indoor environments as active political-ecological spaces. *Progress in Human Geography*, 35: 172–192.

Bijker, W. 1997. *Of Bicycles, Bakelites, and Bulbs*. Boston: MIT Press.

Bijker, W. and J. Law. 1991. *Shaping Technology/Building Society*. Cambridge: MIT Press.

Bird-David, N. 1992. Beyond the "hunting and gathering mode of subsistence": culture-sensitive observations on the Nayaka and other modern hunter-gatherers. *Man*, 27: 19–44.

Bissell, D. 2008. Comfortable bodies: sedentary affects. *Environment & Planning A*, 40: 1697–1712.

Bissell, D. and G. Fuller. 2010. Stillness unbound. Pp. 1–20 in D. Bissell and G. Fuller (eds.), *Stillness in a Mobile World*. London: Routledge.

Blake, M., J. Mellor, and L. Crane. 2010. Buying local food, shopping practices, place, and consumption networks in defining food as "local." *Annals of the American Association of Geographers*, 100: 409–426.

Borgmann, A. 1987. *Technology and the Character of Contemporary Life*. Chicago: University of Chicago Press.

Borgmann, A. 2000. The moral complexion of consumption. *Journal of Consumer Research*, 26: 418–422.

Boyle, P. and K. Halfacree. 1998. *Migration into Rural Areas: Theories and Issues*. Chichester: Wiley.

Brassley, P. 1998. On the unrecognized significance of the ephemeral landscape. *Landscape Research*, 23: 119–132.

Brereton, D. P. 2010. *Campsteading: Family, Place, and Experience at Squam Lake, New Hampshire*. New York: Routledge.

Brewis, J. and G. Jack. 2005. Pushing speed? The marketing of fast and convenience food. *Consumption, Markets, and Culture*, 8: 49–67.

Brinkerhoff, J. and M. Jacob. 1984. Alternative technology and part-time, semi-subsistence agriculture: a survey from the back-to-the-land movement. *Rural Sociology*, 51: 43–59.

Bruner, E. 1993. Epilogue: creative persona and the problems of authenticity. Pp. 321–334 in S. Lavie, K. Narayan, and R. Rosaldo (eds.), *Creativity/Anthropology*. Ithaca: Cornell University Press.

Bulkeley, H. and N. Gregson. 2008. Crossing the threshold: municipal waste policy and household waste generation. *Environment & Planning A*, 41: 929–945.

Bunce, M. 1994. *The Countryside Ideal: Anglo-American Images of Landscape*. London: Routledge.

Campbell, C. 2005. The craft consumer: culture, craft, and consumption in a postmodern society. *Journal of Consumer Culture*, 5: 23–44.

Casey, E. 2001. Between geography and philosophy: what does it mean to be in the place-world? *Annals of the Association of American Geographers*, 91: 683–693.

Caygill, H. 2007. Life and energy. *Theory, Culture & Society*, 24: 19–27.

Chappells, H. and W. Medd. 2008. From big solutions to small practices: bringing back the active consumer. *Social Alternatives*, 27: 44–49.

Chappells, H., W. Medd, and E. Shove. 2011. Disruption and change: drought and the inconspicuous dynamics of garden lives. *Social and Cultural Geography*, 12: 701–715.

Cherrier, H., I. Black, and M. Lee. 2011. Intentional non-consumption for sustainability: consumer resistance and/or anti-consumption? *European Journal of Marketing*, 45: 1757–1767.

Cherrier, H. and J. Murray. 2002. 'Driftin' away from excessive consumption: a new social movement based on identity construction. *Advances in Consumer Research*, 29: 245–247.

Chhetri, P., A. Khan, R. Stimson, and J. Western. 2009. Why bother to downshift? *Journal of Population Research*, 26: 51–72.

Chhetri P., R. Stimson, and J. Western. 2009. Understanding the downshifting phenomenon: a case of South East Queensland, Australia. *American Journal of Social Issues*, 44: 345–362.

Chia, S. 2006. Mining the internet plateau: an exploration of the adoption intention of non-users in Singapore. *New Media and Society*, 8: 589–609.

Chiras, D. 2011. *The Homeowner's Guide to Renewable Energy*. Gabriola Island: New Society Publishers.

Clarke, N. 2008. From ethical consumerism to political consumption. *Geography Compass*, 2: 1870–1884.

Cloke, P. 2003. *Country Visions*. Harslow: Pearson.

Cloke, P. and O. Jones. 2001. Dwelling, place, and landscape: an orchard in Somerset. *Environment & Planning A*, 33: 649–666.

Cole, R., J. Robinson, Z. Brown, and M. O'Shea. 2008. Recontextualizing the notion of comfort. *Building Research and Information*, 36: 323–336.

Connolly, J. and A. Prothero. 2008. Green consumption: life-politics, risk and contradictions. *Journal of Consumer Culture*, 8: 117–145.

Craig-Lees, M. and C. Hill. 2002. Understanding voluntary simplifiers. *Psychology & Marketing*, 19: 187–210.

Crane, N. 2012. Are "other spaces" necessary? Associative power at the dumpster. *ACME: An International e-Journal for Critical Geographies*, 11: 352–372.

Cresswell, T. 2010. Toward a politics of mobility. *Environment & Planning D*, 28: 17–31.

Cresswell, T. 2014. Friction. In P. Adey et al. (eds.), *The Routledge Handbook of Mobilities*. London: Routledge.

Crouch, D. 1989. Patterns of cooperation in the cultures of outdoor leisure—the case of the allotment. *Leisure Studies*, 8: 189–199.

Crouch, D. 1997. 'Others' in the rural: leisure practices and geographical knowledge. Pp. 57–74 in P. Milbourne (ed.), *Revealing Rural Others: Representation, Power and Identity in the British Countryside*. London: Pinter.

Crouch, D. 2003. Spacing, performing, and becoming: tangles in the mundane. *Environment & Planning A*, 35: 1945–1960.

Crowley, J. 2001. *The Invention of Comfort*. Baltimore: Johns Hopkins University Press.

Culton, K. and B. Holzman. 2010. The growth and disruption of a "free space": examining a suburban do it yourself (DIY) punk scene. *Space & Culture*, 13: 270–287.

Cupples, J., V. Guyatt, and E. Pearce. 2007. "Put on a jacket, you wuss": cultural identities, home heating, and air pollution in Christchurch, New Zealand. *Environment & Planning A*, 39: 2283–2898.

Damas, D. 2002. *Arctic Migrants/Arctic Villagers: The Transformation of Inuit Settlement in the Central Arctic*. Montreal: McGill University Press.

Dant, T. 2009. The work of repair: gesture, motion, and sensual knowledge. *Sociological Research Online*, 15: http://www.socresonline.org.uk/15/3/7.html

Daoud, A. 2011. The *Modus Vivendi* of material simplicity: counteracting scarcity via the deflation of wants. *Review of Social Economy*, 69: 275–305.

deCerteau, M. 1984. *The Practice of Everyday Life*. Berkeley: University of California Press.

deLanda, M. 2006. *A New Philosophy of Society: Assemblage Theory and Social Complexity*. London: Continuum.

Deleuze, G. and F. Guattari. 1972. *Anti-Oedipus*. London: Continuum.

Dewey, J. 1919. *Democracy and Education*. New York: The Free Press.

Dickinson, J. and L. Lumsdon. 2010. *Slow Travel and Tourism*. London: Earthscan.

Dillon, M. 2006. *Artificial Sunshine.* Washington: The National Trust.

Douglas, M. 1966. *Purity and Danger.* London: Ark.

Duncombe, S. 1997. *Notes from the Underground: Zines and the Politics of Alternative Culture.* London: Verso.

Dunn, K. and M.S. Farnsworth. 2012. "We ARE the revolution": riot grrrl press, girl empowerment, and DIY publishing. *Women's Studies: An Interdisciplinary Journal,* 41: 136–157.

DuPuis, M. and D. Goodman. 2005. Should we go "home" to eat? Toward a reflexive politics of localism. *Journal of Rural Studies,* 21: 359–371.

Edensor, T. 2006a. Reconsidering national temporalities: institutional times, everyday routines, serial spaces, and synchronicities. *European Journal of Social Theory,* 9: 525–545.

Edensor, T. 2006b. Performing rurality. Pp. 484–495 in P. Cloke (ed.), *Handbook of Rural Studies.* London: SAGE.

Edensor, T. 2010. Introduction: thinking about rhythm and space. Pp. 1–18 in T. Edensor (ed.), *Geographies of Rhythm: Nature, Place, Mobilities and Bodies.* Farnham: Ashgate.

Edensor, T. 2012. Illuminated atmospheres: anticipating and reproducing the flow of affective experience in Blackpool. *Environment & Planning D,* 30: 1103–1122.

Edensor, T., D. Leslie, S. Millington, and N. Rantisi (eds.). 2010. *Spaces of Vernacular Creativity: Rethinking the Cultural Economy.* London: Routledge.

Edwards, C. 2006. Home is where the art is: women, handicraft, and home improvements, 1750–1900. *Journal of Design History,* 19: 11–21.

Elgin, D. 1981. *Voluntary Simplicity.* New York: William Morrow.

Elliott, A. and J. Urry. 2011. *Mobile Lives.* London: Routledge.

Etzioni, A. 1998. Voluntary simplicity: characterization, select psychological implication, and societal consequences. *Journal of Economic Psychology,* 19: 619–643.

Feagan, R. 2007. The place of food: mapping out the "local" in local food systems. *Progress in Human Geography,* 31: 23–42.

Felski, R. 2002. Introduction. *New Literary History,* 33: 607–622.

Fennell, C. 2011. "Project Heat" and sensory politics in redeveloping Chicago public housing. *Ethnography,* 12: 40–64.

Flandrin, J. 1979. *Families in Former Times.* Cambridge: Cambridge University Press.

Gabrys, J. 2009. Sink: the dirt of systems. *Environment & Planning D,* 27: 666–681.

Gallan, B. and C. Gibson. 2011. New dawn or new dusk? Beyond the boundary of day and night. *Environment & Planning A,* 43: 2509–2515.

Gandy, M. 2004. Rethinking urban metabolism: water, space, and the modern city. *City,* 8: 363–379.

Gauntlett, D. 2011. *Making is Connecting: The Social Meaning of Creativity from DIY and Knitting to YouTube and Web 2.0.* New York: Polity.

Gelber, S. 1997. Do-it-yourself: constructing, repairing, and maintaining domestic masculinity. *American Quarterly,* 49: 66–112.

Glassie, H. 2000. *Vernacular Architecture.* Bloomington: Indiana University Press.

Gleick, J. 1999. *Faster.* New York: Pantheon.

Glickman, L. 2009. *Buying Power: A History of Consumer Activism in America.* Chicago: University of Chicago Press.

Graham, S. and S. Marvin. 2001. *Splintering Urbanism: Networked Infrastructures and the Urban Condition.* New York: Routledge.

Graham, S. and N. Thrift. 2007. Out of order: understanding repair and maintenance. *Theory, Culture & Society,* 24: 1–25.

Gregson, N., A. Metcalfe, and L. Crewe. 2007. Moving things along: the conduits and practices of divestment in consumption. *Transactions of the Institute of British Geographers,* 32: 187–200.

Grigsby, M. 2004. *Buying Time and Getting By: The Voluntary Simplicity Movement.* Albany: SUNY Press.

Gunn, S. and A. Owens. 2006. Nature, technology, and the modern city: an introduction. *Cultural Geographies,* 13: 491–496.

Guthman, J. 2003. Fast food/organic food: reflexive tastes and the making of "yuppie chow." *Social & Cultural Geography,* 4: 45–60.

Hackney, F. 2006. Use your hands for happiness: home craft and make-do-and-mend in British women's magazines in the 1920s and 1930s. *Journal of Design History,* 19: 23–38.

Hailey, C. 2008. *Campsites: Architecture of Duration and Place.* New Orleans: Louisiana University Press.

Hailey, C. 2009. *Camps: A Guide to 21st Century Space.* Boston: MIT Press.

Halfacree, K. 1992. *The Importance of Spatial Representations in Residential Migration to Rural England in the 1980s.* PhD thesis, Department of Geography, Lancaster University.

Halfacree, K. 1994. The importance of 'the rural' in the constitution of counterurbanization: evidence from England in the 1980s. *Sociologia Ruralis,* 34: 164–189.

Halfacree, K. 2001a. Constructing the object: taxonomic practices, 'counterurbanisation' and positioning marginal rural settlement. *International Journal of Population Geography,* 7: 395–411.

Halfacree, K. 2001b. Going back-to-the-land again: extending the scope of counterurbanisation. *Espace, Populations, Sociétés,* 1–2: 161–170.

Halfacree, K. 2003. Landscapes of rurality: rural others/other rurals. Pp. 141–169 in I. Robertson and P. Richards (eds.), *Studying Cultural Landscapes.* London: Arnold.

Halfacree, K. 2006. From dropping out to leading on? British countercultural back-to-the-land in a changing rurality. *Progress in Human Geography,* 30: 309–336.

Halfacree, K. 2007a. Back-to-the-land in the twenty-first century: making connections with rurality. *Tijdschrift voor Economische en Sociale Geografie,* 98: 3–8.

Halfacree, K. 2007b. Trial by space for a 'radical rural': introducing alternative localities, representations and lives. *Journal of Rural Studies,* 23: 125–141.

Halfacree, K. 2009. 'Glow worms show the path we have to thread': the counterurbanisation of Washti Bunyan. *Social & Cultural Geography,* 10: 771–789.

Hallam, E. and T. Ingold (eds.). 2007. *Creativity and Cultural Improvisation.* Oxford: Berg.

Hand, M. and E. Shove. 2004. Orchestrating concepts: kitchen dynamics and regime change in *Good Housekeeping* and *Ideal Home,* 1922–2002. *Home Cultures,* 1: 235–256.

Hand, M. and E. Shove. 2007. Condensing practices: ways of living with a freezer. *Journal of Consumer Culture,* 7: 79–104.

Hand, M., E. Shove, and D. Southerton. 2004. Explaining showering: a discussion of the material, conventional, and temporal dimensions of practice. *Sociological Research Online,* 10: http://www.socresonline.org.uk/10/2/hand.html

Hannam, K., M. Sheller, and J. Urry. 2006. Editorial: mobilities, immobilities, and moorings. *Mobilities,* 1: 1–22.

Harper, D. 1987. *Working Knowledge: Skill and Community in a Small Shop.* Chicago: University of Chicago Press.

Harrison, C. and J. Popke. 2011. "Because you got to have heat:" the networked assemblage of energy poverty in Eastern North Carolina. *Annals of the Association of American Geographers,* 101: 949–961.

Harrison, S., S. Pile, and N. Thrift. 2004. *Patterned Ground.* London: Reaktion.

Harvey, D. 1991. *The Condition of Postmodernity.* New York: Wiley-Blackwell.

Harvey, D. 1996. *Justice, Nature, and the Politics of Difference.* Cambridge: Blackwell.

Hawkins, G. 2006. *The Ethics of Waste.* Oxford: Rowman & Littlefield.

Head, L. and P. Muir. 2007. Changing culture of water in eastern Australian backyard gardens. *Social & Cultural Geography*, 8: 889–905.

Heidegger, M. 1971. *Poetry, Language, Thought*. New York: Harper & Row.

Heidegger, M. 1982. *The Question Concerning Technology, and Other Essays*. New York: Harper.

Heinz-Housel, T. 2006. Solar panels, shovels, and the 'net: selective uses of technology in the homesteading movement. *Information, Communication & Society*, 9: 182–201.

Hetherington, K. 1997. *The Badlands of Modernity*. London: Routledge.

Hetherington, K. 2004. Secondhandedness: consumption, disposal, and absent presence. *Environment & Planning D*, 22: 157–173.

Hinrichs, C. 2003. The practice and politics of food system localization. *Journal of Rural Studies*, 19: 33–45.

Hitchings, R. 2007. Geographies of embodied outdoor experience and the arrival of the patio heater. *Area*, 39: 340–348.

Hitchings, R. 2011. Researching air-conditioning addiction and ways of puncturing practice: professional office workers and the decision to go outside. *Environment & Planning A*, 43: 2838–2856.

Hitchings, R. and R. Day. 2011. How older people relate to the winter warmth practices of their peers and why we should be interested. *Environment & Planning A*, 43: 2452–2467.

Hitchings, R. and S. J. Lee. 2008. Air conditioning and the material culture of routine human encasement. *Journal of Material Culture*, 13: 251–265.

Hobson, K. 2006. Bins, bulbs, and shower timers: on the "techno-ethics" of sustainable living. *Ethics, Place & Environment*, 9: 317–336.

Hochschild, A. 1989. *The Second Shift*. New York: Viking.

Hoey, B. 2005. From pi to pie: moral narratives of non-economic migration and starting over in the post-industrial Midwest. *Journal of Contemporary Ethnography*, 34: 586–604.

Hoey, B. 2006. Grey suit or brown Carhartt: narrative transition, relocation, and reorientation in the lives of corporate refugees. *Journal of Anthropological Research*, 62: 347–371.

Hoey, B. 2010. Place for personhood: individual and local character in lifestyle migration. *City & Society*, 27: 237–261.

Holloway, L. 2000. Hell on earth and paradise all at the same time: the production of small-holding space in the British countryside. *Area*, 32: 307–315.

Holloway, L. 2002. Smallholding, hobby farming, and commercial farming: ethical identities and the production of farming spaces. *Environment & Planning A*, 34: 2055–2070.

Holloway, J. 2010. *Change the World without Taking Power: The Meaning of Revolution Today*. London: Pluto Press.

Hornborg, A. 2001. *The Power of the Machine: Global Inequalities of Economy, Technology, and Environment*. Walnut Creek, CA: AltaMira Press.

Huneke, M.E. 2005. The face of the consumer: an empirical examination of the practice of voluntary simplicity in the United States. *Psychology & Marketing*, 22: 527–550.

Ingold, T. 1993. The temporality of the landscape. *World Archaeology*, 25: 152–174.

Ingold, T. 2000. *The Perception of the Environment*. London: Routledge.

Ingold, T. 2005. The eye of the storm: visual perception and the weather. *Visual Studies*, 20: 97–104.

Ingold, T. 2007a. *Lines*. New York: Routledge.

Ingold, T. 2007b. Earth, sky, wind, and weather. *Journal of the Royal Anthropological Institute*, 13: 19–38.

Ingold, T. 2008. Bindings against boundaries: entanglements of life in an open world. *Environment and Planning A*, 40: 1796–1810.

Ingold, T. 2011. *Being Alive*. London: Routledge.

Ingold, T. 2013. *Making: Anthropology, Architecture, Art, and Architecture*. London: Routledge.

Ingold, T. and E. Hallam. 2007. Creativity and cultural improvisation: an introduction. Pp. 1–24 in E. Hallam and I. Ingolds (eds.), *Creativity and Cultural Improvisation*. Oxford: Berg.

Iwata, O. 2006. An evaluation of consumerism and lifestyle as correlates of a voluntary simplicity lifestyle. *Social Behavior & Personality: An International Journal*, 34: 557–566.

Jackson, P., R. Perez, I. Clarke, A. Hallsworth, R. de Kervenoael, and M. Kirkup. 2006. Retail restructuring and consumer choice 2: understanding consumer choice at the household level. *Environment & Planning A*, 38: 47–67.

Jackson, T. 2006. *The Earthscan Reader in Sustainable Consumption*. London: Routledge.

Jacob, J. 1997. *New Pioneers: The Back-to-the-Land Movement and the Search for a Sustainable Future*. University Park: Penn State University Press.

Jelsma, J. 2003. Innovating for sustainability: involving users, politics and technology. *Innovation*, 16: 103–116.

Jewitt, S. 2011. Geographies of shit: spatial and temporal variations in attitudes towards human waste. *Progress in Human Geography*, 35: 608–626.

Jobes, P. 2000. *Moving Nearer to Heaven: The Illusions and Disillusions of Migrants to Scenic Rural Places*. Boulder: Greenwood.

Jones, O. 2011. Lunar-solar rhythmpatterns: towards the material cultures of tides. *Environment & Planning A*, 43: 2285–2303.

Kaika, M. 2004. Interrogating the geographies of the familiar: domesticating nature and constructing the autonomy of the modern home. *International Journal of Urban and Regional Research*, 28: 265–286.

Kaika, M. 2005. *City of Flows*. New York: Routledge.

Kaika, M. and E. Swyngedouw. 2000. Fetishizing the modern city: the phantasmagoria of urban technological networks. *International Journal of Urban and Regional Research*, 24: 120–138.

Khamis, S. 2006. "It only takes a jiffy to make": Nestlé, Australia, and the convenience of instant coffee. *Food, Culture, & Society*, 12: 217–233.

Kimbrell, A. 2002. Introduction. Pp. 1–6 in A. Kimbrell (ed.), *Fatal Harvest*. Sausalito: Foundation for Deep Ecology and Island Press.

Kline, R. 2000. *Consumers in the Country*. Baltimore: The Johns Hopkins University Press.

Kline, R. 2005. Resisting consumer technology in rural America: the telephone and electrification. Pp. 51–66 in N. Oudshoorn and T. Pinch (eds.), *How Users Matter: The Co-construction of Users and Technology*. Boston: MIT Press.

Kloppenburg, J., J. Hendrickson, and G. W. Stevenson. 1996. Coming in to the foodshed. *Agriculture and Human Values*, 13: 33–42.

Kneafsey, M., L. Holloway, L. Venn, E. Dowler, R. Cox, and H. Tuomainen. 2008. *Reconnecting Consumers, Producers, and Food*. London: Bloomsbury.

Kneale-Gould, R. 2005. *At Home in Nature: Modern Homesteading and Spiritual Practice in America*. Berkeley: University of California Press.

Kraftl, P. and P. Adey. 2008. Architecture/affect/habitation: geographies of being-in-buildings. *Annals of the Association of American Geographers*, 98: 213–231.

Lacy, W. 2000. Empowering communities through public work, science, and local food systems: revisiting democracy and globalization. *Rural Sociology*, 65: 3–26.

Latham, A. and D. McCormack. 2004. Moving cities: rethinking the materialities of urban geographies. *Progress in Human Geography*, 28: 701–724.

Latour, B. 2004. How to talk about the body? The normative dimension of science studies. *Body & Society*, 10: 205–229.

Lefebvre, H. 2004. *Rhythmanalysis: Space, Time, and Everyday Life*. London: Continuum.

Lemonnier, P. (ed.). 2002. *Technological Choices.* London: Routledge.

Leonard-Barton, D. 1981. Voluntary simplicity lifestyles and energy conservation. *Journal of Consumer Behavior,* 8: 243–240.

Levine, C. 2008. *Handmade Nation: The Rise of DIY Art, Craft, and Design.* New York: Princeton Architectural Press.

Lewis, T. 2008. *Smart Living: Lifestyle Media and Popular Expertise.* New York: Peter Lang.

Librova, H. 2008. The environmentally friendly lifestyle: simple or complicated? *Czech Sociological Review,* 44: 1111–1128.

Lingis, A. 1992. The society of dismembered body parts. Pp. 1–20 in J. Broadhurst (ed.), *Deleuze and the Transcendental Unconscious.* Coventry: Univ. of Warwick Press.

Lingis, A. 1998. *The Imperative.* Bloomington, IN: Indiana University Press.

Loeffler, R. and E. Steinicke. 2007. Amenity migration in the US Sierra Nevada. *The Geographical Review,* 97: 67–88.

Longhurst, R., L. Johnston, and E. Ho. 2009. A 'visceral' approach: cooking at home with women in Hamilton, New Zealand. *Transactions of the Institute of British Geographers,* 34: 333–345.

Love, T. and A. Garwood. 2012. Electrifying transitions: power and culture in rural Cajamarca, Peru. Pp. 146–163 in S. Strauss, S. Rupp, and T. Love (eds.), *Cultures of Energy: Power, Practices, Technologies.* Walnut Creek, CA: Left Coast Press.

Luna, M. 2008. Out of sight, out of mind: distancing and the geographic relationship between electricity consumption and production in Massachusetts. *Social Science Quarterly,* 89: 1277–1292.

Lupton, E. and J. A. Miller. 1992. *The Bathroom, the Kitchen and the Aesthetics of Waste: A Process of Elimination.* New York: Kiosk.

Luvaas, B. 2012. *DIY Style: Fashion, Music, and Global Digital Cultures.* Oxford: Berg.

Lydon, C., K. Rohmeier, S. Yi, M. Mattaini, and L. Williams. 2011. How far do you have to go to get a cheeseburger around here? *Behavior and Social Issues,* 20: 6–23.

Lyle, J. 1994. *Regenerative Design for Sustainable Development.* New York: Wiley.

MacCracken, G. 1988. *Culture and Consumption.* Bloomington: Indiana University Press.

Mall, A. 2007. Structure, innovation, and agency in pattern construction: the Kolam of Southern India. Pp. 55–78 in E. Hallam and I. Ingolds (eds.), *Creativity and Cultural Improvisation.* Oxford: Berg.

Massey, D. 2004. Geographies of responsibility. *Geografiska Annaler,* 86 B 1: 5–18.

Massumi, B. 2002. *Parables for the Virtual.* Durham, NC: Duke University Press.

May, J. and N. Thrift. 2001. Introduction. Pp. 1–46 in J. May and N. Thrift (eds.), *Timespace: Geographies of Temporality.* London: Routledge.

Mayer, H. and P. Know. 2006. Slow cities: sustainable places in a fast world. *Journal of Urban Affairs,* 28: 321–334.

McCormack, D. 2003. An event of geographical ethics in spaces of affect. *Transactions of the Institute of British Geographers,* 28: 488–507.

McDonald, S., C. Oates, W. Young, and K. Hwang. 2006. Toward sustainable consumption: researching voluntary simplifiers. *Psychology & Marketing,* 23: 515–534.

McDonough, W. and M. Braungart. 2001. *Cradle to Cradle.* New York: FGS.

Meijering L., P. Huigen, and B. Van Hoven. 2007. Intentional communities in rural spaces. *Tijdschrift voor Economische en Sociale Geografie,* 98: 42–52.

Melbin, M. 1987. *Night as Frontier.* New York: Free Press.

Miller, D. 1998. *A Theory of Shopping.* Cambridge: Polity.

Mormont, M. 1987. Rural nature and urban natures. *Sociologia Ruralis,* 27: 3–20.

Moss, L.A.G. (ed.). 2006. *The Amenity Migrants: Seeking and Sustaining Mountains and Their Cultures.* Santa Fe: University of New Mexico Press.

Munro, S. 1997. Ideas of difference: stability, social spaces and the labour of division. Pp. 3–26 in K. Hetherington and S. Munro (eds.), *Ideas of Difference.* Oxford: Blackwell.

Murcott, A. 1982. On the social significance of the "cooked dinner" in South Wales. *Social Science Information,* 21: 677–696.

Nakamura, F. 2007. Creativity or performing words? Observations on contemporary Japanese calligraphy. Pp. 79–98 in E. Hallam and I. Ingolds (eds.), *Creativity and Cultural Improvisation.* Oxford: Berg.

Nansen, B., M. Arnold, M. Gibbs, and H. Davis. 2009. Domestic orchestration: rhythms in the mediated home. *Time & Society,* 18: 181–207.

Newholm, T. and D. Shaw. 2007. Studying the ethical consumer: a review of research. *Journal of Consumer Behavior,* 6: 253–270.

Nye, D. 1999. *Consuming Power: A Social History of American Energies.* Boston: MIT Press.

Nye, D. 2010. *When the Lights Went Out: A History of Blackouts in America.* Boston: MIT Press.

O'Neill, T., C. Jinks, and A. Squire. 2006. "Heating is more important than food:" older women's perception of fuel poverty. *Journal of Housing for the Elderly,* 20: 95–108.

O'Reilly, K. 2000. *The British on the Costa del Sol.* London: Routledge.

O'Reilly, K. and M. Benson. 2009. Lifestyle migration: escaping to the good life? Pp. 1–13 in M. Benson and K. O'Reilly (eds.), *Lifestyle Migration: Exploration, Aspirations and Experiences.* Farnham: Ashgate.

Osbaldiston, N. 2012. *Seeking Authenticity in Place, Culture, and Self: The Great Urban Escape.* London: Palgrave.

Palang, H., G. Fry, J. Jauhiainen, M. Jones, and H. Soovāli. 2005. Editorial: landscape and seasonality—seasonal landscapes. *Landscape Research,* 30: 165–172.

Palen, L. 2010. Living in utility-scarcity: energy and water insecurity in Northwest Alaska. *American Journal of Public Health,* 100: 1010–1018.

Parkins, W. 2004. Out of time: fast subjects and slow living. *Time & Society,* 13: 363–382.

Parkins, W. and G. Craig. 2006. *Slow Living.* Oxford: Berg.

Parr, J. 1999. *Domestic Goods.* Toronto: University of Toronto Press.

Pickering, L. 2010. Toilets, bodies, selves: enacting composting as counterculture in Hawai'i. *Body & Society,* 16: 33–57.

Pink, S. 2007. Sensing Cittàslow: slow living and the constitution of the sensory city. *The Senses & Society,* 22: 59–77.

Portwood-Stacer, L. 2012. Anti-consumption as tactical resistance: anarchists, subculture, and activist strategy. *Journal of Consumer Culture,* 12: 87–108.

Powell, H. 2009. Time, television, and the decline of DIY. *Home Cultures,* 6: 89–108.

Quitzau, M. B. and I. Ropke. 2009. Bathroom transformation: from hygiene to well-being. *Home Cultures,* 6: 219–242.

Renting, H., T. Marsden, and J. Banks. 2003. Understanding alternative food networks: exploring the role of short food supply chains in rural development. *Environment & Planning A,* 35: 393–411.

Rosen, N. 2010. *Off the Grid.* New York: Penguin.

Roush, C. 1999. *Inside Home Depot: How One Company Revolutionized an Industry through the Relentless Pursuit of Growth.* New York: McGraw-Hill.

Rybczynski, W. 1987. *Home.* London: Penguin.

Schilt, K. and E. Zobl. 2008. Connecting the dots: riot grrrls, ladyfests, and the international grrrl zine network. Pp. 171–192 in A. Harris (ed.), *Next Wave Cultures: Feminism, Subcultures, Activism.* New York, NY: Routledge.

Schivelbusch, W. 1995. *Disenchanted Night.* Berkeley: University of California Press.

Schor, J. 1993. *The Overworked American.* New York: Basic Books.

Schor, J. 1999. *The Overspent American.* New York: Basic Books.

Schwartz, D. and W. Schwartz. 1998. *Living Lightly: Travels in Post-Consumer Society.* Oxfordshire: Jon Carpenter.

Schwartz-Cowan, Ruth. 1983. *More Work for Mother.* New York: Basic Books.

Selwyn, N., S. Gorard, and J. Furlong. 2005. Whose internet is it anyway? Exploring adults' (non) use of the internet in everyday life. *European Journal of Communication,* 20: 5–26.

Shaw, D. and T. Newholm. 2002. Voluntary simplicity and the ethics of consumption. *Psychology & Marketing,* 19: 167–185.

Shaw, R. 2010. Neoliberal subjectivities and the development of the night-time economy in British cities. *Geography Compass,* 4: 893–903.

Shove, E. 2003. *Comfort, Cleanliness, and Convenience: The Social Organization of Normality.* Oxford: Berg.

Shove, E., H. Chappells, and L. Lutzenhiser. (eds.) 2009. *Comfort in a Lower Carbon Society.* New York: Routledge.

Shove, E. and D. Southerton. 2000. Defrosting the freezer: from novelty to convenience. *Journal of Material Culture,* 5: 301–319.

Shove, E., F. Trentmann, and R. Wilk (eds.). 2009a. *Time, Consumption and Everyday Life: Practice, Materiality and Culture.* Oxford: Berg.

Shove, E., F. Trentmann, and R. Wilk (eds.). 2009b. Introduction. Pp. 1–15 in E. Shove, F. Trentmann, and R. Wilk (eds.), *Time, Consumption and Everyday Life: Practice, Materiality and Culture.* Oxford: Berg.

Shove, E., M. Watson, M. Hand, and J. Ingram. 2008. *The Design of Everyday Life.* Oxford: Berg.

Silva, E. 2010. *Technology, Culture, Family.* London: Palgrave.

Simpson, P. 2008. Chronic everyday life: rhythmanalysing street performance. *Social & Cultural Geography,* 9: 807–829.

Simpson, P., 2012. Apprehending everyday rhythms: rhythmanalysis, time-lapse photography, and the space-times of street performance. *Cultural Geographies,* 19: 423–445.

Snider, B. 2006. Home heating and the environment. *Statistics Canada,* 11–008: 15–19.

Soderman, B. and R. Carter. 2008. The auto salvage: a space of second chances. *Space & Culture,* 11: 2–38.

Sofoulis, Z. 2005. Big water, everyday water: a socio-technical perspective. *Continuum: Journal Media & Cultural Studies,* 19: 445–463.

Soper, K. 2007. Rethinking "the good life": the citizenship dimension of consumer dissatisfaction with consumerism. *Journal of Consumer Culture,* 7: 205–229.

Soper, K. 2008. Alternative hedonism, cultural theory, and the role of aesthetic revisioning. *Cultural Studies,* 22: 567–587.

Soper, K. 2009. Introduction: the mainstreaming of counter-consumerist concern. Pp. 1–21 in K. Soper, M. Ryle, and L. Thomas (eds.), *The Politics and Pleasures of Consuming Differently.* London: Palgrave.

Soper, K., M. Ryle, L. Thomas (eds.). 2009. *The Politics and Pleasures of Consuming Differently.* London: Palgrave.

Star, S. L. 1999. The ethnography of infrastructure. *American Behavioral Scientist,* 43: 377–391.

Starr, A., A. Card, C. Benepe, G. Auld, K. Smith, and K. Wilken. 2003. Sustaining local agriculture: barriers and opportunities to direct marketing between farms and restaurants in Colorado. *Agriculture and Human Values,* 20: 301–321.

Stewart, K. 2007. *Ordinary Affects.* Durham: Duke University Press.

Stewart, K. 2011. Atmospheric attunements. *Environment & Planning,* 29: 445–453.

Steyn, A. S. and H. S. Geyer. 2011. Urban form revisited: an account of views on the issues. Pp. 62–93 in H. S. Geyer (ed.), *International Handbook of Urban Policy, Volume 3.* Northampton: Edward Elgar Publishing.

Strang, V. 2004. *The Meaning of Water.* Oxford: Berg.

Strauss, S., S. Rupp, and T. Love. 2012. Powerlines: cultures of energy in the twenty-first century. Pp. 1–58 in S. Strauss, S. Rupp, and T. Love (eds.), *Cultures of Energy: Power, Practices, Technologies.* Walnut Creek, CA: Left Coast Press.

Strebel, I. 2011. The living building: towards a geography of maintenance work. *Social and Cultural Geography,* 12: 243–262.

Strengers, Y. and C. Maller. 2012. Materialising energy and water resources in everyday practices: insights for securing supply systems. *Global Environmental Change,* 22: 754–763.

Swyngedouw, E. 1999. Modernity and hybridity: nature, *regeneracionismo,* and the production of the Spanish waterscape, 1890–1930. *Annals of the Association of American Geographers,* 89: 443–465.

Taggart, J. and P. Vannini. 2014. Life off grid: considerations for a multi-sited, public ethnographic film. Forthcoming in C. Bates (ed.), *Video Methods.* New York: Routledge.

Tam, D. 2008. Slow journeys: what does it mean to go slow? *Food, Culture, & Society,* 11: 207–218.

Thompson, P. 2013. *Remember Who You Are: Poems from Petpeswick.* Musquodoboit Harbour: Goat Rock Press.

Thoreau, H. D. 2008. *Walden, Civil Disobedience, and Other Writings.* New York: Norton.

Thrift, N. 1996. *Spatial Formations.* London: SAGE.

Thrift, N. 2004. Intensities of feeling: toward a spatial politics of affect. *Geografiska Annaler,* 86B: 57–78.

Thrift, N. 2008. *Non-Representational Theory.* London: Routledge.

Tobey, R. 1997. *Technology as Freedom.* Berkeley, CA: University of California Press.

Tomlinson, A. 1990. Home fixtures: doing-it-yourself in a privatised world. Pp. 57–73 in A. Tomlinson (ed.), *Consumption, Identity and Style: Marketing, Meanings, and the Packaging of Pleasure.* London: Routledge.

Torkington, K. 2012. Place and lifestyle migration: the discursive construction of "glocal" place- identity. *Mobilities,* 7: 71–92.

Trubek, A. 2008. *The Taste of Place.* Berkeley: University of California Press.

Tufekci, Z. 2008. Grooming, gossip, Facebook, and Myspace. *Information, Communication, and Society,* 11: 544–564.

Turner, K. 2006. Buying, not cooking: ready-to-eat food in American working-class neighborhoods, 1880–1930. *Food, Culture, & Society,* 9: 12–39.

Urry, J. 2000. *Sociology Beyond Societies.* New York: Routledge.

Urry, J. 2008. *Mobilities.* New York: Wiley.

Urry, J. 2011. *Climate Change and Society.* New York: Polity.

Vannini, P. 2011. Constellations of ferry (im)mobility: islandness as the performance and politics of isolation and insulation. *Cultural Geographies,* 18: 249–271.

Vannini, P. 2012. *Ferry Tales: Mobility, Place, and Time on Canada's West Coast.* New York: Routledge.

Vannini, P. 2013. Popularizing ethnography: reflections on writing for popular audiences in magazines and blogs. *Qualitative Research,* 13: 442–451.

Van Vliet, B., H. Chappells, and E. Shove. 2005. *Infrastructures of Consumption.* London: Routledge.

Vaughan, P., M. Cook, and P. Trawick. 2007. A sociology of re-use: deconstructing the milk bottle. *Sociologia Ruralis,* 47: 120–134.

Vellinga, M., P. Oliver, and A. Bridge. 2007. *Atlas of Vernacular Architecture of the World.* New York: Routledge.

Warde, A. 1999. Convenience food: space and timing. *British Food Journal,* 101: 518–527.

Wilhite, H., H. Nakagami, T. Masuda, Y. Yamaga, and H. Haneda. 1996. A cross cultural analysis of household energy use behavior in Japan and Norway. *Energy Policy,* 24: 795–803.

Williams, C. 2004. A lifestyle choice? Evaluating the motives of do-it-yourself consumers. *International Journal of Retail and Distribution Management*, 32: 270–278.

Williams, R. 2008. Night spaces: darkness, deterritorialization, and social control. *Space & Culture*, 11: 514–532.

Winther, T. 2012. Space, time, and sociomaterial relationships: moral aspects of the arrival of electricity in rural Zanzibar. Pp. 164–181 in S. Strauss, S. Rupp, and T. Love (eds.), *Cultures of Energy: Power, Practices, Technologies*. Walnut Creek, CA: Left Coast Press.

Whatmore, S. 2006. Materialist returns: practicing cultural geography in and for a more-than-human world. *Cultural Geographies*, 13: 600–609.

Whitehead, A. N. 1934. *Nature and Life*. Chicago: University of Chicago Press.

Wright, L. 1964. *Home Fires Burning: The History of Domestic Heating and Cooking*. London: Routledge and Kegan Paul.

Wyatt, S. 2005. Non-users also matter: the construction of users and non-users of the internet. Pp. 67–80 in N. Oudshoorn and T. Pinch (eds.), *How Users Matter: The Co-Construction of Users and Technology*. Boston: MIT Press.

Young, J. 1973. The hippie solution: an essay in the politics of leisure. Pp. 182–208 in I. Taylor and L. Taylor (eds.), *Politics and Deviance*. Harmondsworth: Penguin.

Zavestovski, S. 2002. The social-psychological basis of anticonsumption attitudes. *Psychology & Marketing*, 19: 149–165.

INDEX

Page numbers in italics indicate photographs.